LEONARDO

LEONARDO

Maria Costantino & Aileen Reid

Brompton

First published in 1991 by
Brompton Books Corp.
15 Sherwood Place
Greenwich, CT 06830

ISBN 0-86124-839-2

Printed in Hong Kong

Page 1: *Self-Portrait*, c. 1516

Page 2: *Lady with an Ermine (Cecilia Gallerani)*,
c. 1485

Contents

Leonardo da Vinci: His Life and Patrons

MARIA COSTANTINO

ALTHOUGH it might be possible to avoid speculation or theorizing about the events of Leonardo's later life, it is difficult to avoid this when dealing with the first thirty years. Few facts are available and from Leonardo's early youth he seems to have been a legendary figure; because this process of mystification and deification began at such an early stage, even the commentary of a near-contemporary such as Giorgio Vasari cannot be relied upon with complete confidence.

Tuscany and Florence, 1452-82

Born illegitimately at Anchiano, a village close to the town of Vinci, on 15 April 1452, Leonardo was the son of Ser Piero, a notary or lawyer, and Caterina, who is usually described as a peasant girl. Around these bare facts grew the story of Leonardo growing up in the Tuscan countryside, enjoying farm life and, according to Walter Pater in his book *The Renaissance* (1893), watching the lizards and glow worms and other strange small creatures which haunt an Italian vineyard. A further legend, since there is no contemporary description or firmly identifiable portrait, is of Leonardo's physical beauty. The emphasis placed on the painter's beauty by Vasari and other chroniclers does however lead us to assume that this legend has some basis in fact.

What we do know for certain is that by 1469 Leonardo was in Florence with his father, who had become a notary to the Signoria, and they were living in a rented house on the Piazza San Firenze, not far from the Palazzo Vecchio. It seems that for his first six or seven years in Florence Leonardo was employed in the workshop of Andrea di Cione, better known to us as Andrea del Verrocchio (*c* 1435-88).

RIGHT: Verrocchio's Colleoni monument in Venice may have influenced his pupil Leonardo's conception of the Sforza (page 84) and Trivulzio (page 143) monuments.

BELOW: This view of Florence by Leonardo's biographer Giorgio Vasari shows the siege which led to the final collapse of Republican rule in 1530. The city center is dominated by Brunelleschi's cathedral dome, while between the cathedral and the river is the Palazzo Vecchio, site of Leonardo's lost *Battle of Anghiari* (pages 104-09).

RIGHT: *The Proportions of the Human Head*, silverpoint on blue prepared paper, 8¾×6 inches (21.3×15.3 cm), Windsor Castle, Royal Library 12601. © 1990 Her Majesty The Queen. In measured drawings of human and animal bodies (page 87), Leonardo was pursuing a line of enquiry complementary to but different from his anatomical drawings and dissections. In making these measurements he was trying to divine fundamental rules of proportion in nature, and as such they are often closer to his mathematical than his anatomical studies.

Since little is known about Leonardo's life or education before this time, we can only assume that he followed the traditional course of study for boys of his age. As the son of a notary, albeit illegitimate, Leonardo would have received a basic schooling. His later struggles with Latin suggest that he did not receive continuous instruction in this subject. His education must, therefore, have been restricted to basic numeracy and literacy, both subjects important for life in the Florentine commercial world. In Florence, as in most other towns, a boy in the private or municipal lay schools, or in the Humanist Schools, was educated in two stages.

From the age of six or seven for about four years, he would study at the primary school, or *botteghuzza*, where he would be taught the fundamentals of reading and writing with, perhaps, some elementary business and notarial letters. After a further four years, from the age of ten or eleven, most would advance to the *abbaco* or secondary school. Here the boys would read more advanced texts including Dante and Aesop. But on the whole the emphasis was on mathematics. A few students might continue their education at universities, but, for most, the mathematics they had learnt at the *abbaco* was the height of their skill. The mathematics the boys learnt was adapted to fit the needs of the merchant classes from which most of these boys came. But we must also remember that many of the Renaissance artists whose names are most familiar to us were also business people who had themselves undergone the same education in the lay schools, who knew and used the geometry and arithmetic they had learnt.

The universal mathematical tool of the Renaissance was the 'Merchant's Key,' also known as the Rule of Three or the Golden Rule. Various printed accounts of the Rule of Three exist from the mid fifteenth century, but to demonstrate the union between painter and merchant, one account, *De abbaco*, by the painter Piero della Francesca is appropriate. Piero explains that the Rule of Three says that we must 'multiply the thing we want to know about by the thing that is dissimilar to it, then, we divide the product by the remaining thing.' The example Piero gives is the equation: 7 bracci of cloth are worth 9 lire; what is the value of 5 bracci? The solution is to multiply the quantity you want to know about (5) by what the 7 bracci of cloth are worth (9): thus $5 \times 9 = 45$; divide the product by 7 and the result is the cost of 5 bracci of cloth, ie 6 3/7.

This equation demonstrates how a merchant might use mathematics, but what use was it to a painter such as Piero della Francesca? Apart from when an artist needed to work out the cost of, say, wood for a certain commission, the Rule of Three was how Renaissance artists dealt with proportions. Modern-day mathematics would express Piero's equation as $7:9 = 5:6\ 3/7$, but it was also the manner in which Leonardo studied the proportions of the human head. Alongside his *Study of the Proportions of a Head* (page 9) he wrote:

From *a* to *b* (that is from the roots of the hair in front to the top of the head) is equal to *cd*, that is from the bottom of the nose to the meeting of the lips in the middle of the mouth; from the inner corner of the eye *m* to the top of the head *a* is equal to the distance from *m* down to the chin *s*; *s*, *c*, *f* and *b* are equidistant each from the next.

Any belief we may have had that Leonardo was a mathematical genius is quickly dispelled when we realize that this study was based on mathematical knowledge common to every fifteenth-century merchant or student.

Having entered Verrocchio's studio, for the next six or seven years Leonardo followed the traditional course of apprenticeship. His instruction would have begun, following the medieval traditions, with all kinds of tasks, such as preparing pigments and brushes. As an apprentice learned, he would move on to more complicated tasks such as transferring cartoons to panels and perhaps painting drapery or other less significant areas in paintings. Only after he had displayed his skill and knowledge would an apprentice rise to be an assistant to his master, able to complete entire works from sketches or instructions. According to Vasari, Leonardo was an assistant working on *The Baptism of Christ* (page 35) for the church of San Salvi. According to Vasari, Verrocchio gave up painting when he saw one of the angels Leonardo had painted; Vasari would have us believe that Verrocchio stopped painting because his student was more capable than he was. It seems more likely, however, that in a commercial workshop like Verrocchio's, the master was able to give up painting and concentrate on other works like sculpture once he was convinced that he could safely entrust painting commissions to his assistant. Verrocchio was fortunate, indeed, for not only did he have Leonardo as an assistant, during the 1470s he also had in his studio the young painters Pietro Perugino (c. 1450-1523), Lorenzo di Credi (1459-1537), Domenico Ghirlandaio (1449-94), Francesco Botticini (1446-97) and Cosimo Rosselli (1439-1507). Verrocchio's studio was rivalled in Florence only by that of the brothers Pietro and Antonio Pollaiuolo, and was dominated by a communal spirit. A work of art was not yet the expression of a single personality and the spirit of craftsmanship is expressed by the fact that even at the height of his career, Verrocchio and his studio produced woodcarvings and designs for tapestries as well as major painting commissions.

ABOVE: Lorenzo di Credi (1459-1537) *Adoration of the Shepherds*, oil on wood panel, 88⅛×77⅛ inches (224×196 cm), Galleria degli Uffizi, Florence. Lorenzo was a pupil in Verrocchio's studio at the same time as Leonardo. His style follows very closely what is understood by the 'Verrocchio style' (see pages 35 and 141).

ABOVE: Pietro Perugino (c. 1450-1523) *Madonna and Child with Ss John the Baptist and Sebastian*, 1493, oil on wood panel, 70×64½ inches (178×164 cm), Galleria degli Uffizi, Florence. Perugino's mastery of a sense of peaceful sweetness in his painting enjoyed great popularity in Florence around the turn of the fifteenth century. Perugino, another of Verrocchio's pupils, is also remembered as Raphael's master.

OVERLEAF: Domenico Ghirlandaio (1449-94) *Apparition of the Angel to Zacharius*, 1485-90, fresco, S Maria Novella, Florence. Ghirlandaio was one of Verrocchio's older pupils and later was master of Michelangelo. Although this is a biblical scene it also portrays the good and the great of contemporary Florentine society. The lefthand two of the four figures at the lower left have been identified as the Neoplatonic philosopher Marsilio Ficino (1433-99) and the poet Cristoforo Landino who lauded Bernardo Bembo's platonic friendship with Ginevra de' Benci (page 46).

11

ABOVE: Francesco Botticini (1446-97) *Madonna and Child with St John the Baptist and an Angel*, Galleria Palatina, Florence. Botticini was among the most conservative of Verrocchio's pupils.

In 1472 Leonardo's name was inscribed on the roll of the Guild of St Luke as a painter: 'Leonardo di Ser Piero da Vinci dipintore.' He was then 20 years old and having paid his guild fees, he could have set up his own independent workshop. The guilds acted in a manner similar to trade unions: they were responsible for the guidelines for training within the professions – whether law, medicine or art – and only when a student had completed a period of time of instruction and mastered various skills could he join the guild.

Leonardo, it seems, chose to spend at least four more years with Verrocchio, during which time he was responsible

for a number of works. As well as probably taking part in arranging pageants for Lorenzo de' Medici and Giuliano de' Medici in 1469 and 1475, Leonardo was also involved in the arrangements for the festivities to welcome Galeazzo Maria Sforza, Duke of Milan, to Florence in 1471. It is also believed that Leonardo was asked to make a watercolor cartoon for a tapestry to be woven in Flanders and destined for the King of Portugal but which never reached the weaving stage. Two paintings of the Virgin attributed to Leonardo – the *Benois Madonna* (page 54) and the *Madonna with a Vase of Flowers* (page 49) are also believed to date from this period in Verrocchio's workshop. The

RIGHT: Leonardo's registration as a painter with the Guild of St Luke was recorded in 1472.

BELOW: This landscape drawing of the valley of the Arno is dated 5 August 1473 and is Leonardo's earliest dated drawing. His interest in the natural phenomena of rivers, lakes and plants, as well as his mastery of a simple and assured drawing style, is evident here.

earliest dated work that can be positively attributed to Leonardo is from August 1473, a drawing of a landscape in pen and bister with some watercolor in shaded areas (below).

On 8 April 1476 a note was dropped in the *tamburo*, a box outside the Palazzo Vecchio into which people could place accusations, whether signed or anonymous. The anonymous note dropped in the *tamburo* accused Leonardo and three other young Florentine men of engaging in homosexual acts with a 17-year-old artists' model, Jacopo Saltarelli. Though no witnesses came forward, the matter went to court twice in two months. In distress, Leonardo petitioned Bernardo di Simone Cortigiano, an influential head of the Florentine guilds, with the words: 'You know I have told you before, that I am without any friends' (Codex Atlanticus 4v). After the intervention of the other defendants' families, and by Verrocchio himself, Leonardo was acquitted on the proviso that he was never again the subject of an accusation. He was

15

ABOVE: Lorenzo de' Medici (1449-92) inherited from his grandfather, Cosimo, an interest in Platonic philosophy. His Platonic Academy at the Medici villa at Careggi was not a teaching institution in the Classical or modern sense, but provided a meeting place for many of the great humanist thinkers of the age.

lucky: a couple of decades later, the same charge in Florence could have resulted in the death penalty, as Savonarola believed that all homosexuals should be burnt.

Much has been made about Leonardo's sexuality. Two barely legible lines from a sheet (Uffizi) of studies of heads and machines from 1478 support the thesis that he was homosexual: 'Fioravante di Domenico...in Florence is my most cherished companion, as though he were my...' The nature of Leonardo's sexuality was further explored by Sigmund Freud in *Leonardo da Vinci and a Memory of Childhood*. In a discussion on the flight of birds, Leonardo made the following note:

Among the first recollections of my childhood it seemed to me that, as I lay in my cradle, a kite came to me and opened my mouth with its tail and struck me several times with its tail between my lips (Codex Atlanticus 162r).

To Freud this was a revelation of Leonardo's passive homosexuality. In his analysis, Freud erroneously translated 'nibbio' (kite) into 'vulture' and proceeded to base his theory on the fact that in Egyptian hieroglyphics 'vulture'

and 'mother' were both represented by the figure of a vulture since they were phonetically linked: both were pronounced 'mut.' Pshycosexual analysts anxious to shed light on the meaning of the strange smile on the lips of Leonardo's female subjects or the drawings he made of his right hand have even been able to see the outline of a vulture in the drapery of the Virgin's clock in the *Virgin and Child with St Anne* in the Louvre (page 120).

After the accusations in 1477, Leonardo left Verrocchio's studio and began working independently. The courts of Italy in the late fifteenth and early sixteenth centuries were more akin to warring, feudal cities. They were also important as centers which conjoined power and culture. The prince of the court, whether pope, cardinal or duke, could attract those in search of favors and patronage and held sufficient power and authority to distribute public honors and offices. The prince could also repel, since his power necessarily generated enemies. The major court in the fifteenth century in Italy was the court of Milan under the Sforza family, followed in power and prestige by Papal Rome, the court of

BELOW: This portrait of Lorenzo 'il Magnifico' de' Medici was made posthumously but clearly reflects those traits of character which enabled Lorenzo to remain effective ruler of Florence for 23 years. Although he was a patron of artists as well as writers and philosophers, definitive proof that he was a patron of Leonardo is elusive.

LAVRENTIVS MEDICES PETRI FILIVS.

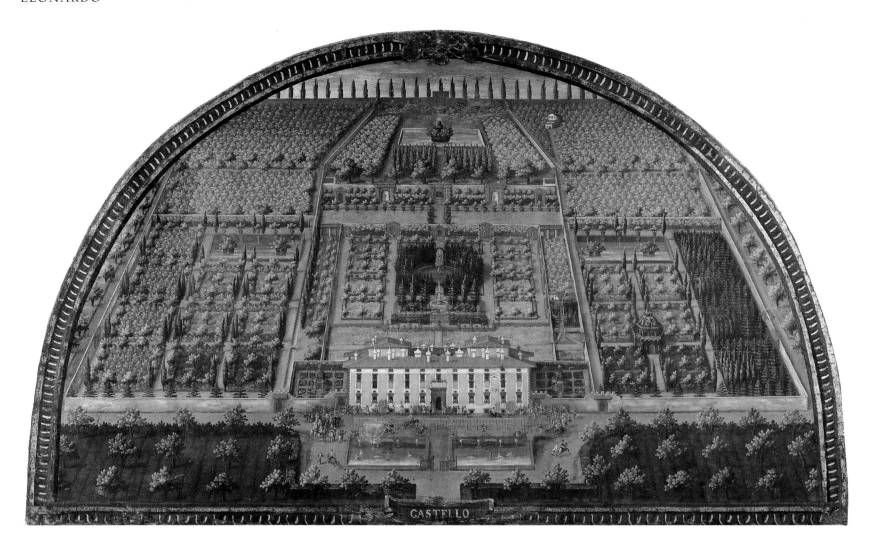

CASTELLO

Ferrara under the d'Este family and at Mantua under the rule of the Gonzaga. In Milan the residence was the castle in the middle of the city: a walled fortress capable of withstanding wars, riots and revolutions, complete with moats, 62 drawbridges and, by 1500, some 1800 machines of war and between 800 and 1200 mercenary troops.

The Medici court in Florence under Lorenzo was dominated, however, by Neoplatonic thought. Lorenzo himself was a poet and philosopher as well as the founder of the world's first academy of art. According to Anonimo Gaddiano in the Codice Maggliabec-chiano, Leonardo was set to work in the gardens of the Piazza San Marco where the academy was to be established. In a note in the Codex Atlanticus (288), on a sheet of calculations and a drawing of a pair of scales, Leonardo mentions the gardens and the work on which he could have been employed:

The Labors of Hercules for Piero F Ginori. The Garden of the Medici.

Florence, however, was still nominally a Republic and as such the majority of the artists continued to operate on the time-honored system of payment for goods produced or services rendered. It seems that Leonardo was ill-suited to the business-like atmosphere of Florence: in the nine years since his re-gistration with the Guild of St Luke, he had produced little saleable material.

From the minutes of the Florentine executive council, the Signoria, a com-mission for an altarpiece for the chapel of San Bernardo in the Palazzo Vecchio was first awarded to Piero Pollaiuolo on 24 December 1477, but seventeen days later the commission was re-awarded to Leonardo. On 16 March 1478 Leo-nardo received the first payment of 25 florins and started work. Work on the altarpiece was not far advanced when Leonardo abandoned the painting, and a resolution passed on 25 May 1483 by the Signoria transferred the project to Domenico Ghirlandaio. The altarpiece was finally finished in 1485, but it was completed by Filippino Lippi.

In 1478, the same year that Leonardo received this commission, Giuliano de' Medici (brother of Lorenzo) was murdered by Francesco de' Pazzi in Santa Maria del Fiore (Florence Cathe-dral) during High Mass. Pazzi and his collaborators were arrested and hanged, except for one Bernardo Baroncelli who escaped to Turkey. The Sultan of Turkey obliged Florence by extraditing Baroncelli and on 29 December 1479, Baroncelli and his wife were publicly hanged. Beside the sketch of the dead Baroncelli, now in the Musée Bonnat, Bayonne, Leonardo wrote this description:

A tan-colored skull cap, a doublet of black serge, a black jerkin, lined and the collar covered with a black and red stippled vel-vet. A blue coat lined with fur of foxes' breasts. Black hose.
Bernardo di Bandino Baroncelli.

A further commission was given to Leonardo in March 1481 and again he was to leave it unfinished. The monas-tery of San Donato at Scopeto near Florence had requested that Leonardo paint an *Adoration of the Magi* and Leo-nardo's notary father, Ser Piero, duly drew up the contract in which Leo-nardo agreed to deliver the painting in 24 months. His payment was to be one third of an inheritance the monastery had been bequeathed: the father of one of the monks had left his estate to the monastery with a proviso that his grand-daughter should receive a dowry of 150 florins. Leonardo was to pay the dowry in instalments while the monks held the right to buy back the land granted to Leonardo for 300 florins, three years after Leonardo had completed the painting.

Shortly after the contract was agreed and signed, the monastery advanced Leonardo money to buy paints. In July Leonardo requested a further 28 florins and between July and September the monastery also provided him with fire-wood, wheat and wine. On 28 Septem-ber 1481 three monks delivered a barrel of wine to Leonardo's house. Shortly after, Leonardo left Florence without completing the *Adoration of the Magi* or paying for the girl's dowry.

LEFT: Gardens were a feature of great importance to the country villas of fifteenth-century Florentine gentry. Leonardo mentions the Medici gardens in one of his manuscripts and some of his drawings relate to this or similar work (pages 179 and 180).

RIGHT: This grisly, on-the-spot recording was made by Leonardo in 1479 at the hanging of Bernardo Baroncelli who had conspired unsuccessfully to assassinate Lorenzo de' Medici. The notes on the drawing record the style and color of Baroncelli's clothing.

LEFT: This detail from an anonymous fifteenth-century altarpiece known as the *Pala Sforzesca* shows Ludovico Sforza, Duke of Milan, who ruled the city from 1476 to 1500. He provided Leonardo with the sort of patronage which allowed him to work in the rather erratic manner which suited him. Many important works including the *Last Supper* (pages 88-89) and the *Madonna of the Rocks* (page 71) were produced during Leonardo's 18-year stay in Milan.

RIGHT: The murder of Galeazzo Maria Sforza in 1476 was the event which brought his younger brother Ludovico to power. Galeazzo's son and heir died mysteriously in 1494.

Milan, 1482-99

Many explanations have been offered as to why Leonardo left Florence. Some say it was his restless spirit that drove him on to Milan. Others cite his apparent lack of recognition by Lorenzo de Medici: in 1481 Pope Sixtus IV had summoned the finest artists in Tuscany to decorate the Vatican. After consultation with the Medici, Botticelli, Ghirlandaio, Luca Signorelli, Pietro Perugino and Pinturicchio were summoned to Rome, but not Leonardo. Lorenzo had not, in fact, ignored Leonardo altogether. In 1478, during one of Ludovico Sforza's visits to Florence, Lorenzo is said to have recommended the artist for the monument the Duke of Milan was planning to erect as a tribute to his father, Francesco Sforza. Furthermore, the Medici needed to remain on good terms with the court of Ludovico Sforza (Il Moro, as he was known, because of his dark complexion). The rightful Duke of Milan, Gian Galeazzo Sforza, was only 13 years old and his uncle, Ludovico Sforza, Duke of Bari, was virtual ruler. With designs on becoming the king of Italy, Ludovico was attempting to create the finest court in Europe. Milan was one of the great trade centers, ideally situated on the plain of Lombardy and the Artiglio Canal. Ludovico also coveted and exploited Milan's physical proximity to its political ally of France. At any time, Milan cold call upon the king of France to use his forces against any Italian city that threatened Ludovico's power.

Thus Leonardo went to the city of Milan, accompanied by Atalante Migliorotti, a renowned lutenist, and Tomaso Masini, also known as Zoroastro de Peretola. In Milan Leonardo was provided with a comfortable life in a court that boasted some 200 servants and where he was allowed to roam through the gardens of the castle and the surrounding countryside. In return, Leonardo provided designs for machines of war, and in time his name was added to the list of Sforza engineers. By the time he was summoned to Pavia in 1490 to advise on the completion of the cathedral, Leonardo had earned the title of *ingeniarius ducalis*.

Before he had left Florence, Leonardo had listed in his notebook the works in his possession:

A head, full face, of a young man with fine flowing hair
Many flowers from nature
A head, full face with curly hair
Various St Jeromes
A Head of the Duke (possibly Francesco Sforza?)
Many designs for knots
4 studies for the panel of Sant'Angelo
A small composition of Giuliano da Fegline
A head of Christ done with the pen
Eight St Sebastians
Many angels
A chalcedony [a kind of crystal]
A head in profile with fine hair
Some bodies in perspective
Some machines for ships
Some machines for waterworks
A portrait of Atalante (Migliorotti) raising his head
The head of Geronimo da Fegline
The head of Gian Franco Boso
Many throats of old women
Many heads of old men
Many complete nude figures
Several arms, legs, feet and poses
A Madonna, finished
Another almost (finished) which is in profile
The head of Madonna ascending to Heaven
The head of an old man with a very long neck
A head of a gypsy
A head with a hat on
A representation of the Passion made in relief
A head of a girl with tresses gathered in a knot
A head with the hair dressed

However, by the time of Leonardo's celebrated letter of self-commendation to Ludovico Sforza, such artistic attainments as those listed above had become secondary. In his letter Leonardo says that he has plans for portable bridges, water-raising devices, battering rams and devices for scaling high walls, plans for cannon, warships, catapults and armored cars. Only at the end of his letter does he assure Il Moro that he can:

execute sculpture in marble, bronze or clay, and also painting, in which my works will stand comparison with that of anyone else, whoever he may be.

Leonardo also added that he could undertake the bronze equestrian statue of Ludovico's father (see pages 84, 85, 86 and 87).

Where Leonardo gained his technical knowledge is uncertain, as is the date of his letter. There are some gaps in the chronology of Leonardo's life between 1482 and 1487, and although it has been suggested that he visited the Near East

LEFT: Beatrice d'Este married Ludovico Sforza in 1491. Her sister Isabella d'Este was a great patron of the arts, but Beatrice herself died in childbirth in 1497.

RIGHT: The Castello Sforzesco in Milan was the fortress home of the Sforzas from 1450. Leonardo decorated several rooms there for Ludovico Sforza, including the Sala delle Asse (page 100).

where Kait Bey, Sultan of Egypt, was engaged in warfare, the commissions Leonardo received in Milan suggest otherwise. We know, in fact, that on 25 April 1483 Leonardo and the brothers Evangelista and Giovanni Ambrogio da Predis signed a contract with Prior Bartolomeo Scorlione, Giovanni Antonio Sant'Angelo and other members of the Confraternity of the Immaculate Conception, agreeing to produce an altarpiece with an elaborate carved frame for the brotherhood's chapel in the church of San Francesco Grande in Milan. The contract names Leonardo as *maestro* over the da Predis brothers and states that the fee was set at 800 Imperial Lire (200 ducats), the initial sum of 100 lire to be paid on 1 May 1483 and the balance in monthly instalments of 40 lire beginning in July. The final payment was to be made in January or February of 1485 when, on completion, the three painters would be entitled to a

bonus determined by the members of the brotherhood. It was further stipulated that the altarpiece was to be completely finished no later than the Feast of the Immaculate Conception (8 December) 1485.

The subject of the central panel painted by 'the Florentine' was to be a Virgin and Child with a group of angels and two prophets. On each of the side panels there were to be four angels singing and playing musical instruments. As Leonardo was assigned the central panel (the future *Madonna of the Rocks*), Evangelista undertook the gilding, coloring and retouching, Ambrogio the side panels with angels, while the wooden retable into which the painting was to fit was carved by Giacomo de Mairo. In fact decorating the frame alone used up all the 800-lire fee and, although they had completed the project, Leonardo and Ambrogio (Evangelista had died in 1490) peti-

tioned the Duke in 1493 or 1494 for an additional payment since they had only technically received 100 lire. But their petition was dismissed, as well as their request that the central panel by Leonardo be sold. Ambrogio appealed again in 1503, this time to Louis XII of France, but as Leonardo was no longer in Milan at this time, the case was deferred again. On 27 April 1506 the altarpiece was judged to be unfinished, and although absent from Milan, Leonardo had to finish the panel within two years, for which he would receive 200 lire. The complex history of the two extant versions of the *Madonna of the Rocks* is discussed in Chapter 2, below. Leonardo's trouble with the Milanese contracts reinforces what was apparent in his working practices in Florence – that he was not suited to conducting his works along business lines.

Also dating from Leonardo's early period in Milan, around 1482 to 1483, are two paintings: the unfinished *Portrait of a Musician* (page 80), the only portrait Leonardo ever painted of a man, and believed to be a portrait of Franchino Gaffurio, the choirmaster at Milan Cathedral, and *Lady with an Ermine* (page 76), a portrait of Cecilia Gallerani, who had become Ludovico Sforza's mistress in 1481.

Around 1483 Leonardo began work on the equestrian statue of Francesco Sforza, a project he is believed to have been involved with for some sixteen years (page 84). Leonardo, while apprenticed to Verrocchio, had assisted with the Colleone Monument in Venice and so the job of designing, casting and erecting the bronze monument fell to the Florentine 'engineer.'

In the preface to his *De Divina Proportione* (1497) Luca Pacioli, a mathematician who had been invited to Milan by Ludovico Sforza, noted that the bronze horse would measure twelve 'bracci' (about 56 feet) from the hoof to the top of Francesco's head, and would

weigh nearly seventy tons. Although the project was technically feasible, Ludovico's hope of seeing his father immortalized was dashed when war expenses bit into the funds. Leonardo received no money for his efforts and the clay model of the statue crumbled under the target practice of French archers in 1500.

In 1485 Leonardo produced his first designs for the construction of a flying machine. In Manuscript B, folio 89 recto, he recommends that the test flight, for safety's sake, be carried out over water. In the same year Leonardo watched the eclipse of the sun and devised a method of observing these events without injuring the eyes (Manuscript Trivulziana folio 6 recto). In April he was asked by Ludovico Sforza to paint a Madonna for presentation to Matthias Corvinus, King of Hungary, if we assume that it was Leonardo who was the 'unsurpassed painter' mentioned in a letter to Malfeo di Treviglio, Milan's ambassador in Buda.

Between 1487 and 1488 Leonardo was engaged in constructing a model for the 'triburio,' the central cupola planned for the dome of Milan Cathedral. Aided

by carpenter Bernardo Maggi da Abbiata, Leonardo submitted the model with a letter to the works department, in which he compares the building in need of repairs to a sick body, and the architect to a doctor. In addition to his architectural plans, Leonardo proved equally adept at planning masques and devising stage machines for court occasions. For the wedding of Gian Galleazo Sforza and Isabella of Aragon scheduled for early 1489, Leonardo devised a portico covered in greenery to be erected in the gardens of the Castello Sforzesco. The festivities were halted when the bride's mother died, but the marriage finally took place in 1490 and was celebrated by the Leonardo-designed 'Masque of the Paradiso.' In the hall of the ducal palace a mountain was constructed and crowned by a giant egg. A series of characters representing mankind sang the praises of the Sforza family; the egg revolved and opened to reveal the seven planets and twelve signs of the Zodiac personified, which were followed by the Graces, the Virtues, Nymphs, Mercury, Jupiter and Apollo.

A series of planned marriages which served predominantly to cement

Milan's political alliances culminated in Ludovico Sforza's marriage in 1491 to Beatrice d'Este, the sister of aesthete Isabella d'Este, who had herself married into the Gonzaga family who ruled Mantua. To celebrate the marriage Leonardo staged a pageant sponsored by Galeazzo di Sanseverino, who was Ludovico Sforza's son-in-law and a captain in the Milanese army.

It seems that Ludovico found favor with Leonardo for this type of work. What projects the artist probably thought were of greater interest, such as his schemes for underground sewerage systems, running water supplies and a clean-air project for Milan, the Duke shrugged off and, furthermore, he failed at times to pay Leonardo the sums due on other commissions.

At this time rumors were being circulated that Leonardo was an alchemist and, worse, a heretic for dissecting bodies. Had Leonardo not correctly challenged Galenus on the number of vertebrae in the human body and the number of chambers in the heart – knowledge acquired with Ludovico's consent from his dissections at Milan hospital – such rumors would not have occurred. They were, however,

CAROLVS VIII GAL·REX

LEFT: In 1500 Milan fell to French forces representing King Charles VIII. Although Leonardo was offered French patronage he returned to Florence.

to Milan and the possibility of a French invasion became probable.

To counter these threats, Ludovico offered his support to Charles VIII of France in his claim to take control of Naples from the Spanish ruler Ferrante of Aragon. In the midst of these political intrigues, fueled further by the rumors that he had poisoned his nephew Gian Galeazzo, Ludovico continued undaunted, and commissioned decorations for the Sala delle Asse at the Castello and for his favorite monastery in Milan, the Dominican Santa Maria della Grazie. This latter was Leonardo's famous painting of the *Last Supper*, for which Ludovico paid him 2000 ducats.

There is a further irony linked to this, one of the most famous of all paintings: the New Year of 1497 saw the pregnant Beatrice d'Este celebrating by dancing and drinking. The next day she miscarried and was dead. For many superstitious Milanese, Beatrice's death and the *Last Supper* were linked: in the early stages of development, Leonardo's fresco had accompanied a crucifixion by Montorfano, with the donor portraits of Ludovico, Beatrice and their two children. When this painting was painted over, Beatrice's death was seen as a portent of evil things to come.

Despite his wife's death and the consecration of the *Last Supper* to her memory, Ludovico lost no time in taking Lucrezia Crivelli, one of Beatrice's attendants, as his mistress.

The relationship between Ludovico and Leonardo, however, was more strained: there were several quarrels, probably about the casting of the equestrian statue and over money owed to Leonardo. After two years without payment, in March 1498 Ludovico paid Leonardo all that he owed him and added the gift of a vineyard, probably in the hope that his military engineer would not leave Milan. As a member of the court, Leonardo could have found

aggravated by rumors once again of Leonardo's homosexuality. In July 1491 Leonardo took the ten-year-old Gian Giacomo Caprotti do Orene, nicknamed Salai, or 'little devil,' into his household as a servant and occasional model, since according to Vasari, Salai was a rather beautiful boy. He was also well nicknamed: no sooner had Leonardo engaged him than Salai stole his money. Despite Salai being a thief, obstinate, greedy and a liar, Leonardo also probably detected the makings of an artist and Salai was destined to stay with his master until Leonardo died.

What the effect these rumors had on Leonardo we can only speculate. More important to his work was the effect of Il Moro's marriage. It seems that his wife, Beatrice d'Este, was not pleased that Leonardo had painted the portrait of her husband's mistress, Cecilia Galleani. Beatrice shrewdly contrived to rid the court of Cecilia by arranging a marriage for her. At the same time, she

gave Leonardo a final deadline for the completion of the equestrian statue. Although planned as a bronze, the final model was carried out in clay and unveiled at the wedding of Ludovico Sforza's niece, Maria Bianca, to the Holy Roman Emperor, Maximillian I. Once again this won a political alliance rather than a love match: the bankrupt emperor received 400,000 ducats in exchange for officially investing Ludovico as Duke of Milan. Although now with a powerful, albeit expensive, ally Ludovico found that he needed all the weapons he could lay hands on. His beloved equestrian monument was destined to remain a clay model while the metal originally assigned for its casting was requisitioned for armaments. The French and Italian cities that had designs on Milan were now irked further by Ludovico's claim to the dukedom. The King of Naples, with the help of Beatrice's sister Isabella d'Este in Mantua, challenged Ludovico's right

RIGHT: Isabella d'Este (1474-1539), Marchioness of Mantua, was drawn by Leonardo in 1500, when he stopped in Mantua on his way back to Florence in 1500. The drawing survives in a battered state (page 102), but in spite of Isabella's pressure on him to complete the painted portrait from it, or to send her other works, Leonardo seems not to have produced anything for her. This portrait, attributed to Titian, was made in 1534.

his life in danger. By September 1498, Ludovico 'Il Moro' Sforza was no longer Duke of Milan. An alliance had been formed between France and Venice. Venice had lost parts of her eastern empire to the Turks during sixteen years of war (1463-79) and was now looking to acquiring mainland territory. In spite of Il Moro's alliance with the Emperor Maximillian, he could never overthrow the combined forces of France and Venice. Hoping to spare Milan (and save his dukedom), he invited the French king, now Louis XII, to Italy.

When the French under Trivulzio entered Milan on 28 September, through the city gates opened by Ludovico's officers, Leonardo left with Luca Pacioli to stay with the Melzi family at the Villa d'Adda at Vaprio, and only returned to Milan when it appeared that war was unlikely.

On his return to the city, Leonardo met the French King and his aide, Cesare Borgia, the son of Pope Alexander VI. Borgia offered Leonardo the post of military engineer. Leonardo turned down this offer and was on his way to Mantua and Isabella d'Este: Milan it appears, was not altogether secured. On 5 February 1500, Ludovico, backed by a Swiss mercenary army, re-entered Milan. When the ensuing battle went against him, he tried to escape disguised as a monk but was taken prisoner to Loches, where he was to remain a prisoner until his death ten years later.

By this time Leonardo had left Mantua (having only completed a preliminary sketch for a portrait of Isabella) and by March 1500 he was in Venice.

Venice, Florence and Romagna, 1500-1506

After leaving Milan when the triumphant French entered the city, Leonardo stopped off at Venice en route to Florence. The government of the Serenissima, already hit hard by the battle against the Turks at Lepanto in August 1499 and concerned that the Turks would now make an attack on Venice by land, took the opportunity of seeking Leonardo's advice. A fragment of a draft letter in Codex Atlanticus (234 verso) to the governing council of the city details Leonardo's travels through the areas under threat from the Turks (the Isonzo Valley in the Friuli) and outlines his scheme to flood the area as a defensive measure. But by Easter 1500 Leonardo was back in Florence. During his eighteen-year absence the Medici had been banished from the city. Charles VIII's invasion of Italy to claim the Kingdom of Naples precipitated the overthrow of the Medici in 1494 and reintroduced a Republic under the leadership of the stern – some would say fanatic – Dominican prior Girolamo Savonarola who was later to be ousted and burnt at the stake.

Leonardo's father was now a procurator of the Servite monastery of Annunziata where the monks had

RIGHT: Girolamo Savonarola was called to Florence in 1490 by Lorenzo de' Medici and soon became the city's most popular preacher. After the fall from power in 1494 of Lorenzo's son Piero, Savonarola exerted powerful political influence. His support of a limited democracy modeled on the Venetian Council of 3000, ensured him wider popular support for a while. His denunciation of worldliness and corruption in the church contributed to this popular support but also to his excommunication by the Pope in 1498, which in turn led to his trial and execution. The system of government survived, however, until 1512, and decoration for the Council's chamber provided commissions for both Leonardo (pages 104-09) and Michelangelo.

FAR RIGHT: Cesare Borgia (1476-1507), son of Pope Alexander VI, set out to reconquer, by any means necessary, former dependencies of the Papal States on the Adriatic coast. Although noted for his brutality, Cesare was a brilliant soldier and loyal patron of Leonardo, whom he employed as his architect and engineer in the first years of the sixteenth century.

commissioned Filippino Lippi to complete two paintings for the high alter of their church. Probably because his father was the procurator, the commission was transferred to Leonardo. (Vasari, however, tells us that Lippi voluntarily gave up the commission when Leonardo expressed an interest in it.) In September Leonardo was hard at work, but not, it seems, on the altarpiece. He did in fact complete a first cartoon of the Virgin and Child with St Anne (now lost) and the *Madonna of the Yarnwinder* (page 110) for Florimund Robertet, secretary of state to Louis XII. It seems that Leonardo spent much time on mathematical problems.

On 12 May 1502 Leonardo was asked to appraise four jewelled vases that had once belonged to Lorenzo de' Medici and that were now being offered for sale to Isabella d'Este. By the end of the month, Leonardo was employed by Cesare Borgia as architect and chief engineer and as such he studied the area around Piombino for possible ways of reclaiming swamp land.

Cesare Borgia shared Ludovico Sforza's desire to rule all Italy. His father Pope Alexander VI had made Cesare the Marshal of the Papal Troops and appointed him Duke of Romagna, thereby ousting the legitimate rulers of the area in the name of the Catholic Church. Florence was subdued by the powerful neighbor through a treaty naming Cesare as 'Condottiere' of the Republic. His lively intellect, now coupled with a less attractive facet to his character, his driving ambition, made him capable of murder. Indeed Cesare retained in his service a personal assassin, one Grifonetto, who carried out executions on Cesare's behalf. Leonardo travelled everywhere with Cesare on his campaign missions through Emilia Romagna and the Marches and produced maps and surveys for his employer. Leonardo's method for drawing maps was first to chart the river systems and then to pilot the locations of towns. Lastly he would insert the mountains to indicate the watershed. This procedure resulted in accurate maps suggestive of the nature of the terrain.

At the same time Leonardo was exploring areas of personal interest: plant life, fossils and the movement of water. While studying the watershed around the area of Chiana and the region of the upper Arno, Leonardo searched for shells to find out if the area had at one time been submerged by the sea.

During this period Leonardo met Niccolò Machiavelli, the ambassador of the Florentine Treasury and the first writer to develop the theory and program of political realism. As such, Machiavelli admired Cesare Borgia's exploits in Emilia Romagna since the Duke at least imposed some order and justice in an area where different regions were held as papal fiefs and whose governments were often little more than lawless despotisms. In his book *The Prince* Machiavelli named his ideal statesman Valentino, after Cesare Borgia, Duke of Valentinois 'by the Grace of Louis XII.'

On the death of his father, Pope

LEFT: This rather fanciful representation of the 'accidental' poisoning of Pope Alexander VI and his son Cesare Borgia, reflects the uncertainty of the times in which Leonardo lived and worked.

RIGHT: Niccolò Machiavelli (1469-1527) is remembered today for *The Prince*, an uncompromising promotion of political subterfuge, a study informed by his own varied political fortunes. As secretary of the Grand Council of Florence, Machiavelli was signatory to Leonardo's contract for the *Battle of Anghiari* and supplied details to Leonardo about the battle to assist with the painting.

According to Vasari, Leonardo also painted the *Mona Lisa* here (page 131), reputedly a portrait of the wife of Francesco Giacondo which remained unfinished for some years.

The contract for the cartoon for the *Battle of Anghiari* stipulated that Leonardo was to receive 15 florins per month beginning on 20 April 1504, but if the cartoon was unfinished by February 1505, all monies paid to him would have to be returned and he would, furthermore, forfeit the cartoon to the Signoria. Even though the deadline was met and Leonardo started work on the painting proper, nothing, or virtually nothing, remains of the *Battle of Anghiari* save for a detailed record of the project and later artists' copies. The pigments Leonardo used – oil on a type of stucco base – were from a formula he had found through reading Pliny and required heating by torches to encourage them to dry. Because technique was not a success the painting was never completed, the cartoon subsequently vanished and copies by later artists (pages 105 and 107) show only the central portion of the original composition.

The failure of the *Battle of Anghiari* and the plans to divert the Arno (the only result of which was the creation of a new area of swampland which led to an outbreak of malaria in 1504 in which many Florentines died) did not endear Leonardo to Soderini. His association with Cesare Borgia probably didn't help and matters were probably exacerbated by his reputation as homosexual. As the treasury was being depleted by war, payments to Leonardo ceased.

In the spring of 1506, at the request of Charles d'Amboise, Lord of Charmont-sur-Loire and Governor of the city in the name of Louis XII, Leonardo was back in Milan. When he returned to Florence in the fall of 1507, it was to do legal battle with his brothers over an uncle's will and to settle with the Friars

Alexander VI, Cesare Borgia returned to Rome. In the meantime, Leonardo returned to Florence. Ironically, had Cesare laid siege to Tuscany, Florence might well have fallen precisely because of the skill of Leonardo's work in map-making, strategic and engineering plans for Cesare. One of his plans was for blocking the River Arno, effectively cutting off the city in order to starve it into submission.

Back in Florence Leonardo was set to work as Chief Military Engineer in the war against Pisa. In 1406 Pisa had been sold to the Florentines, but in 1494, under the protection of Charles VIII of France, the city had renounced its subordination and skilfully defended its independence. In 1503 the Republic of Florence embarked on a new campaign against Pisa. Between 24 and 26 July Leonardo was in the Florentine camp where plans were being laid to divert the Arno and cut off Pisa from the sea, a plan supported by Machiavelli. The huge numbers of men needed for the construction of a canal system and the

overall cost of the scheme meant that the project was abandoned in October 1504. It would be five years before Pisa finally succumbed to Florentine domination once more.

In October 1503 Leonardo rejoined the Guild of St Luke in Florence where he was listed by profession, not as an engineer but as 'City Painter.' On 18 October the mayor of Florence, Piero Soderini, ordered that a large fresco be painted in the Palazzo Signoria's Grand Council Hall, the Sala del Gran Consiglio, and both Leonardo and Michelangelo were called upon to produce designs. Michelangelo's subject was the Battle of Cascina, an episode in the wars between Pisa and Florence when bathing Florentine soldiers were surprised by the enemy and dashed for their weapons left on the river bank. Leonardo's choice of theme was the 1440 triumph of Florence over the Milanese mercenaries at the Battle of Anghiari. Work on the cartoon for the Battle of Anghiari was carried out in the Sala del Papa near Santa Maria Novella.

LEFT: Pope Julius II (1503-13), although a great wager of war, was also of singular importance as a patron of the arts. Although Leonardo did not apparently enjoy his patronage, it was Julius II who commissioned the Sistine ceiling from Michelangelo.

pressure on Venice mounted, the Republic ceded some of the lands formerly held by the Borgias. Venice refused to give up other important areas, and although backed by Swiss and Romagna mercenaries, Venice was swiftly relieved of Trieste, Gorizia, Pordenone, Fiume and some territory in Hungary. At this point Julius and Maximillian successfully mustered anti-Venetian sentiments and the result was the famous League of Cambrai of December 1508 which allied all the major western powers against Venice.

The Venetians have boasted of their powers to spend 36 millions of gold in ten years in the war with the Empire, the Church and the Kings of Spain and France at 300,000 ducats a month. (Leonardo in Codex Ambrosiana 218r)

In a reversal of policy where he now saw Louis XII as the great enemy, Julius resolved to rid Italy of the French through a coalition – the so-called Holy League of 1511 – which allied the Pope, Spain and Venice with additional resources from the English and Swiss. In 1512 Massimiliano Sforza (son of Ludovico) entered Milan with the Emperor, the Pope and the Venetians and finally drove out the French.

Leonardo thus found himself in rather a tricky position: he would obviously not be popular with Massimiliano since he had fled Milan and Ludovico at the first sign of trouble.

In September 1512, a bloodless revolution in Florence returned Lorenzo 'Il Magnifico' de' Medici as head of state. The following March, Giovanni de' Medici was hailed as Pope Leo X. Giuliano de' Medici, brother of the Pope was named Gonfaloniere and a Prince of Florence and had the strength of both the papal forces and the armies of Spain behind him.

On 24 September 1513 Leonardo and his companions Salai and Francesco Melzi were on their way to Rome.

of San Francesco over the disputed commission for the *Madonna of the Rocks*. Once all litigation was complete, Leonardo returned to the French court at Milan, where he remained until 1512.

The Second Period in Milan, 1506-13

Leonardo left Florence in May 1506 with the *Battle of Anghiari* unfinished, promising the Signoria that he would return within three months. In August the French Chancellor at Milan, Geoffroy Charles, contacted Florence with the announcement that Charles d'Amboise wished to extend Leonardo's stay in Milan.

Once again Leonardo was at work on a large-scale monument, this time for the Milanese nobleman Gian Giacomo Trivulzio. Trivulzio had made financial provision for a monumental tomb to be erected in the church of San Nazarro. This commission, it would seem, offered Leonardo some compensation for the destruction of his masterpiece-

never-to-be, the equestrian monument to Francesco Sforza. But like the Sforza monument, the Trivulzio monument, although carefully planned and calculated, was never completed. This time in Milan, however, did see an incredible increase in Leonardo's output of botanical studies.

The Trivulzio monument was never completed, most likely because the duchy of Milan was preparing itself against possible hostilities on its eastern borders. When Pope Alexander VI died in 1503 and was succeeded by Julius II (after an interim papacy of the Piccolomino Pius II), Cesare Borgia found himself cut off from the papal treasury and opposed to Julius, an old adversary of the Borgias. As Cesare's Romagna dukedom fell apart, Venice was on hand to pick up the pieces. Since the lands now claimed by Venice technically belonged to the papacy, Pope Julius, in preparation to smite Venice, entered into an alliance with Emperor Maximillian and Louis XII. As

ject before he had even started. While Michelangelo was viewed as being a master of both painting and sculpture, Leonardo was seen as an able engineer, and in Rome, now the center of artistic production in Italy, the powers and patrons in the city were interested less in intellectual matters and more in immortalizing themselves in displays of opulence and beauty.

The year 1515 would prove to be another turning point for Leonardo, as it would be for most of Italy. The first day of the year brought the news of the death of Leonardo's former patron Louis XII of France. Succeeding him, François I set out to regain the Duchy of Milan for France, where the son of Massimiliano Sforza had ruled since 1512, supported by Swiss infantrymen.

Allied with the Venetians, François I quickly took control of Genoa and was victorious on the field in Lombardy against the anti-French League forces which included Emperor Maximillian, Ferdinand of Spain, the Swiss Cantons, Massimiliano Sforza and, from July 1515, Pope Leo X as well. In September, against cavalry, artillery and some 20,000 Swiss pikemen, François won the Battle of Melegnano (Marignano).

On 14 December 1515 François and Pope Leo held secret discussions in Bologna, and according to statements in the Vatican archives which show that he received 33 ducats for expense, Leonardo was in the retinue. It was in Bologna that he was probably first introduced to the French king (Leonardo had already been familiar with him through the earlier French court at Milan and his work for Charles d'Amboise). François offered Leonardo a pension and a small château at Cloux near Amboise on the Loire river. With Giuliano de Medici's death in 1516, Leonardo lost his patron and faced with disdain the prospect of working for Leo X, Leonardo entered France with the title 'Foremost Painter and Engineer

Rome and Amboise, 1513-19

Once in Rome, Leonardo was lodged in the Belvedere, the summer palace at the top of the Vatican hills. Also in Rome were Donato Bramante (1444-1514), Raphael (1483-1520) and Michelangelo (1475-1564), artists who seemed to be preferred since commissions for Leonardo from the Pope were few. Leonardo was, however, given a dispensation allowing him to continue his studies in anatomy which involved dissections of cadavers, a practice normally forbidden by papal decree, but possibly allowed since the church believed Leonardo was searching for the seat of the soul. Nevertheless, his letters to 'Il Magnifico' show that Leonardo's studies were being misinterpreted: rumors were being spread by one Maestro Giorgio, a German

employed by Leonardo, that he was a sorcerer, rumors which ultimately convinced the Pope to ban all further dissections.

Of the commissions he did receive, one which interested Leonardo greatly was the project for draining the Pontine Marshes around Rome. By transforming the Afonte river into a controlled canal system, the marshes could be drained and reclaimed allowing for more urgently needed building land.

When Pope Leo finally awarded Leonardo a commission for a minor painting, the Pope noted that he never expected the work to be finished. According to Vasari, when Pope Leo learnt that Leonardo was experimenting with a varnish, he is said to have commented that Leonardo would never get any painting done because he was thinking about the end of the pro-

LEFT: This chalk drawing of an old man is traditionally accepted as a self-portrait of Leonardo around 1516.

RIGHT: Francis I, King of France (1515-47), was only 22 when he invited Leonardo to France as painter to the King.

BELOW: This vision of Leonardo dying in the arms of Francis I, by François Menageot, is in the Musée de l'Hôtel de Ville d'Amboise. Although the scene probably has no basis in fact, the story dates from the sixteenth century, and reflects Leonardo's great status by the time of his death.

and Architect to the King of France and Technician of the State of France.' Once again Leonardo was a celebrity, adored by the French court whose king visited him in his studio for discussions.

At the age of 65, no longer able to paint because of crippling rheumatism and the effects of a stroke, Leonardo continued to design pageants, canal systems and even royal residences. In September 1517, for the celebrations held by Marguerite d'Angoulême at Argenton, he devised a mechanical lion, which when struck on the chest, opened to reveal a display of French lilies, and in May 1518 staged a mock battle at Amboise to celebrate the marriage of Lorenzo de' Medici (Leo X's nephew) to Madelaine de la Tour d'Auvergne (niece of François I).

Now in declining health and after a hard winter, on 23 April 1519 Leonardo dictated his last will and testament to a royal notary at Amboise. To Francesco Melzi, Leonardo bequeathed his books, instruments and the remaining portion

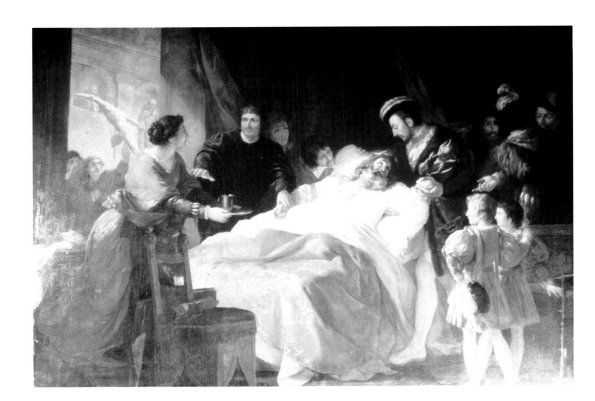

of his pension; to his servant Batista he left half his vineyard outside Milan; to

the faithful Salai he left the remaining part of the vineyard; and to the poor of Saint Lazarre of Amboise he left 70 soldi.

Leonardo da Vinci died on 2 May 1519 and was buried the following August in the monastery of Saint Florentine in Amboise. But this would not be his final resting place: his mortal remains were scattered during the Wars of Religion.

One story has it that Leonardo died in the arms of his patron François I. Although almost certainly groundless, this has contributed to the tangled webb of myth and legend that has been spun over the years around the few facts known of Leonardo's life. Because this myth-building began in Leonardo's lifetime, the true story of Leonardo's life is probably lost for all time, and it is thus ill-advised to discuss his art with reference to his supposed psychological makeup, or, indeed, to divine his personality from his paintings and drawings.

The Paintings and Sculpture

AILEEN REID

IT comes as some surprise to many to learn that only a handful of paintings are attributed to the author of the world's most famous work of art. That Leonardo painted so few paintings (though, of course, only a proportion survive) may at first seem odd. It is not as though he was occupied on major sculptural or architectural works, or even on large-scale fresco cycles, as were his most famous contemporaries, Michelangelo and Raphael. Perhaps then he was supervising military or aquatic engineering projects? After all, he claimed skill in these fields in his letter of introduction to Ludovico Sforza in 1481, and there are hundreds of drawings (pages 148-169) to support this. Yet drawings are all most of these schemes were, and many of them could only ever have been drawings. The existence of such a large number of Leonardo's drawings and notes in part explains the small number of paintings. It is fair to say that pictorial questions were only a part of the whole system of enquiry that occupied Leonardo's mind, and many of these questions could be resolved more speedily in drawings. And even specifically in painting, much of what interested Leonardo – such as composition or tonal relations – was resolved when the underpainting had been completed. This helps explain the relatively high proportion of surviving paintings in this state: the *Adoration of the Magi* (page 56), *St Jerome* (page 68) and the *Virgin and Child with St Anne and St John the Baptist* (page 116).

The First Florentine Period, 1452-82

Although the earliest surviving paintings convincingly attributed to Leonardo date from the early 1470s, it is reasonable to assume he may have began painting before he arrived in Florence and was apprenticed to Verrocchio. Leonardo himself was infuriat-

ingly reticent about his life, so that for biographical information we have to rely on the testimony of his pupils, contemporaries such as the Anonimo Gaddiano, or near-contemporaries such as Giorgio Vasari, a painter who published the first edition of his *Lives of the Artists* in 1555. Vasari is a tantalizing informant, however, as although he provides us with a far more detailed account of the lives of Renaissance artists than any other contemporary commentator, where his information can be compared with documented facts, he is not always accurate. Thus any insubstantiated fact from Vasari must be regarded with a degree of scepticism. Into this category comes the story of Leonardo painting a shield for his father. Piero da Vinci was asked by one of his employees in Vinci to have painted for him in Florence a shield which he had made himself from the wood of a fig tree. Piero took it to Leonardo in Florence who, after some thought, decided he would paint the shield to produce an effect on the viewer analogous to the effect of seeing the Medusa's head. To achieve this he collected together lizards, locusts, bats, butterflies, crickets and snakes which he composed into a vile and terrifying creature which 'emitted a poisonous breath and turned the air to fire.' This monster he depicted emerging from the cleft of a rock, belching forth fire, smoke, and venom. When his father came to collect the shield, Leonardo set it up illuminated in an otherwise dark room, and so terrifying was the effect that his father shied back in horror from it when he first saw it. When Piero had recovered his composure, he was so impressed that he quietly bought his employee another painted shield, and sold his son's creation to some merchants for 100 ducats. Later the same merchants sold the shield to the Duke of Milan for 300 ducats.

Although most of this story must be

apocryphal, it strikes an essentially authentic note because it demonstrates Leonardo's early mastery of that skill essential to the High Renaissance artist, exact truth to nature or the 'seen' world. And this would certainly have been a quality he sought consciously. In 1490 he expressed the view that art from the fall of the Romans up to Giotto (c. 1266-1337) was in decline and that a similar decline occurred in the century or so between Giotto and Masaccio (1401-c. 1428). What distinguished Giotto and Masaccio was simply their obedience to nature:

Masaccio showed with perfect works how those who take for their guide anything other than nature – mistress of the masters – exhaust themselves in vain.

But the story of the shield also demonstrates Leonardo's love of the first-hand study of creatures of all kinds, of fantastic beasts, and, though this can only be inferred, of the snaking, intertwining forms which feature time and again in his paintings and drawings (pages 100, 137, 139 and 223).

A more reliable source for information about Leonardo's early work is the inventory he himself made in 1482. In it he apparently attempts a succinct but comprehensive record of his work up to that time:

Many flowers copied from nature; a head, full face with curly hair; certain St Jeromes; measurements of a figure; designs of furnaces; a head of the Duke; many designs of busts; 4 drawings for the picture of the Holy Angel; a little narrative of Girolamo da Fegline; a head of Christ done in pen; 8 St Sebastians; many compositions of angels; a chalcedony; a head in profile with beautiful hair-style; certain forms in perspective; certain gadgets for ships; a head portrayed from Atalante, who raises his face; the head of Girolamo da Fegline; the head of Gian Francesco Boso; many necks of old women; many heads of old men; many complete

ABOVE: Andrea del Verrocchio (c. 1435-88)
Baptism of Christ, c. 1473-78, oil on wood,
69⅝×59½ inches (177×151 cm), Galleria degli
Uffizi, Florence.

ABOVE: *Study of Drapery for the Legs of a Seated Figure*, c. 1473, brush on linen, heightened with white, 10⅜×9 inches (26.3×22.9 cm). Musée du Louvre, Paris. This drawing is similar to the legs of the Virgin in the *Annunciation* (page 38), but is not a direct study for the painting.

LEFT: This detail of an angel's head from Verrocchio's *Baptism of Christ* (page 35) is one of Leonardo's earliest painted works.

nudes; many arms, legs, feet and postures; a Madonna finished; another almost finished, which is in profile; the head of Our Lady who ascends to heaven; the head of an old man with an enormous chin; a head of a gypsy; a head wearing a hat; a narrative of the Passion made in relief; a head of a young girl with plaited tresses; a head with a headdress.

The painting which is traditionally accepted as Leonardo's earliest surviving painted work is the left-hand angel

in Verrocchio's *Baptism of Christ* (Uffizi, Florence; pages 35 and 36), painted for the monastery of San Salvi. Vasari, in his life of Verrocchio, records Leonardo's assistance in the painting and even during Leonardo's lifetime it was claimed as a work of his. The scene portrayed is that of Christ's baptism by John the Baptist, as related near the beginning of all the Gospels. According to the Gospels, as Christ arose from the waters of the River Jordan, God appeared in the form of a dove from the

ABOVE: *Annunciation*, c. 1473, oil on wood panel, 38⅜×85½ inches (98×217 cm), Galleria degli Uffizi, Florence.

heavens and announced 'This is my Beloved Son, with whom I am well pleased.' Verrocchio, like many painters before him, including Piero della Francesca (National Gallery, London), depicts the baptism not as one of immersion as implied by the Gospels, but shows Christ's feet barely covered by the river and St John baptizing Him from a shallow vessel. The painter is thus able to elide the moment of baptism with the appearance of the dove. The angels at the left, one of whom holds a towel for Christ's use after the baptism, are a further departure from scriptural authority but were by the 1470s a longstanding convention, and found in numerous representations of the baptism.

Even without documentary evidence, a comparison of the two angels in the *Baptism* would immediately suggest they were by different hands. In the cheek, nose and eyes of the left-hand figure color and tone shade with a melting delicacy when compared with the harsh modelling of face and hands in the other angel, yet this exploration of the subtle nuances of surfaces establishes far more surely the three-dimensional solidity and spatial presence of Leonardo's figure. In the way we read the painting this angel's solid location in space is important, as the positioning of his right leg parallel to an imaginary orthogonal in the painting serves to lead our eye, in a manner recommended by Alberti, to the focus of the

picture, the figure of Christ. But Leonardo's contribution to the *Baptism* is almost certainly not confined to the angel. A comparison of the background vision of mountains and lakes, with their atmospherically rendered aerial perspective, and the famous Arno drawing of 1473 (page 15), leaves little doubt that Leonardo was also the author of this background. This is especially evident when compared with other natural features in the painting which are clearly not by Leonardo, such as the palm tree or the rocks at the left, which are stiff and conventionalized and wholly unremarkable for the late fifteenth century.

Dating of this painting has varied from around 1470 to around 1476. The

principal basis for asserting that it is earlier than, say, the Munich *Madonna and Child with a Vase of Flowers* (page 49), or even the Uffizi *Annunciation* (above), is that Leonardo only painted part of it and that these other paintings are all his own work. In itself this argument is insufficient to establish the *Baptism* as earlier than these other works as Leonardo, although he completed his apprenticeship to Verrocchio in 1472, continued to live in his former master's house until 1476, and could certainly have collaborated on a major painted commission such as this. Professor Kemp has argued convincingly (1981) that the way the angel is painted has more in common with Leonardo's more mature style than

the *Annunciation*, the portrait of *Ginevra de' Benci* or the Munich Madonna, so it is discussed here first without any intention to ascribe it a definitive date in Leonardo's oeuvre.

Whereas Leonardo's part in the *Baptism of Christ* has been accepted since 1510, the *Annunciation* was only attributed to him in 1869. It came from the monastery of San Bartolomeo at Monteolivieto near Florence and was traditionally attributed to Domenico Ghirlandaio (1449-94), probably another pupil of Verrocchio and later master to Michelangelo. Another theory had it that the painting was begun by Ghirlandaio and completed by Leonardo, although this is contradicted (not conclusively; it could have been made *from*

LEFT: *Study of a Sleeve, c. 1473*, pen and brown ink, 3¼×3⅝ inches (8.2×9.3 cm), Courtesy of the Governing Body, Christ Church, Oxford. This is almost certainly a study for the right sleeve of the angel in the *Annunciation*, (page 38).

BELOW: *Study of the Drapery of a Figure Kneeling to the Right*, c. 1473, Cabinet des Dessins, Musée du Louvre, Paris.

RIGHT: *Study of Drapery for a Seated Figure*, c. 1473, brush on linen, heightened with white, 10¼×7 inches (26×18 cm), Cabinet des Dessins, Musée du Louvre, Paris.

RIGHT: Andrea del Verrocchio (c. 1435-88) *Madonna and Child*, c. 1469, 42×30 inches (106.7×76.3 cm), oil on wood panel, National Gallery of Scotland, Edinburgh. This painting shows many of the characteristics of the 'Verrocchio style': the demure, downcast eyes of the Virgin, the delicate yet precise local color, and the general air of sweet calm. These were qualities much emulated by Verrocchio's pupils such as Perugino (page 11) and Lorenzo di Credi (pages 10 and 51), but rarely apparent in Leonardo's paintings. The precisely worked-out perspective of the architecture, however, reveals that Leonardo's studies, such as that for the *Adoration of the Magi* (page 63), were certainly not unprecedented.

not *for* the painting) by the existence of a drawing, which is certainly by Leonardo, for the right sleeve of the angel, complete with its fluttering ribbon (page 40, above). Two other Leonardo drawings relate to this painting, although each differs in too many small details to be considered as direct studies for it. Once is a finished drawing of a lily (symbol of purity; page 219), such as is held by the archangel, the other a study of drapery akin to that worn by the Virgin (page 37). This is an example of a type of finished drawing that Leonardo seems to have made throughout his career and which Vasari describes as having been taken from clay models draped in plaster-soaked cloth (pages 40 and 41). It perhaps accounts for the rather stiff and, appropriately, sculptural quality of the draperies, which resemble those of the Leonardo angel in the *Annunciation* which may, therefore, date from around the same time.

The scene is the Annunciation to the Virgin by the angel Gabriel described in Luke I, 26-38. The figures are set in the enclosed courtyard garden (for *hortus conclusis*, another symbol of virginity) of a villa, vaguely Florentine in character. Certain features seem to derive from the work of Verrocchio, including the decoration of the lectern's base which resembles the decoration of Verrocchio's Medici tomb in San Lorenzo, Florence, or the rigidly correct perspective of the building and pavement which is also found in a Verrochio *Madonna and Child* (page 43) of around 1468. (Although it should be pointed out that this painting has occasionally been attributed to Domenico Ghirlandaio and even, once, to Leonardo himself.) The rigidity of the perspectival scheme and the way the figures relate to it and to each other account for a great deal of the sense of awkwardness and immaturity there is in the painting. The angel is portrayed in a very con-

ventional pose, parallel to the picture plane which is strongly affirmed by the enclosure wall. The strongly marked perspective serves only to suggest a second axis intersecting this plane, rather than a unified three-dimensionality, so that the figure of the Virgin, the painting's only spatially convincing element (and not a theoretical construction, such as the lectern base), sits uneasily in the picture as a whole. This disunity may also derive partly from the picture having been painted over a number of years, just as the *Baptism* owes its lack of cohesion to its varied authors.

Nonetheless, these flaws are compensated for by qualities which are already Leonardesque, such as the landscape background, which, with its misty but towering mountains and lake or sea stretching into infinity, looks backward to the *Baptism* and the Arno drawing and forward to the *Madonna of the Rocks* (page 71), the *Virgin and Child with St Anne* (page 120), and the *Mona Lisa* (page 131), among others. There is also a sense of vibrancy and movement in the swathe of flower-bedecked grass which looks forward to the vegetation in such works as the *Madonna of the Rocks* (page 71) and the *Leda* (page 136). This reflects not only Leonardo's botanical interests, as evinced by his drawings (pages 219-227), but also his sense of the underlying and unifying life forces present, which accounts for the contrast between Leonardo's representations of plants and flowers in his paintings and those in roughly contemporary works by other artists such as Botticelli's *Primavera* (Uffizi, Florence), where the flowers are decoratively strewn like botanical specimens on a green carpet. In order to see why this painting should not be dismissed as an unworthy forerunner to the *Madonna of the Rocks* et al, it is worth comparing it with another *Annunciation* (pages 44-5) once thought

to be by Leonardo. It was painted as a predella panel for an altarpiece in Pistoia Cathedral, painted by Verrocchio. The composition is certainly more coherent than the Uffizi *Annunciation*, with the figures more securely located in their surroundings, but there is something unrelievedly quattrocento about both the attitudes of the figures and the way they are painted. The Virgin is in an attitude of *humilitatio* or submission, the penultimate of five stages of spiritual and mental conditions applicable to the Virgin Annunciate laid out by Fra Roberto Caracciolo da Lecce in 1491 (after the *Annunciation* was painted, but probably typical of fifteenth-century teaching). *Humilitatio* corresponds to the moment when the Virgin, having accepted the words of the angel, kneels, declaring: 'Behold the handmaid of the Lord' (Luke I, 38). The Virgin in the Uffizi *Annunciation* is much more difficult to classify in such a scheme, but it is the lack of either volume or subtlety of modelling in the

Louvre figures which more surely gives the lie to the contention that this is Leonardo 'conscious of the need to pay a tribute to a tradition out of which he is emerging' (Pedretti, 1973); Leonardo did not feel that need with the *Baptism*, why should he feel it here? A more likely explanation is that the Louvre *Annunciation* is the work of Verrocchio's most faithful pupil, Lorenzo di Credi (1459-1537), whose work has a rather insubstantial, delicate sweetness and enamel-like colors more akin to the work of Filippino Lippi (c. 1457-1504), or even Botticelli, than Leonardo.

If the *Annunciation* now in the Uffizi can be dated from the evidence of its style, and from the style of the associated drawings, to around 1473, then it has been assumed that Leonardo must have begun work on the portrait of *Ginevra de' Benci* (page 46) shortly after this. This is because portraits of Florentine women were frequently commissioned on the occasion of marriage and Ginevra de' Benci was married to Luigi

di Bernardo Niccolini in January 1474. However, doubt has always surrounded this painting which has been known only since it was recorded in the collection of the Prince of Liechtenstein in 1733. This is not so much because Vasari describes Leonardo as painting a portrait of Ginevra in his second Florentine period (1500-1506), when the subject would have been in her forties, but because the painting is unusually accomplished when compared with the *Annunciation*. Moreover, recent research (Fletcher, 1989) has identified the device painted on the back of the panel as the personal device of Bernardo Bembo, Venetian ambassador to Florence in 1475-76 and 1478-80. Bembo's intense but platonic friendship with Ginevra has long been recognized and was celebrated at the time in poetry by Alessandro Braccesi and Cristoforo Landino (see page 12). This platonic quality is reinforced by the motto added to the device which reads 'Virtutem forma decorat' (beauty

adorns virtue). There is evidence linking Leonardo with Ginevra's brother Giovanni and, although there is no conclusive proof linking Leonardo and Bembo, Bembo sustained a friendship with Lorenzo de' Medici, one of Verrocchio's major patrons. It is thus not improbable that Bernardo would have commissioned a portrait of Ginevra from a talented young artist, in which case the painting could date from any time up to 1490.

Assessment of the painting is complicated by the fact that it has lost about a quarter of its height from the lower edge. This can be established conclusively by the cropping of the device on the back of the panel and by the existence of a beautiful silverpoint drawing (page 47) of hands which would fit well with the missing portion of painting. Although the hands with their well-defined curving fingers relate to a contemporary Verrocchiesque type exemplified by the sculpture of the *Lady with the Primroses* (page 141), they are closer

to those in the *Lady with an Ermine (Cecilia Gallerani)* (page 76) of around 1485, which, along with the maturity of the drawing, suggests a date later than 1474. But more compelling than any of these factors as an indication of the maturity of the artist when he painted this portrait is the strong but subtle characterization of the sitter. This subtlety can be demonstrated by the varying connotations that have been put on the directness of her gaze. Is this 'sternness' and 'coldness' (Friedenthal, 1960)? If so, is it symptomatic of Leonardo's supposed lack of sympathy for women (and by implication, his homosexuality, though of course this supposes the simplistic and usually mistaken equation of male homosexuality with misogyny)? Or, in that we know that Ginevra was an unusually well-educated woman and an accomplished poet, does this forthrightness express her independence of spirit in a society that was patriarchal, culturally as well as politically? Equally, the suggestion

ABOVE: *Portrait of Ginevra de' Benci*, c. 1476, oil on wood panel, 15¼×14½ inches (38.8×36.7 cm), National Gallery of Art Washington, Ailsa Mellon Bruce Fund.

RIGHT: *Study of a Woman's Hands*, c. 1476, silverpoint on pink prepared paper, 8½×6 inches (21.5×15 cm), Windsor Castle, Royal Library 12558. © 1991 Her Majesty The Queen. It has plausibly been suggested that this is a study for the hands of Ginevra de' Benci, from the lost part of the panel.

210.

RIGHT: *Madonna and Child with a Vase of Flowers*, c. 1475, oil on wood panel, 24½×18¾ inches (62×47.5 cm), Alte Pinakothek, Munich.

of remoteness or other-worldliness could refer to the platonic nature of her relationship with Bembo, particularly if he commissioned the portrait. The fact that all of these varied interpretations of this painting, and no doubt many others, are plausible, establishes this portrait as a worthy precedent for the *Mona Lisa* with her undeniable if, to late twentieth-century eyes, hackneyed aura of mystery.

Although the 1482 inventory mentions various portraits, no item has been successfully linked with the Ginevra portrait, and it seems to be the only surviving secular painting of the first Florentine period. Conversely, two Madonna and Child paintings of the period are mentioned in the inventory and are documented by surviving drawings of various types, as part of a group of five projects of the same subject. The *Madonna and Child with a Vase of Flowers* (right) is sometimes identified with the 'finished' Madonna of the 1482 inventory, but there is no consensus on whether it is by Leonardo. If it is by Leonardo there are such strong associations with what is understood by the Verrocchio style – the delicacy and restraint of the Virgin, with her downcast eyes (cf page 43 or the *Dreyfus Madonna*, page 50) and her calm, even static, pose – that it must have been painted when he was still strongly associated with his master and other pupils such as Lorenzo de Credi, to whose work this painting seems particularly close in the claustrophic sense of space. If the *Annunciation* gives an impression of two-dimensionality, then this painting, like Lorenzo di Credi's Uffizi *Annunciation*, with its curiously diverse perspective in the background, gives the impression of a *trompe l'oeil* with a confined space painted to convince us that it extends much further, such as in Palladio's Teatro Olimpico in Vicenza. Even the background of shimmering lakes and towering mountains of the *Madonna and Child with a Vase of Flowers*, which, with its attention to botanical variety, is the most individually Leonardesque feature, fails to dispel this impression.

One explanation for these incongruities could be that Leonardo began the painting but that it was finished by a fellow-pupil such as Lorenzo (in which case it probably is not the 'finished' Madonna of the inventory). Certainly, Leonardo throughout his life seems to have had difficulty finishing paintings, the reason for which I have already speculated on, and this fate seems to have befallen his earliest recorded independent commission. In January 1478 Leonardo received a first payment for an altarpiece in the Chapel of St Barnard in the Palazzo Vecchio in Florence. We may infer from the lack of further payments, from the existence of the 1485 altarpiece by Filippino Lippi and, not least, from the lack of any record of Leonardo's painting having been delivered, that he did not progress very far with it. Perhaps the *Adoration of the Shepherds* drawing, discussed below (page 57) was a study for it. Or perhaps it may be identified with one of the five Madonna projects from this period. One of these, for a Madonna and Child with St John, is known only from a single drawing but this is interesting for the foretaste it provides, in the subject and, specifically, in the way the infant St John begins to climb on the Virgin's knee towards the infant Christ, of a work of thirty years later (page 116). Quite a different type of drawing is the delicate silverpoint of a head of a woman (page 52) which is usually identified as a study for the *Madonna Litta* (page 53), and which may represent the 'Our Lady, almost finished, who is in profile,' this being the nearest to a profile pose of any of these early Madonnas. Technically the drawing compares with the drawing of hands, discussed above, and in terms of the artist's

ABOVE: School of Verrocchio *Madonna and Child with a Pomegranate*, c. 1470-75, oil on wood panel, 6⅛×5 inches (15.7×12.8 cm, National Gallery of Art, Washington, Samuel R Kress Collection.

BELOW: Lorenzo di Credi *Annunciation*, 1470s,
oil on wood, 34⅝×28 inches (88×71 cm),
Galleria degli Uffizi, Florence.

understanding of and ability to represent the psychological state of the Virgin it surely cannot date from before about 1480. Where the Ginevra portrait impresses by the variety of interpretations that can be put on her gaze, the drawing delicately but precisely connotes the relation of mother-love and veneration of the Virgin to the invisible Christ child. There is in the drawing and the Ginevra portrait, equally, a strength of characterization quite different from the *Madonna with a Vase of Flowers* and the delicacy of Verrocchio and his other pupils. All this strength is

lost in the painting, the *Madonna Litta*, which I believe is a copy of at least 10 years later. Not only is there none of the psychological subtlety of the drawing, but also the landscape is tame and lifeless compared with even the *Annunciation*, and the figures are neither anatomically plausible nor located solidly in space, even compared with the *Baptism of Christ*. However, there is a sense of *déjà vu* about the way the child is painted and the slick modelling of the Virgin's face and hands which suggests to me that in the 1490s a technically competent follower of Leonardo,

ABOVE: *Madonna and Child with a Cat*, c. 1478, pen and ink, 5³⁄₁₆×3¾ inches (13.2×9.5 cm), Courtesy of the Trustees of the British Museum, London.

ABOVE RIGHT: *Madonna and Child with a Cat*, c. 1478, pen, ink and wash, 5³⁄₁₆×3¾ inches (13.2×9.5 cm), Courtesy of the Trustees of the British Museum, London. These two drawings appear on either side of one sheet of paper. The righthand one appears to have been pressed through from the other side with a stylus, and then inked and washed in.

LEFT: *Benois Madonna*, c. 1478, oil on wood panel, 18⅞×12¼ inches (48×31 cm), Hermitage Museum, Leningrad.

familiar with his more mature style, copied one of his earlier works.

In order to see why the *Madonna Litta* fails to convince as a work by Leonardo himself (even, as has been suggested, as a work completed or overpainted by a follower), one need only compare it with either the *Benois Madonna* (left) or the drawings for a *Madonna and Child with a Cat* (above). The cat may refer to a story of a cat giving birth at the time of the Nativity or it may simply represent one of Leonardo's many zoological interests, and a further item in the interlocking composition of figures. What is so unusual is the wild interplay of lines drawn and redrawn in a frenzied search for the ideal form. So frenetic has been this activity that the artist has pressed the favored lines through to the back of the paper and begun again there, washing in the final form (above right). Professor Kemp (1981) sees the adoption of this much freer drawing style as the source of a 'watershed' in the development of Leonardo's artistic vision which first finds painted expression in the *Benois Madonna*, for which the *Madonna and Child with a Cat* drawings could be early studies. I would suggest that they are all expressions of the same rapidly developing vision and that the frantic drawing method is a symptom not a cause of this change of vision.

In the *Benois Madonna* we find what it is that Leonardo is searching for in the drawings. It is that sense of the figures having a true relationship to each other and in space, that is so lacking in the *Madonna and Child with a Vase of Flowers* and the *Madonna Litta*. The Child sits solidly on the Virgin's knee and she, in turn, sits solidly in space. This solidity is achieved not just by the convincing rendering of draperies and flesh, which we have already seen, but by the way the figures are unified as a solid mass by the single light source, so different from the diffuse and diffused light of the *Madonna and Child with a Vase of Flowers*.

But more than that is the sense we get of the artist painting not just across the figures but all round, that revelation of vision so clearly demonstrated in the drawings. Further evidence that this painting belongs to a new phase in Leonardo's art can be seen in the treatment of the Virgin's right leg as a diagonal lead in to the picture and support for the Christ Child who provides a perpendicular compositional counterthrust. Variations on this theme formed the basis of the compositional dynamism in many of Leonardo's later pictures (page 56 and 71) and it is especially close to the *Virgin and Child with St Anne* (page 120) of about thirty years later.

LEFT: *Adoration of the Magi*, 1481, oil on wood panel, 96⅞×95⅝ inches (246×243 cm), Galleria degli Uffizi, Florence. Leonardo left this painting, commissioned as an altarpiece for the monks of San Donato a Scopeto in Florence, unfinished when he left for Milan in 1481 or 1482.

Leonardo's first large group painting, which gives a foretaste of such large and complex mature works as the *Last Supper* (pages 88-89) and the *Battle of Anghiari* (pages 104 and 107), is the unfinished *Adoration of the Magi*, now in the Uffizi in Florence. This painting is interesting for a host of reasons which I will discuss but not least because it is the earliest of Leonardo's surviving paintings which can be identified with a particular commission. In 1479 a saddler provided an endowment for the monastery of San Donato a Scopeto just outside Florence's city walls, which would provide an altarpiece for the High Altar and a dowry for the donor's granddaughter. Ser Piero da Vinci, Leonardo's father, was notary to the monastery, and it may be that he arranged for his son to receive the commission and assume responsibility for the payment of the dowry. The contract arranging all this was drawn up in March 1481 and required delivery of the painting within 24 months, with a possible extension of a further 6 months. Unfortunately for the monks of San Donato, the painting was never finished, perhaps because of Leonardo's departure for Milan, and payments were not made after 28 September 1481. Perhaps they hoped that Leonardo would one day return to finish the painting, but eventually an altarpiece of the same subject was commission from Filippino Lippi, which was delivered in 1496.

From surviving drawings it appears that Leonardo worked on an idea for an *Adoration of the Shepherds* (Luke II, 16) in the late 1470s, which may be preparatory to the commission for the Chapel of St Bernard in the Palazzo Vecchio referred to earlier. A compositional drawing for this exists which suggests it would have been quite a conventional quattrocento composition with the Virgin and Child flanked symmetrically by parallel groups of figures. Although the

RIGHT: Gentile da Fabriano (1360-c. 1427) *Adoration of the Magi*, 1423, tempera on wood, 118⅛×111 inches (300×282 cm, including pinnacles and predelle), Galleria degli Uffizi, Florence. Gentile's vision of the Adoration was as influential in its day as was Leonardo's sixty years later.

Adoration of the Magi seems from the surviving compositional drawings and drawings of individuals and groups of figures, to have changed and developed considerably from the original conception of it as Leonardo worked on it, it seems from the start to have been an altogether more complex and ambitious work than the *Adoration of the Shepherds* ever would have been. Additionally, the story of the Adoration of the Magi was especially popular in Florence at this time which further suggests the *Adoration of the Shepherds* was a separate project, some of whose ideas still seemed relevant to Leonardo when he was devising the *Adoration of the Magi*. The popularity of the subject may derive from the fact that the date of the Adoration, January 6th, was the same in the ecclesiastical calendar as the Baptism of Christ, the central event in the life of St John the Baptist, patron saint of Florence. Certainly a pageant was organized every year in Florence on that day which reflects many earlier painted representations of the Adoration such as Gentile da Fabriano's (?1360-c. 1427) celebrated version of 1423 (right) in the Strozzi chapel of Santa Trinità in Florence (now in the Uffizi) or an Adoration (also now in the Uffizi; page 60) by Lorenzo Monaco (c. 1370-1425). This would help explain the populousness of such representations which has no scriptural derivation.

There exist only two general compositional studies for the *Adoration*, but comparison of these is most revealing about the complexity of the development of the final scheme. The earlier (page 62) is sketchily executed but contains certain important elements which appear in the painting, such as the ruined background architecture of vaults and staircases, with the stable rising within it, and the disposition of the group of Virgin and Child and adoring figures to the right. But the whole lacks coherence in the relation of the

ABOVE: Lorenzo Monaco (c. 1370-1425)
Adoration of the Magi, early 1420s, tempera on
wood, 56¹¹⁄₁₆×69¹¹⁄₁₆ inches (144×177 cm),
Galleria degli Uffizi, Florence.

figures to each other and to their setting, and in the rather inexpertly
managed perspective scheme. This last
failing is triumphantly overcome in the
other general study for the painting
(page 63). Here Leonardo avoids the
rather laborious treatment of perspective of the *Annunciation* (page 38) to
create a scene that is entirely convincing spatially. This he achieves partly by
placing the vanishing point off-center
on the horizon line (perhaps according
to the golden section, whereby the relation of the part to right of the vanishing point to the part to the left is the
same as the left part of the whole width
of that line); partly because he defines
space not just by the orthogonals but
also by dividing the ground up according to a scheme devised by Alberti and
here demonstrated by the tiled floor;
and partly by peopling this mathemat-
ically exact formula with vibrant figures
and exotic beasts. And yet, for all that
he must have learnt much in making
this precisely worked-out study, Leonardo diverged from it in the final
painting. That having made such a
systematically thought-out study he
then produced something related but
quite different means that we must look
very closely at the ways in which the
painting differs from the drawings to
understand it.

The principal difference in the background is the banishing to the right
background of the stable, which
figured largely in the first study and
which in the second looms as a ghostly
but essential compositional element
countering the diagonals of the staircases with its vertical posts, Leonardo
may perhaps have rearranged things
thus to leave the central space open to
accommodate the triangular foreground group of Virgin, Child and
kings within the semicircle formed by
the accompanying figures, a geometrical contrast of principal and secondary
players. This geometry overcomes the

LEFT: *Compositional Sketch for the 'Adoration of the Magi,'* c. 1481, pen and ink over metalpoint, 11¼×8½ inches (28.5×21.5 cm), Cabinet des Dessins, Musée du Louvre, Paris.

ABOVE: *Perspective Study for the Background of the 'Adoration of the Magi,'* c. 1481, pen and ink over metalpoint, with wash, 6½×11½ inches (16.5×29 cm), Galleria degli Uffizi, Florence.

incoherence of the first preliminary drawing and serves to orchestrate and not to interfere with the relationship of the groups of figures. The semicircular device further serves to separate the foreground scene from the background of ruined architecture and embattled groups of figures. The significance of this is usually interpreted as the contrast of the old pagan world and the new Christian world just begun. Certainly the ruins which are apparently classical may refer specifically to the Basilica of Maxentius in Rome, known at the time of this painting as the Temple of Peace. The Romans claimed this building would endure until a Virgin gave birth, and it fell, according to legend, on the night of Christ's birth. A further example of elements in the

painting serving the twin purposes of composition and symbolism are the trees at the center. These provide a vertical anchor contrasting with the semicircle of figures and with the diagonals both of the architecture and of the central group of figures which makes up for the loss of the stable from the perspective drawing. One of the trees is easily identified as a palm which is symbolic of peace and victory and which has associations with the Virgin by virtue of the Song of Solomon VII, 7, 'You are stately as a palm tree,' which is taken to prefigure the Virgin. The other tree is some difficult to identify and thus to interpret. Professor Kemp (1981) has suggested it might be an ilex tree, traditionally the tree which furnished the wood for Christ's cross, but an

ABOVE: *Battle between Horsemen and Dragon*, c.
1481, pen, ink and wash, 5½×7½ inches
(13.9×19 cm), Courtesy of the Trustees of the
British Museum, London. This battle
developed into a battle between horsemen in
the background of the *Adoration of the Magi*
(page 56).

alternative suggestion has been that it is a carob tree; not only was it traditionally believed that it was a carob from which Judas hanged himself, but also the 'locusts' on which John the Baptist fed were in fact carob pods, in which case we would have a further allusion to Florence's patron saint.

But some of the iconography is less easily explicable. The Egyptian column in the left background was presaged in the perspective drawing by a camel and may be intended to suggest a prophetic element of the mystic philosophy of Hermes Trismegistus made popular by Marsilio Ficino (see page 12) whose circle had lauded the platonic love of Bernardo Bembo and Ginevra de' Benci already discussed. It is difficult also to fathom the significance of the battling figures in the background, such as the horses at the right. These began life as a battle between a horse and a dragon (left) but perhaps this tells us more about the artist's penchant for mythical beasts, already demonstrated in Vasari's tale about the shield, than about the painting's iconography. What this group does provide us with, however, is a foretaste of the extraordinary turbulent dynamism of another complex equine composition of twenty years later, the *Battle of Anghiari* (pages 104-105). Not all the ideas which Leonardo worked out in the studies for the *Adoration* made it to the painting; some, such as a disputational group of figures at a table, were to resurface fifteen years later in the composition of the *Last Supper* (pages 88-89).

It is difficult to make a valid judgment about this painting for the obvious reason that it is unfinished. Much of the background, especially, is in no more finished state than many of Leonardo's drawings; one has only to compare, for instance, the tree growing from the top of the ruined vaults at the extreme left with the trees in the celebrated Arno drawing of 1473 (page 15)

to see that they use the same reductionist technique to depict foliage. And even the more highly finished foreground of *tarraverde*, brown bitumen and white lead is only a tonal ground preceding the application of color. This notwithstanding, it is quite evident that this painting represents a great advance in the artist's vision and accomplishment over any of his previous paintings. Although the whole is rendered coherent by the geometrical devices already discussed, such is the skill with which these are used, they give the appearance of naturally arising out of, and not of existing to control, the disposition of figures. But more important than this is the way these figures are characterized both as individuals and as members of groups. There is every variety of facial type, young and old, facial expression, gesture and bodily attitude. But this richness is so orchestrated as to re-emphasize the focus of the painting on the Virgin and Child. This focus, whether it is seen in terms of supplicants at an altar or as figures on a stage, was enormously influential. Vasari tells us that Raphael stood before it, speechless with admiration, and certainly, in Raphael's *School of Athens* in Rome, there are echoes of figures from the *Adoration*. The immediate impact of the painting on Leonardo's contemporaries can be seen by comparing an earlier (admittedly much earlier) *Adoration*, that of Gentile da Fabriano (page 58), with either the version (page 66) executed by Filippino Lippi in 1496 for the monks of San Donato a Scopeto to replace the unfinished version by Leonardo, or another by Domenico Ghirlandaio of 1485-88 for the Ospedale degli Innocenti in Florence (page 67). Both reveal, in the focus on the Virgin and Child achieved by a limited group of surrounding figures, including at least one king who leans forward imploringly from a kneeling position, qualities

ABOVE: Filippino Lippi (1457-1504) *Adoration of the Magi*, 1496, Tempera on wood panel, 101½×95⅝ inches (258×243 cm), Galleria degli Uffizi, Florence. This painting was produced to take the place of Leonardo's *Adoration* (page 56) which he left unfinished on his departure for Milan in 1482.

RIGHT: Domenico Ghirlandaio (1449-94) *Adoration of the Magi*, 1480, oil on wood panel, Ospedale degli Innocenti, Florence. Ghirlandaio, like Filippino Lippi, appears to have been influenced by Leonardo's unfinished *Adoration* in his composition.

MCCCCLXXXVI

Loria mexcelsis œ o.

LEFT: *St Jerome*, c. 1481, oil on wood panel, 40½×29½ inches (103×75 cm), Vatican Museum, Rome. This painting was rediscovered, in two parts, in the nineteenth century.

which were to leave Raphael speechless thirty years later.

The only other painting which may be dated with any certainty to the first Florentine period is the *St Jerome* (left) now in the Vatican Museum in Rome. This work has been known only since the nineteenth century when, so the story goes, it was discovered by Cardinal Fesch in two pieces, one of which was serving as a table top. This accounts for the damage and some of the retouching in the painting. Although it has been ignored by some scholars (Kemp, 1981), Leonardo mentions 'Saint Jeromes' in his list of around 1482, and various qualities in the painting leave little doubt that *St Jerome* is by Leonardo. Not only are there obviously Leonardesque features like the misty landscape background to the left, but also the technique is very similar to the *Adoration of the Magi*. It appears to have been abandoned at a similar stage of execution, with some of the underdrawing complete, such as the saint's torso and face, which look forward to some of Leonardo's anatomical drawings (pages 195 and 196), and some merely sketched in, such as the church in the right background. Also like the *Adoration* is the solid placing of the figure in his setting and the com-

positional use that is made of the attendant figure, in this case the lion, in focusing attention on the centrally important figure by the way his body curves around towards St Jerome. But what is so extraordinary about the painting is the conviction of the saint's anguish. Surely no other depiction of this subject comes near to equalling the emotional intensity of Leonardo's Saint Jerome. Even roughly contemporary paintings of St Jerome in the desert, by Botticelli in a predella panel for the altarpiece of San Marco in Florence, or by Filippino Lippi (Uffizi, Florence), seem quiet and contemplative by comparison. Some critics (Eissler, 1962) have interpreted this concentration on the intensity of the saint's emotional and physical feelings as a symptom of Leonardo's homosexuality. Certainly the 'red in tooth and claw' treatment of St Jerome contrasts with the cool remoteness of female figures, as we have seen with Ginevra de' Benci and as we shall see with *Leda* (page 140) and others, but the blending of psychoanalysis and art, whether it is used to interpret paintings or to flesh out the psychobiographies of artists, is a dangerous game, especially when the elapse of five hundred years has introduced so many uncertainties.

RIGHT: *Madonna of the Rocks*, c. 1483, oil on wood, transferred to canvas, 78⅜×48 inches (199×122 cm), Musée du Louvre, Paris. This painting is now widely accepted as that commissioned in 1483 from Leonardo and Ambrogio and Evangelista da Predis by the Confraternity of the Immaculate Conception in Milan. It seems that when the Confraternity refused to pay the painters a further fee, they sold the painting privately. The version in the National Gallery in London was presumably made later to fulfill the original contract.

Leonardo in Milan, 1482-99

As we have already discovered, there is no doubt that Leonardo had left Florence and was living in Milan by 1483. What is less certain is why he left. From the number of paintings which survive, and from the perhaps not significantly greater number which we may infer from his drawings that he produced, it is clear that Leonardo had succeeded in establishing himself as a painter after his registration with the Guild of St Luke in 1472. No painter who had not demonstrated his skill or who was not well regarded would have been given such a major commission as the *Adoration of the Magi*. The suggestion has been made on a number of occasions that Leonardo went to Milan because the Aristotelian thinking in northern Italy was more in tune with his own philosophy than the Neoplatonism which held sway under the patronage of the Medici in Florence. A more prosaic suggestion has been that he was sent as an emissary by Lorenzo de' Medici to Ludovico Sforza with the gift of a lute. Certainly, Leonardo seems to have been accompanied to Milan by a 16-year-old musician, Atalante Migliorotti (the 'Atalante who raises his face' of the inventory?), but given the lack of evidence about Leonardo's relationship to the Medici this seems an unsatisfactory explanation.

Perhaps a more convincing explanation, not least because the portrayal of Leonardo as anti-Platonic and of Milan as a singlemindedly Aristotelian city is oversimplistic, is that Leonardo had an eye to the main chance. Although he had clearly managed to find himself commissions in Florence, there is no evidence that Leonardo, unlike Verrocchio, enjoyed the direct patronage of the Medici. All the income he had must have been derived from such ad hoc commissions as that from the monks of San Donato a Scopeto. But even if he had enjoyed the patronage of the Medici, Leonardo would have known that Florence was still nominally a republic and that the Medici could never offer the kind of patronage enjoyed by artists, writers and musicians at the courts of Milan, Ferrara and Mantua. Certainly, Leonardo's letter of introduction to Ludovico Sforza so strongly promotes the diversity of his own attainments, that we may infer that Leonardo was well aware of what the Sforza court could do for him. From the fact that in the late 1490s Leonardo petitioned Ludovico for two years' back pay, we may assume that he had enjoyed the status of a paid employee of the court. This undoubtedly would have suited his need to work in his own way and in his own good time.

But the first definite proof that exists which shows that Leonardo was in Milan was not a commission from the Sforza court. A contract of 25 April, 1483 required Leonardo and two Milanese painters Ambrogio and Evangelista da Predis, to furnish an altarpiece for the church of S. Francesco Grande in Milan for the Confraternity of the Immaculate Conception. Not only were they to supply the central panel of 'Our Lady with Her Son,' but also the panels in the wings and painted and gilded decoration for an already existing carved framework. However, all did not go smoothly in the execution of this work, as may be inferred from the existence of two versions, in the Louvre (page 71) and in the National Gallery in London (page 112). It appears from surviving documents that the money which the three painters were offered was used up in painting the framework and that they were unsuccessful in persuading the confraternity to pay more than an extra 25 ducats for the central panel which seems already to have been completed by the early 1490s. From their claim around that time that they had already been offered 100

ABOVE: Attributed to Leonardo *Head of a Young Woman*, 1480s?, drawing on board, 10⅝×8¼ inches (27×21 cm), National Gallery, Parma.

LEFT: Detail of the head of the Virgin from the *Madonna of the Rocks* (page 71).

ducats for the painting it seems likely that they sold the original painting to the highest bidder. However, it appears that they did begin a replacement for the Confraternity in the 1490s, before Leonardo left Milan, and it is presumably this version that they were required by a court order of 4 April 1506 to complete for the Confraternity, and which was in place in S Francesco

Grande by 18 August 1508. It seems likely that this latter painting, which I will return to, is the version in the National Gallery in London, and which Leonardo was permitted to remove temporarily from the church to copy in 1508. This copy may be one of the known copies of lesser quality or it could be that it has been lost or, consistent with the spirit of the

73

ABOVE: Detail of the Angel's head from the *Madonna of the Rocks* (page 71).

RIGHT: Detail of the infant Christ from the *Madonna of the Rocks* (page 71).

commission, perhaps it was never completed. There can never be a definitive explanation of the two *Madonna of the Rocks* paintings. One critic, at least (Clark, 1939, 1947), believed that Leonardo brought the Louvre version with him from Florence as an example of his skill as a painter when he went to Milan seeking the patronage of Ludovico Sforza, and that the version in London was the original 1483 commission. For reasons I will go into, this does not seem plausible to me, but it illustrates that widely varying explanations for the existence of two paintings of the same subject are possible in the absence of comprehensive proofs, documentary or otherwise.

The subject matter of the *Madonna of the Rocks* is interesting because, unlike the *Annunciation* or the *Adoration of the Magi*, it does not illustrate a specific incident in the Gospels, and is therefore open to a variety of interpretations. It may be that it shows an incident popularized by the fourteenth-century theologian Pietro Cavalca when the infants St John and Christ met as the Holy Family were fleeing to Egypt. Certain elements in the painting support this as its subject. The angel could be the Angel Uriel who, in Cavalca's rendition of the tale, protected the child-hermit St John. There are also elements of symbolism and prefiguration in the painting both of the Baptism and of the

LEFT: *Lady with an Ermine (Cecilia Gallerani)*, c. 1485, oil on wood panel, 21¼×15⅜ inches (54×39 cm), Czartoryski Museum, Kraków.

Crucifixion. The pool in the foreground would be an obvious prefiguration of the Baptism, while such elements as the sharp leaves of the iris may allude to the sword of sorrows which pierced the Virgin's heart at the Crucifixion. The clear way in which the relationships of the figures to one another are indicated – the directing of our attention by the angel to the infant St John; the way St John leans forward towards Christ emphasizing his devotion; the gesture of blessing directed by Christ to St John – suggest that a specific narrative is intended.

But the painting can be seen as more than an illustration of this apocryphal story. At no time was the cult of the Virgin Mary stronger than in the fifteenth century, and at the particular time and place of this painting's creation, the doctrine of her own Immaculate Conception, (briefly, for Christ to be entirely 'immaculate' his Virgin mother must herself be born of a virgin; the problem of the impossibility of logically concluding this doctrine appears not to have diminished the enthusiasm of its adherents) was especially popular. The Confraternity which commissioned the work was founded in 1478 to promote and celebrate the Feast of the Immaculate Conception (which was not approved by the Pope until 1480). As we have seen in the *Adoration of the Magi*, not only are symbols of the Virgin, such as the palm, a feature of paintings at this time, but also the Song of Songs is a popular source for Marian prefiguration, and so it could be with the rocky setting of the figures: 'O my dove, in the cleft of the rock, in the covert of the cliff, let me see your face' (Song of Songs, II, 14).

What makes this painting such a landmark in the development of Leonardo's painting is neither the way in which it is composed nor the symbolism nor the narrative. Rather it is the treatment of light and shade and the way they, rather than the color, control and emphasize the emotional dynamism of the painting. Nothing could be further from the docility and sweet coloration of Verrocchio (page 43) or Lorenzo di Credi, where the local color of objects is delicate yet uncompromised by powerful suggestions of light and shade. Put crudely, there is no part of their paintings where the precise colors of objects are not explicit. That this is not the case in the *Madonna of the Rocks* is notable not only for how it affects the painting's impact, but also as the earliest expression of a theory that Leonardo was to explore in some detail in his notes. The theory which he began to expound soon after this painting must have been made was, basically, that in shadow the individual quality of colors is lost such that where objects' edges are in shadow they should not be delineated, or separated from other objects of different color, presumably for the reason that this is not what we see but what we know. Only in bright light is the true color of an object seen. The results of this can clearly be seen in this painting in the unifying quality of the shadowed areas which lend still greater emphasis to the brightly illuminated areas of the scene, this quality of emphasis being one Leonardo repeatedly recommended in his notes on painting. But the importance to him of the tonal values in a painting, which we have already seen in the *Adoration of the Magi*, is not just that they can serve to unify the narrative or the chromatic diversity of the picture, but also that it is tone rather than color which determines three-dimensionality and relief in a painting. It is the understanding and mastery of this simple fact which so fundamentally separates Leonardo from his immediate artistic predecessors.

Further effects of light and surface quality are evident which mean that the *Madonna of the Rocks* is more than an

LEFT: Hugo van der Goes (1420-c. 1482) *Portinari Altarpiece* (central panel of the *Adoration of the Shepherds*), oil on wood panel, 99⅝×119¹¹⁄₁₆ inches (253×304 cm), Galleria degli Uffizi, Florence. Certain interests of Netherlandish and Flemish painters, such as the accurate portrayal of individual character, were shared by Leonardo. The *Portinari Altarpiece* was one of the best-known of northern paintings in the Florence of Leonardo's time, when it was displayed in one of the chapels of Sta Trinità, for which it had been commissioned.

exercise in chiaroscuro. It is not just shadow which has a mitigating effect on color and form, but distance and atmosphere. Thus it is that the distant mountains and water become increasingly unfocused and unified in color. In tandem with these general effects of light and atmosphere Leonardo explores the localized effects of light and reflection on the variegated surfaces of the painting. The way the light plays on the surface of the angel's curls, or the soft shading of the Christ Child's cheek is offset by reflected light from his strongly illuminated shoulder, provide the strongest link with similar features in earlier paintings such as the *Annunciation* (page 38) or the left-hand angel in Verrocchio's *Baptism of Christ* (page 35). However, here these effects are much more diverse and play a role in the overall scheme of tonal values: color as well as light is reflected and the attention to the play of light on objects plays across the whole of the painting.

Although Leonardo probably worked on the *Madonna of the Rocks*, one version or another, sporadically throughout the 1480s and 1490s, it seems unlikely that he produced no other paintings before his next major work, the *Last Supper* (pages 88-89), begun around 1495. As we shall see from his drawings, he certainly was busy with designs for weapons, with designing festivities and pageants, with anatomical and engineering studies, with making notes for his treatise on painting, as well as with 'The Great Horse' (page 84), but it seems unlikely that Ludovico would have been content to allow such a gifted painter as Leonardo to remain idle in this sphere while he was in his pay. It is said that no painting by Leonardo of Ludovico himself, nor of his wife Beatrice d'Este (whom he married in 1491), survives. It is recorded that Leonardo was commissioned to paint their portrait in the refectory of S Maria delle Grazie;

LEFT: *Portrait of a Musician*, c. 1485, oil on wood panel, 17×12¼ inches (43×31 cm), Pinacoteca Ambrosiana, Milan. The subject of this portrait has been positted as court musician and musical theorist Franchino Gaffurio (1451-1522), although it is also far from certain that the painting is by Leonardo.

Ludovico needed to sustain his claims as Duke of Milan (he was only the fourth son of Francesco Sforza), and a portrait by such an artist as Leonardo might have been seen to represent a potent emblem of power. However, perhaps he considered the hieratic remoteness of such an image as the *Pala Sforzesca* as fulfilling this role more effectively. What is more certain is that Leonardo painted the portraits of two of Ludovico's mistresses, Cecilia Gallerani and Lucrezia Crivelli. The former portrait is usually identified with a painting now in Kraków, the *Lady with an Ermine* (page 76).

Cecilia Gallerani was, like Ginevra de' Benci, an extraordinarily accomplished and learned individual. As well as being a writer and poet herself, Cecilia Gallerani wa a patron of the arts. She was Ludovico's mistress for ten years until her marriage in 1491; from the fact that by 1498 when Isabella d'Este asked to borrow her portrait, she was reluctant to lend it on the grounds that it was no longer a good likeness, we may infer that it dates from the early part of her association with Ludovico. There are several indications beyond the obviously fine quality of the painting which suggest that this is Leonardo's portrait of Cecilia Gallerani. Ludovico's court poet Bernardo Bellincioni described how in Leonardo's portrait of Cecilia she appears not to speak but to listen, and this perfectly describes the attitude of the sitter in this painting, as she turns around to her left to an unseen speaker. This gesture of turning, and more specifically of turning to look over the shoulder, is one that Leonardo increasingly used to enhance the dynamism and movement of his paintings, complementing the swirling movement to depict form which began with the drawings for a *Madonna and Child with a Cat* (page 55). This sense of arrested movement is expressed further in the ermine held by Cecilia, whose back arches beneath her touch and which seems rapt at the same source. The significance of the animal is not just that it is traditionally, as well as in the bestiary which Leonardo compiled, a symbol of purity and moderation, but also that its name in Greek is galay, a punning reference to the sitter's name.

A comparison of *Lady with an Ermine* with the *Portrait of Ginevra de' Benci* (page 46) reveals how Leonardo had developed as an artist and could apply those lessons he had learnt in creating the *Madonna of the Rocks*. Where the Ginevra portrait impresses by the variety of interpretations that can be put on the directness of the sitter's gaze, Leonardo's Cecilia Gallerani is very precisely characterized, and those qualities of calm and sweetness are seemingly captured at a very precise moment. This concentration on particulars of character and, probably, of the sitter's appearance, is matched by the obvious interest and relish the artist takes in depicting the varying qualities of the dress, the necklace and the fur of the ermine. This interest is related to Leonardo's studies of light, the reflection of which helps differentiate surface qualities and which we saw played out in the *Madonna of the Rocks*. Once again he uses the device of having the brightly illuminated figure emerge from a murky background and once again the use of secondary or reflected light, as on Cecilia's right hand or her chin, accounts for many of the naturalistic qualities of the painting. These effects of light are not achieved just by intuition or by trial and error. Leonardo made an extensive study of the effects of light falling on objects and from these observations extrapolated rules for the depiction of objects in varying light conditions. Principally he noticed, perhaps not astonishingly, that surfaces are most strongly illuminated where they are struck by a perpendicular light source, and that this intensity

RIGHT: *La Belle Ferronière*, c. 1495, oil on wood panel, 24¾×17¾ inches (63×45 cm), Musée du Louvre, Paris. It is recorded that Leonardo painted a portrait of Lucrezia Crivelli, Ludovico Sforza's mistress of the 1490s; this could be that painting.

diminished as the directness of illumination diminished. But beyond this he made observations of the effects of light passing through apertures, of the difference between reflexions on water and on solid objects and how both of these differed from light reflected from one surface to another. Such was the accuracy with which Leonardo made these observations and translated them into paint that the naturalness of the effect loses nothing and there is no sense of a formula having been applied.

But are these newly developed qualities derived solely from this understanding of light? It could be argued that many of the painting's finest qualities – the concentration on the sitter's personality and appearance, the interest in the texture of surfaces – are more characteristic of Netherlandish than Italian painting at this time. With the emphasis in art history on Italy, and especially Leonardo, as the catalyst of the High Renaissance, the idea that northern painting, which was to adopt more slowly the principal ideas of the Renaissance, could have had a part in shaping its painting has been little explored. Netherlandish painting had been known in Florence since the 1440s and at least one major Flemish painter, Rogier van der Weyden, a pupil of Jan van Eyck, had visited Italy in 1450 for the Jubilee of Rome. Moreover at least two paintings were commissioned from him by the Medici. But perhaps the Netherlandish painting that was the most influential in Florence in the time of Leonardo was Hugo van der Goes's altarpiece (pages 78-79) for Tommaso Portinari. This was painted in Bruges in 1476-78 for the Portinari

chapel in Santo Egidio in Florence. Here, in the accurately observed botanical specimens in the foreground, in the landscape backgrounds and in the portrait of Portinari himself, in the left-hand wing of the altarpiece, are those same qualities of individual characterization and interest in variegated qualities of light and surface – that fascination with showing things the 'way they are' – that was one of Leonardo's major preoccupations and which he developed in his *Lady with an Ermine*.

These considerations certainly color any assessment of two other portraits from around this time whose authorship by Leonardo has been asserted. It is perhaps unfair to judge too harshly the *Portrait of a Musician* (page 80) as it is unfinished, but it seems to lack that extraordinary sense of accurate characterization which makes the *Lady with an Ermine* so arresting. There is something unnervingly stiff about the man's pose and disembodied (not just because the rest of the arm is not present) about the hand that holds the piece of music. The portrait is sometimes thought to represent Franchino Gaffurio, court musician, composer and musical theorist at the Sforza court, in which case, Leonardo, who was not just court painter but had considerable musical ability, would have known the sitter well. Nonetheless, there is such a strong similarity between the treatment of the eyes here and those of the angel in the *Madonna of the Rocks* (page 71), not to mention the way the light glimmers on his tumbling locks, that one cannot dismiss out of hand Leonardo's authorship. A female portrait traditionally known as *La Belle Ferronière* (right), on

the other hand, has that disturbingly accurate suggestion of individual personality which the *Lady with an Ermine* has, and which is made all the stronger here by the directness of the sitter's gaze which has the effect of establishing a private communication with the viewer. The ultimate expression in Leonardo's oeuvre of this relationship is, of course, the *Mona Lisa* (page 131). Because of the rather conventional pose of the figure, the dull way such details as her snood and jewelry are painted, and the old-fashioned device of the sill in front of her suggest that this is the work, not of Leonardo, but of his pupil Giovanni Antonio Boltraffio (1467-1516). Yet surely those intangible qualities of psychological accuracy and the incomparably subtle modelling of the face are clearer indicators of authorship than questions of composition or detail. Later great painters, such as Titian in his supposed *Self-Portrait* (National Gallery, London), were to use the sill device, for example.

But who is *La Belle Ferronière*? La Belle Ferronière was the nickname of a mistress of Henry II of France, and the name was also erroneously given to the painting. But it is known that as well as painting Ludovico Sforza's mistress of the 1480s, Cecilia Gallerani, Leonardo painted a portrait of Lucrezia Crivelli who was Ludovico's mistress in the 1490s. A court poet praised Leonardo's skill in that portrait in omitting to portray Lucrezia's 'soul,' because, as her soul was 'owned' by Ludovico, Leonardo has achieved 'greater truth.' For this reason alone it is tempting to doubt that *La Belle Ferronière* is by Leonardo!

As part of his campaign to establish his claims as Duke of Milan, and to aggrandize the Sforza family in general, Ludovico wished to create a monument to his father Francesco (1401-66), the first Sforza to rule Milan. By the time Leonardo came to Milan in 1482 the decision had already been taken that Francesco Sforza would be commemorated in a bronze equestrian statue. As early as 1482, in his letter of introduction to Ludovico, Leonardo had expressed the opinion that he could undertake work on the bronze horse. However, the first subsequent

indication we have of Leonardo working on the horse is in a letter of 1489 from the Florentine ambassador to Lorenzo de' Medici. He suggests that although Ludovico had commissioned Leonardo, he was not confident that he would succeed, and that Ludovico would like Lorenzo de' Medici to suggest some alternative Florentine sculptors. What exactly this means is hard to tell. Perhaps Leonardo had been working on the project ever since he had come to Milan and Ludovico was wearying of the slowness or was mindful of Leonardo's reputation for not completing work. Or perhaps it was simply that he wanted further sculptors to assist with the technical problems inherent in casting a bronze sculpture of great scale.

Leonardo's first ideas for the monument seem, from surviving drawings, to have been for a rearing horse. To provide a support for the great weight of the rearing horse and to symbolize Sforza triumph over adversaries, a crouching figure was to be placed under the front hooves of the horse. Leonardo's decision of around 1490 to portray instead a walking horse seems to have been taken for aesthetic rather

ABOVE AND LEFT: Two views of a sixteenth-century *Rearing Horse*, bronze, height 8⅝ inches (22 cm), Museum of Fine Arts, Budapest. This small maquette relates very closely to Leonardo's early studies for the Sforza monument which had the horse rearing. Leonardo later favored a 'walking horse,' whether for aesthetic or technical reasons is not certain.

than technical reasons as, although a rearing horse would have been immensely difficult to achieve in bronze, the idea was not unprecedented, and if anyone could do it, Leonardo could. In 1490 Leonardo saw and admired greatly a classical statue of a walking horse at Pavia. His desire to emulate the artistic vitality of this work, and perhaps to invest his own with classical associations highly attractive to the Sforza dynasty, seems to underly his new conception of the monument. The formulation he settled on was of a high-stepping horse, one front leg raised in the manner of the Marcus Aurelius statue in Rome. The drawings for the monument and Leonardo's own notes reveal that he made a great many drawings from life of some of Ludovico's own horses (page 86), seeking in these to find

underlying proportions as he had in his studies of the human head (page 9). By the winter of 1492-3 a full-scale clay model of the statue, three times life size, had been made. Although this aroused widespread wonder and admiration, and in spite of the detailed technical notes Leonardo made about the casting of such a huge bronze, the statue was never made. In November 1494 Ludovico sent the bronze intended for the statue to Ferrara to his father-in-law, Ercole d'Este, to be made into cannon to repel the invading French. The clay horse languished in Milan until 1499 when newly arrived French bowmen used it for target practice, an act of destruction which it is perhaps only slightly too fanciful to suppose influenced Leonardo's decision not to accept French patronage at this time.

LEFT: *A Horse in Profile to the Right and its Forelegs*, c. 1497, silverpoint on blue prepared paper, 8½×6¼ inches (21.4×16 cm), Windsor Castle, Royal Library 12321. © 1991 Her Majesty The Queen. Leonardo made such studies to further his knowledge of anatomy, as well as studies for the 'Great Horse' monument to Francesco Sforza (page 84).

RIGHT: *Measured Drawing of the Near Foreleg of a Horse*, c. 1495, pen and ink, 9⅞×7⅜ inches (25×18.7 cm), Windsor Castle, Royal Library 12294. © 1991 Her Majesty The Queen.

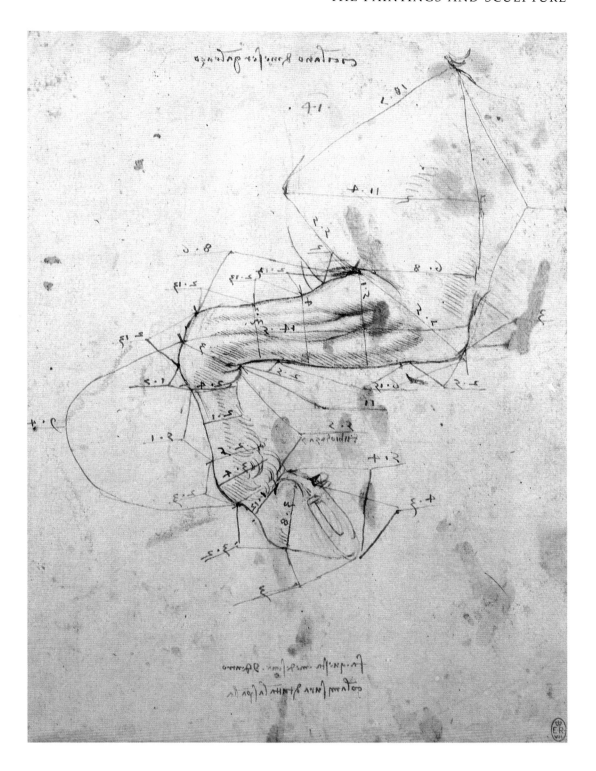

The Last Supper

If Ludovico Sforza took care to promote the cultural life of his court, he certainly did not neglect its and his own spiritual well-being. During the 1490s he adopted as his court church the Dominican S Maria delle Grazie in Milan. At his direction the east end of the church was reconstructed by Donato Bramante, later to be the architect of the new St Peter's in Rome. Bramante's design is a massive centralized space based on simple geometric forms, and the degree of similarity to Leonardo's various schemes for centralized churches (page 176) may not be coincidental. Ludovico intended the church as a family mausoleum – a memorial to his wife, Beatrice d'Este, was erected here after her early death in 1497 – and as a dynastic memorial to the Sforzas, but he was also interested in the monastic function of the foundation.

Every Tuesday and Thursday he dined in the refectory with the abbot of S Maria delle Grazie and it was for the end wall of this room, facing the abbot's table, that he commissioned the *Last Supper*. An image of the *Calvary* on the opposite end wall is dated 1495 and we know from documents that Leonardo was at work on the *The Last Supper* in 1497. A unique contemporary description of Leonardo at work on the painting was written by Matteo Bandello who, as a young monk visited his uncle, the abbot of S. Maria delle Grazine, in 1497:

Many a time I have seen Leonardo go early in the morning to work on the platform before the *Last Supper*; and there he would stay from sunrise till darkness, never laying down the brush, but continuing to paint without eating or drinking. Then three or four days would pass without his touching the work, yet each day he would spend

several hours examining it and criticizing the figures to himself. I have also seen him, when the fancy took him, leave the Corte Vecchia when he was at work on the stupendous horse of clay [the 'Great Horse'; pages 84-85], and go straight to the Grazie. There, climbing on the platform, he would take a brush and give a few touches to one of the figures: and then suddenly he would leave and go elsewhere.

This description is of far more than anecdotal value and, moreover, offers more than an insight into Leonardo's working methods. It conveys some of the time spent in contemplation that was needed to formulate the extraordinary leaps forward in artistic vision that he made, of which the *Last Supper*, for all its decayed appearance, is a prime example. But it also gives some indication of how, if Leonardo should become distracted during one of these contemplative periods, works could

PREVIOUS PAGES: *The Last Supper*, 1495-97, tempera on gesso, pitch, and mastic, 15 feet 1 inch × 28 feet 10½ inches (460×880 cm), S Maria delle Grazie, Milan.

LEFT: Detail from the *Last Supper* (pages 88-89), showing, from the left, Ss Bartholomew, James the Less, and Andrew. The pointing knife may alude to St Bartholomew's martyrdom by flaying.

remain unfinished. The decay and the working method described by Bandello are, however, linked. The *Last Supper* was Leonardo's first wall painting. Because of the large scale and the nature of the wall surface, from a practical point of view he could not work in the oils which would have allowed him to make changes as he went along and generally to work in the erratic way described. But the *buon fresco* method with which he would have been familiar from his earliest days in Florence, although the obvious choice for a large-scale wall painting, allowed no changes to be made and was unsuitable from an artistic point of view. This led him to develop his own medium of tempera on stone. This required a strong base of gesso, pitch and mastic, to seal the wall against damp and provide a ground for the paint. Unfortunately the medium was most unsuccessful in the first of these requirements and as a result the paint began to detach from the ground within a few years of the painting's completion. By May 1556 when Vasari visited the monastery, damage was so extensive that the painting appeared to him to be no more than a 'mass of blots.' This was almost certainly an exaggeration as more than half a century after this, before the first of many restorations, Rubens waxed lyrical about the painting:

In a word, as a result of deep thought he has attained such a degree of perfection that it seems to me impossible to speak in adequate terms of his work, let alone imitate it.

Apart from the natural decay that the painting's medium caused to befall it, the first damage that occurred to it was the insertion of a doorway through the lower central part of the tablecloth in 1652. Although this was subsequently filled in again the damage is still clearly visible. Throughout the eighteenth and nineteenth centuries restoration

LEFT: Detail of the *Last Supper* (pages 88-89), showing, from the left, St Peter, Judas (in front), and St John. Details such as this reveal the extent to which the *Last Supper* has suffered through the paint detaching itself from the wall.

attempts were made on the *Last Supper* to arrest the paint loss that was ruining it. The first of these was undertaken in 1726 by the painter Michelangelo Bellotti whose chief mistake was in supposing that Leonardo had worked in oil paint. He retouched many of the areas that had been laid bare by the paint loss and gave his finished restoration a coat of oil varnish. This work, in common with all subsequent restorations, failed to tackle the central problem of the humidity which was causing the paint loss. In 1770 another painter, Giuseppe Mazza, was called in by the monks of S Maria delle Grazie to see what could be done. Not only did he resort to scraping off Bellotti's restorations, but also he seems to have repainted more extensively than was consistent with a restoration of the artist's original intentions. The Irish painter James Barry was so horrified with what he found Mazza doing to the *Last Supper* when he visited it in 1770 that he remonstrated to the abbot, and Mazza's work was halted. Most of the subsequent efforts at restoration, including the most recent, consisted of trying to prevent the paint from detaching from the ground. The main exception was the scheme of 1821 of a painter-restorer Stefano Barezzi to detach the *Last Supper* from its support in order to house in more favorable conditions. This scheme is not as insane as at first appears, as Barezzi had succeeded, as restorers continue to this day to succeed, in detaching frescoes in one piece and transporting them elsewhere. The central flaw in his attempts on the *Last Supper* was that it is not a fresco. A fresco can be detached because it consists of two quite substantial layers of plaster, the *intonaco* which is a rough base layer applied to the wall and on which a sketch of the final fresco may be made, and the *arriccio*, a much finer layer that would be applied over the dry *intonaco* in *giornate*, sections corresponding to a day's work:

RIGHT: Detail from the *Last Supper* (pages 88-89), showing, from the left, Christ, St Thomas, St James the Greater, and St Philip.

in *buon fresco*, the technique used by the greatest fresco painters, the plaster would only be painted on while it was wet. The *arriccio* layer is of a different texture from the *intonaco* which explains why it can be detached in a piece from it. Leonardo's technique in the *Last Supper* was quite different from this and so it could not be detached. Barezzi only discovered this after he had damaged a sizeable portion of the table-cloth and one of Christ's hands.

The work of over-zealous restorers is not the only problem that the painting has had to contend with over the centuries. Milan's strategic importance to European affairs has seen it frequently involved in war. In 1796 Napoleon's troops entered Milan and in spite of his personal orders to the contrary, the refectory was used for purposes as diverse and unsuitable as a hay-store and a magazine, and as quarters for troops and prisoners. But the worst treatment the refectory suffered happened only in 1943. One night in August 1943 the roof and one of the walls of the refectory were completely destroyed by a bomb. Luckily a steel framework filled with sandbags had been erected to protect the painting against such an eventuality and the supporting wall withstood the blast. But modern science has yet to solve the problem of humidity which ultimately will destroy the *Last Supper* where World War II could not.

But until that time, we will still be able to enjoy the *Last Supper* in the setting for which it was intended, the refectory of S Maria delle Grazie. The subject was one which was described in detail by all the Gospels, but most concisely in St Matthew, xxvi, 20-30:

When it was evening, he sat at table with the twelve disciples; and as they were eating, he said, 'Truly, I say to you, one of you will betray me.' And they were very sorrowful, and began to say to him, one after

another, 'Is it I, Lord? He answered, 'He who has dipped his hand in the dish with me, will betray me. The Son of man goes as it is written of him, but woe to that man by whom the Son of man is betrayed! It would have been better for that man if he had not been born.' Judas, who betrayed him, said, 'Is it I, Master?' He said to him, 'You have said so.'

Now as they were eating, Jesus took bread, and blessed, and broke it, and gave it to the disciples and said, 'Take, and eat; this is my body.' And he took a cup, and when he had given thanks he gave it to them, saying, 'Drink of it, all of you; for this is my blood of the covenant, which is poured out for many for the forgiveness of sins. I tell you I shall not drink again of this fruit until that day when I drink it new with you in my father's Kingdom.

And when they had sung a hymn, they went out to the Mount of Olives.

By the time that Leonardo painted the *Last Supper* it was, for obvious reasons, already a commonplace subject for wall paintings in refectories. Traditionally, it formed one of many scenes in fresco cycles of Christ's life, particularly the Passion. One such Leonardo would have known is Taddeo Gaddi's *Last Supper* which forms a kind of extended predella to his *Crucifixion* of c. 1350 in the monastery of S. Croce in Florence. By the middle of the fifteenth century, the Last Supper had become popular as an individual scene and was often depicted on a large scale. The logical step from representing the room in which the Last Supper is taking place in perspective, as in Andrea del Castagno's version of 1450 in S Apollonia, to representing that same room as though it were an extension of the room on one of whose walls the painting was made, took place in Florence when Leonardo was still living there. A typical example is that of 1480 by another of Verrocchio's pupils, Domenico Ghirlandaio, in the monastery of Ognissanti in Florence. Here the artist has introduced vaults and responds into his painting which emulate those of the room one of whose walls it occupies. This is one newly established convention in the depiction of this subject that Leonardo adopts, but if we consider the many and various conventions, some of ancient origin, that he did not adopt, we can begin to see what it was that Leonardo was doing in those hours and days of contemplation, and why the *Last Supper* occupies such an important place in his oeuvre and in the history of western art.

Depictions of the Last Supper originate in the *agape* or 'love feast' of Early Christian catacomb paintings, and from the earliest times they express the dual function of the subject: the announcement of the Passion by reference to the betrayal by Judas, and the institution of the Eucharist by allusion to the significance of the bread and wine. Thus paintings of the Last Supper rarely depict a single moment in the story. Leonardo continues this by alluding to a number of moments from the story in the Gospels. Most obviously, and most dramatically, he shows the moment where Christ announces, 'Truly, I say to you, one of you will betray me.' Much of the dramatic tension in the painting derives from the apostle's various reactions to this announcement, a subject I will return to. But, in the way Judas, the figure to the left whose face is obscured, holds his hand over a dish we are reminded of another moment when Christ declares, 'He that dipped his hand in the dish with me, will betray me,' or where Christ gestures to the bread and wine we know the moment of the institution of the Eucharist is indicated. Peter, the figure whose sudden forward movement causes Judas to lean away, his face in darkness, and thus reveal himself as betrayer, holds a knife which may also refer to his cutting off the soldier's ear at the time of Christ's arrest.

What is unusual about Leonardo's *Last Supper* is that he achieves this complex narrative with a composition that is apparently simple and unadorned. Certain conventions had arisen in the previous century for differentiating the apostles in depictions of the Last Supper. The most popular was placing Judas on the other side of the table from the other apostles, or to have St John reclining on Christ's chest. Ghirlandaio made use of both of these devices in his *Last Supper* in Ognissanti in Florence of 1480. Other pictorial devices such as placing the apostles on both sides of the table, had maintained popularity with artists from Giotto in the Scrovegni Chapel in Padua at the beginning of the fourteenth century, to Fra Angelico in the monastery of San Marco in Florence in the mid fifteenth century. The effect of this is to allow the artist to contain the space needed to display the thirteen figures and to create a convincing sense of depth, but it had the major drawback of having several of the figures seen from behind, from where it was impossible to characterize them individually. It is this latter problem which made this scheme unsuitable to Leonardo's purposes, because it is the precise depiction of individual character and response that lends the *Last Supper* so much of its power. Although the painting is now so damaged that it is virtually impossible to make out the individual figures' faces, four finished drawings, of Judas (page 98), St Philip, St James the Greater (page 97) and St Bartholomew, survive which reveal that Leonardo carefully considered each individual figure. This was not only so that we will be able to recognize each figure, in the same way that earlier depictions did, but also that we will see their various individual reactions to the announcement, 'one of you will betray me.'

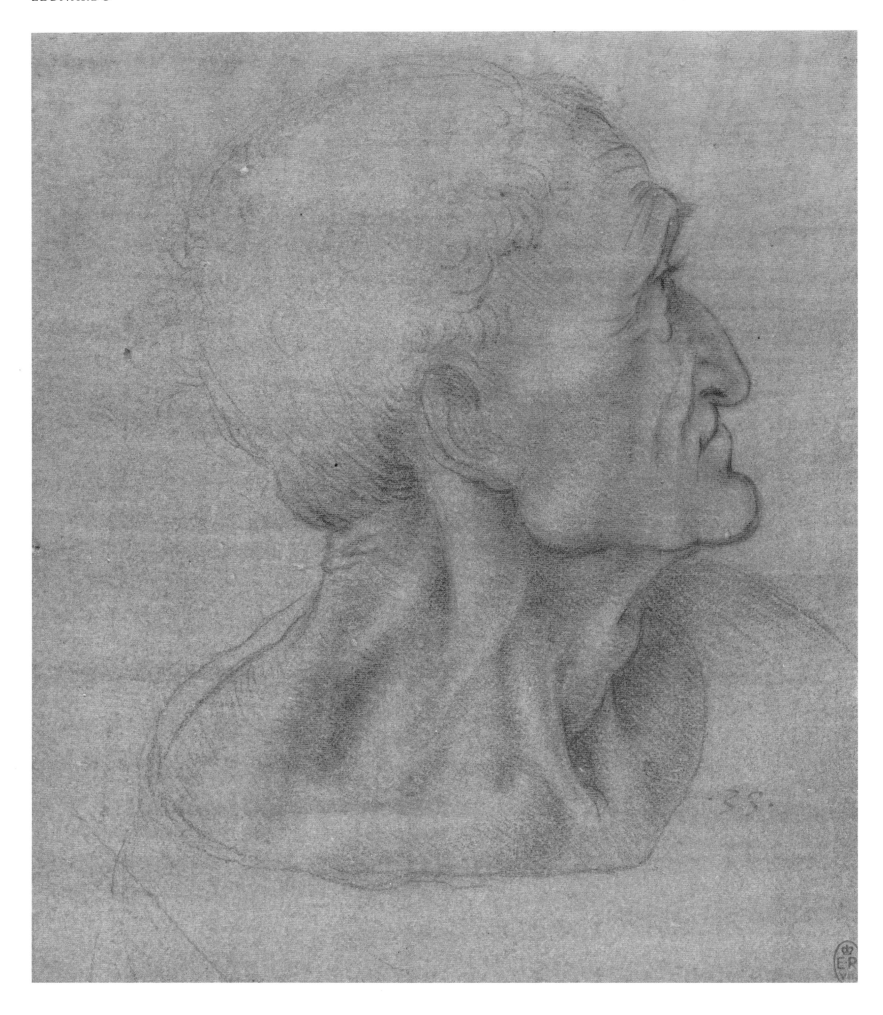

This concentration on the immediate aftermath to the announcement of the betrayal was a novel and startling departure from representations of the Last Supper up to this time, whose traditional focus was Judas. Here the Juddas figure is, quite literally, shadowy, and if our attention is drawn to him it is because his face is dark and impassive where the other disciples are brightly lit and highly animate. Leonardo's decision to represent this emotive moment in the Last Supper must reflect his study of the physiological *modus operandai* of emotions in the human body, their outward manifestations in men's faces and actions and the need for artists to understand these processes in order to represent them accurately. Such sentiments recur in his notebooks: 'Painted figures must be done in such a way that viewers are able easily to recognize through their attitudes the thoughts in their minds, and if you show a good man speaking make his attitudes suitable accompaniments to good words. And . . . if you have to portray a bestial man, do him with fierce actions.' Again and again in his *Treatise on Painting* Leonardo stresses the varying expression that varying emotions have on people and how these may be affected by such factors as the power of emotion or the age of the person. We have already seen the use he made of this in the *Adoration of the Magi* but never before or after the *Last Supper* did he contain and direct this variety of response so powerfully.

We can understand how this is achieved if we notice two principal deceptions which the artist perpetrates on us. The first is the deceptive simplicity of the composition. The symmetrical disposition of the disciples on either side of Christ, all on one side of the table, is potentially dull, lacking as it does the variety of representations going back to Giotto which arranged the figures on either side of the table. The setting, too, is unrelievedly symmetrical with three windows, the center one of which frames Christ's head. And yet, of course, there is nothing simple or bland about the arrangement of the disciples themselves. They are arranged in two groups of three on either side of Christ. In the first group at the left of the painting are Bartholomew, James the Less and Andrew A clear link echoing the flow of emotion towards Christ is provided by James the Less who stretches behind Andrew to touch Peter, in the group closer to Christ, on the arm. He echoes this action in leaning forward to whisper in the ear of John, whose head is bent down and towards Peter. This action, and the brightly lit faces of Peter and John, serve to emphasize the exclusion of Judas who leans in shadow away from the flow of action through from Bartholomew to John. On the other side, from the outside, are St Simon, St Jude (who share a feast day) and St Matthew, who sweeps round to them in disbelief. Matthew's grandly

gesturing arm provides a link with the next group of Philip, standing, James the Greater, his arms spread wide, and Thomas, with his finger raised, a gesture Leonardo used throughout his work from the *Adoration of the Magi* (page 56) to the *St John the Baptist* (page 142), and which here demonstrates Thomas's doubt.

Thus the composition of the *Last Supper* is far from simple. Despite the complexity of the groups of disciples, the viewer's attention is concentrated on their reactions, which are at once varied yet easy to read because of the compositional restraint. Because of the accuracy with which the artist represents varying emotion, and also because of the convincing perspective scheme, we get the impression that the *Last Supper* is a scientifically naturalistic depiction of thirteen men dining at a table. Yet this too, like the apparent simplicity of the composition, is a deception. Most obviously, the perspective of the room in which the Last Supper is taking place only works from approximately twice the height of the eye-view of someone standing in the refectory of S Maria delle Grazie. The reason for this is clear when we realize that to have represented the scene at that height on the wall from a perspective correct for a viewer in the refectory would mean that the top of the table would have been invisible, in which case the Eucharistic allusion of Christ's gesture to the bread and wine would have been lost. More subtle is the proportion of the figures and their relation to the table. Not only is Christ appreciably larger in scale than the other figures but also the table is far too small for thirteen men to be seated at it.

The point of these departures from a scientific naturalism is that they serve to concentrate our attention on the essentials of the scene – the Christ figure in the center, gesturing to the bread and wine, calm in contrast to the

disciples varying gestures of alarm, despair and disbelief – and thus absorb the viewer effortlessly in the drama of the scene where a literal representation would have distracted us, dissipating the flow of energy and emotion. It is this essential rather than literal truth to 'the appearance of things' which distinguishes Leonardo's great group compositions, the *Adoration of the Magi*, the *Last Supper* and the *Battle of Anghiari*, of which the *Last Supper* is the only complete, albeit battered, survivor.

If the *Last Supper* represents Leonardo's best-known commission of the 18 years or so that he spent at Ludovico's court, then the *Sala delle Asse* (Room of the Boards) at the Castello Sforzesco in Milan must be the least known. Although it has not decayed to the same extent as the *Last Supper* it was very heavily restored at the beginning of the twentieth century, such that it is hard to say now how much was by Leonardo and how much by a pupil. However, as we shall see, the restorer seems to have been faithful to the original conception of the ceiling decorations, and we do know from documentary sources that Leonardo worked on the ceiling. It is in a large square room situated in the northern tower of the Castello and formed the introduction to a suite of private rooms intended for Ludovico and his wife Beatrice d'Este. Beatrice died in childbirth in January 1497 and this event presumably influenced the decoration of these rooms. Certainly, we know from a document of 20 April 1498 that Leonardo was occupied in decorating a *Saletta Negra* (small black room) which has obviously mournful associations. Nothing survives of this decoration, but further contemporary references to Leonardo working on 'The "large room of the boards" in the tower' may safely be related to the vegetal wall and vault decorations that have survived there, and much better preserved than the Last Supper.

LEFT: The *Sala delle Asse* in the Castello Sforzesco, Milan. Although this painting has been heavily restored, the interest in natural forms and the intertwining of the foliage with the golden thread, as well as representing a device of Beatrice d'Este, Duchess of Milan, were typical interests of Leonardo.

What is initially most striking about the decorations is their exuberant naturalism. They consist of a veritable riot of trunks, branches and foliage which, on closer inspection, conform to the vaulted structure of the ceiling. There are 18 trunks around the room, the principal eight of which – those rising from the four corners and from the centers of the four walls – rise up to join at the center of the ceiling. Secondary and tertiary branches grow from these and form a mass of linkages across the vaults much like the ribs, liernes and tiercerons in the vaults of some northern late Gothic Cathedral, a simplified scheme of which Leonardo would have known well in the late fourteenth-century nave of Milan Cathedral. Considerable ingenuity is expended in rendering this scheme naturalistic, notably the way the trunks around the two windows are 'pruned' so as to follow their form. The foliage is equally convincing (though substantially repainted) as are the roots which nestle among stone-

work at the base of the walls. We cannot be surprised at this scrupulous naturalism given what we know about Leonardo's studies of nature in all its forms, but there seems to be more to it than that. This 'tent of nature' is, in fact, a vehicle for a variety of motifs and devices significant to the patron, Ludovico Sforza.

Painting the patron's personal device into the decoration of a room was not unusual in northern Italian palaces at this time, nor was the use of foliage as decoration. But the *Sala delle Asse* is exceptional for the way the artist has contrived to insinuate the patron's emblems and devices into the tree forms in a way that is as subtle as the vision is naturalistic. In fact the whole scheme of decoration can be seen as a Sforza emblem, the image of a tree with roots being one of Ludovico's personal devices. Others, such as the central oculus containing the joint arms of Ludovico and Beatrice, or the four shields, one in the center of each wall,

101

LEFT: *Isabella d'Este*, 1500, black chalk, heightened with red chalk, 24¾×18⅛ inches (63×46 cm), Cabinet des Dessins, Musée du Louvre, Paris. This drawing is usually accepted as that which Leonardo made of Isabella d'Este during his brief stay in Mantua in 1500.

RIGHT: Although Girolamo Savonarola's had been executed in 1498, memories of his stern régime were still fresh when Leonardo arrived back in Florence in 1500.

alluding by inscription to events of the 1490s relevant to Sforza power in Milan, are more obvious and conventional uses of devices. But as the shield that caps the whole room suggests, the decoration is intended to commemorate not just Ludovico and his anticipated dynasty, but also his union with Beatrice d'Este. One feature of the decoration is a gold chord which entwines around the boughs like gilded bindweed; just as the trees can be interpreted as an allusion to Ludovico, so can this chord be seen to recall the late Beatrice. The device of interlocking gold threads was one which Beatrice had adopted from her sister, Isabella d'Este, and which she had worked into her clothing in the form of filigree or gilded knotting. The *Sala delle Asse* serves thus as a demonstration of Sforza power and the artist's ingenuity as well as a poignant memorial of the recently dead Beatrice d'Este.

The confidence that the Sforzas had a brilliant future in Milan, secured through the marriage of Ludovico's niece to the Emperor Maximilian, which is expressed in the *Sala delle Asse* soon proved to be misplaced. In August 1499, following the invasion of Lombardy by Louis XII of France who had a claim to Milan, Ludovico left Milan. Leonardo stayed on for three months after the arrival in Milan of the French king in October and seems to have entered into negotiations with him to continue as court painter. These, however, came to nothing and Leonardo seems to have left Milan for Matua late in 1499. It is likely that it was at this time that Isabella d'Este, who had shown a great interest in his work and had borrowed his portrait of Cecilia Gallerani, sat for a portrait to him. All that survives of this is a badly damaged drawing (page 102), which may or may not be by Leonardo. It is pricked for transfer by pouncing and shows Isabella's head in profile with her body

turned towards us and her hands folded in front of her, both formulas familiar to us from Leonardo's earlier female portraits. This and the softness and delicacy of the features look forward to the *Mona Lisa* (page 131) and support the contention that this is by Leonardo, for all that it may have been reworked by other hands. Leonardo did not stay long in Mantua and by 13 March 1500 he was in Venice offering advice to the Venetian Republic on defenses against an anticipated Turkish invasion. Here, again, his stay was brief, and by the end of March he was back in Florence after an absence of nearly twenty years.

The Second Florentine Period

The Florence that Leonardo arrived back in at the beginning of 1500 was markedly different, politically if not artistically, from the one he had left in

1482. The Medici had been overthrown in 1494 and their rule replaced by a stern régime under Girolamo Savonarola. His execution in 1498 had done little to mitigate against the sober atmosphere that prevailed in Florence, although the survival of the Grand Council of 3000 did, by requiring a suitably decorated chamber for the Council, indirectly foster the arts and, as we shall see, Leonardo's work in particular. But the level of patronage in Florence had been severely limited by sumptuary edicts under Savonarola, and although opportunities for freelance commissions arose, Leonardo was, as he had demonstrated in Florence before, constitutionally unsuited to earning a living in this way. This situation may account for his disrupted existence over the next eight years, and the two years he spent in Florence in 1500-02 were the longest stay in one place during that time.

103

LEFT: Pieter Paul Rubens (1577-1640) *Copy after Leonardo's 'Battle of Anghiari'*, c. 1604, black chalk, pen and ink, heightened with gray and white, 17¾×25 inches (45.2×63.7 cm), Cabinet des Dessins, Musée du Louvre, Paris. Although Rubens made this drawing from a sixteenth-century woodcut after Leonardo's *Battle of Anghiari*, he has succeeded, in a way that many artists who copied direct from the painting failed, in expressing many of the qualities commonly found in Leonardo's paintings.

The Battle of Anghiari

Although Leonardo never enjoyed in Republican Florence the same kind of security from which he benefitted as court painter in Milan, he was certainly not neglected by the state. With its new form of government, consisting of a chamber of 3000 franchized citizens, it was deemed appropriate that a suitably large and magnificent meeting hall be built to house them. In 1495 Antonio da Sangallo the Elder (1455-1537), assisted by Cronaca (Simone del Pollaioulo, 1454-1508) had designed a vast hall 178 feet long, 77 feet wide and 60 feet high to house this body. Given the recent departure of the Medici and the Republic's consequent need to demonstrate its durability, this room became a vehicle for decorations demonstrating Republican power. This extended even to the woodwork and panelling decorated with Roman motifs redolent of Republican rule. But many of the allusions had more specific relevance to the Florentine Republic. In the middle of the long west wall was to be an altarpiece by Filippino Lippi containing Ss Anne, John, Bernard, Zenobius, Reparata, Victor, Peter and Paul. Many of these saints had long-standing Florentine associations as we have already seen with St John the Baptist, but St Anne was a particular symbol of Republican sentiments as it was on her feast day (26 July) in 1343 that the citizens of Florence had risen against the hated tyrant, the Duke of Athens. Similarly Christ the Saviour was venerated as it had been on St Saviour's day in 1494 that the Medici had been expelled from Florence. For this reason a marble statue of Christ as Saviour was commissioned from Andrea Sansovino (c. 1470-1529) in 1502 to stand on the east wall opposite the altarpiece.

Leonardo's involvement had similar associations. Some time in the fall of 1503 Leonardo was commissioned to

RIGHT: Copy of the fight for the standard from the center of the *Battle of Anghiari*, c. 1550, oil on wood panel, 6×8⅜ inches (15.1×21.3 cm), Palazzo Vecchio, Florence.

BELOW: Studies for the central and left groups of the *Battle of Anghiari*, c. 1503-04, pen and ink, 5¾×6 inches (14.5×15.2), Galleria dell'Accademia, Venice.

execute a large wall painting depicting the Battle of Anghiari, while the young Michelangelo was commissioned to do an equivalent version of the Battle of Cascina. Both battles were famous Florentine victories and accounted for the popularity of Saint Victor on whose feast day (actually the following day) in 1364 the Battle of Cascina had taken place, and Ss Peter and Paul, on whose feast days (29-30 July) the Battle of Anghiari had taken place in 1440. As well as being encouraging victories these battles were seen as especially relevant to the Republic as the-then vanquished Pisa and Milan still represented the enemies at large.

The exact disposition of the various decorations in this huge room is now impossible to determine as none of the constituent parts was completed and redecoration of the room (today known as the Salone dei Cinquecento) begun by Giorgio Vasari in the 1560s obliterated what had been completed by the time the Medici returned to power in 1512. The huge dimensions of the room mean that Michelangelo's and Leonardo's paintings could have been on either the east or the west wall (or even one on each). The most convincing suggestion as to their location is on the east wall, opposite the altarpiece wall and either side of both the Christ the

Saviour statue and the loggia built on the east wall to house the Gonfaloniere of Florence and his eight Priors. From what we know of the distribution of light effects in Michelangelo's cartoon we can suppose that his was to the left of whichever wall they were on, nearer the windows.

Although the *Battle of Anghiari*, like so many of Leonardo's paintings, was never completed and what he did complete was lost by around 1560, we do have a considerable body of documentary evidence to allow us to follow the progress of his work, as well as his own preparatory drawings and copies of varying dates to give a good idea of the

painting's appearance. Although no original contract for the painting survives, we do know that on 24 October 1503 Leonardo was given keys to a large room in S Maria Novella in which to work and specifically, we may infer, to produce a full-size cartoon for the work. It seems odd that a suitable room in or near the Palazzo della Signoria could not have been found as S Maria Novella is more than half a mile from the Palazzo della Signoria, and a full-size cartoon would not have been an easy item to transport any distance. By the time a contract was signed in May 1504 Leonardo had been supplied with paper and other materials, as well as

scaffolding. The contract, signed by Machiavelli and clearly mindful of Leonardo's reputation for not finishing work, stipulated that either must complete the cartoon by February 1505 or, alternatively, must then begin painting the part of the cartoon he had completed, in which case the deadline for completing the cartoon would be extended.

Throughout 1504 and on past the deadline of February 1505 he received supplies for making whitewash, flour for sticking the cartoon to the wall, wall plaster, Greek pitch, linseed oil, Alexandrian white and Venetian sponges. What this motley assortment of mat-

erials suggests is that he was once again devising a novel technique, following the failure of his experiments with the *Last Supper*. The presence of pitch and linseed oil on the list suggests that he intended to paint pitch over a smooth plaster layer as the ground for an oil-based paint. Payments to Leonardo and two assistants, Raffaello d'Antonio di Biagio and Ferrando de Llanos, throughout the spring and summer of 1505 suggest that work progressed on the *Battle of Anghiari*. However Leonardo left for Milan in May 1506 and work was abandoned much to the chagrin of the Gonfaloniere of Florence, Piero Soderini. Wooden boards were

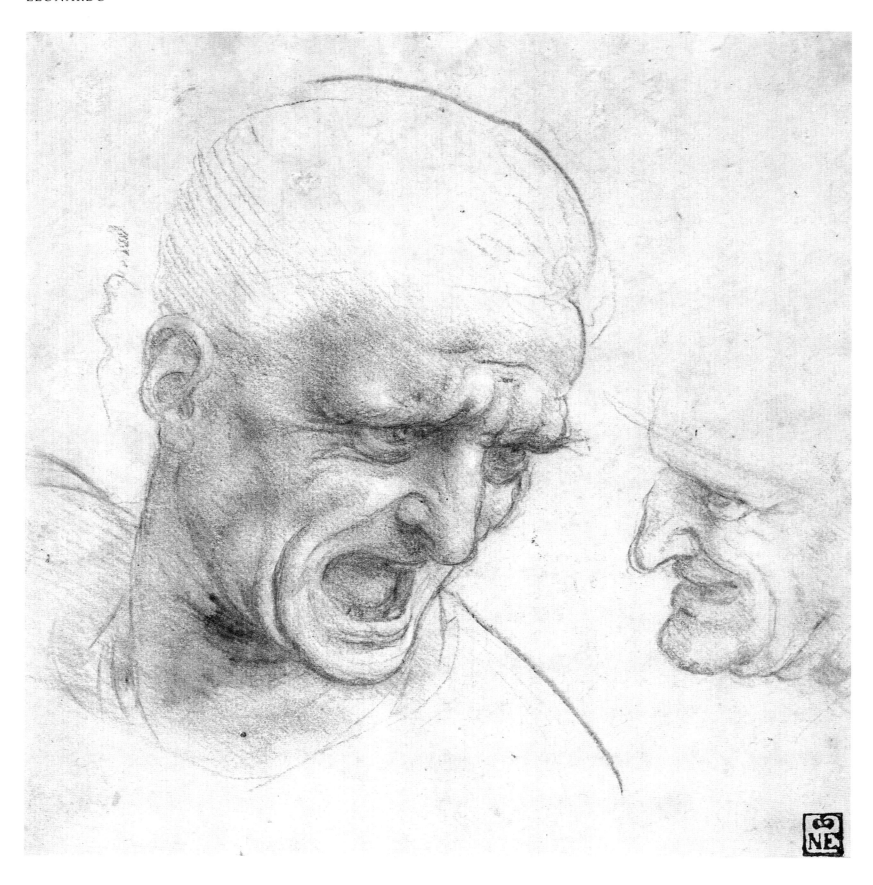

erected to protect the painting in 1513 and several copies were made of it before it finally disappeared in 1560 when Giorgio Vasari frescoed the Sala del Consiglio. It is from these copies and from some preparatory drawings that we know something of this lost masterpiece.

We do know that the area available to Leonardo to depict the battle measured around 22 feet in height and 60 feet wide (c. 7×18 metres), which means that even if the group of four horsemen was considerably larger than life it would have occupied only a small proportion of the whole wall painting. In the vibrant preparatory drawings (page 106) we see Leonardo working out various scenes and refining the elements of those which he chose. Study of these drawings has led to the suggestion that some of the other scenes might have been of battling foot soldiers, of horsemen impaling fallen soldiers, of assembled Florentine and Papal troops led by the Patriarch of Aquilea and of a bridge over a river. Such a large painting offered the opportunity for representing various significant moments in the battle without confusing or overcrowding the narrative. But it seems likely that the scene which we know from the copies and which Leonardo chose to paint first must have been the dramatic climax of the whole painting. And it was also the dramatic climax of the battle, when the Florentine troops successfully defended the standard, or *gonfalone*, of Florence from capture by the Milanese, an act symbolic of the protection of Florence's sovereignty, both at the time of the Battle of Anghiari and in Leonardo's own day.

The scene of the fight for the standard is extraordinarily compact, with the four horsemen and three subsidiary figures interlocked in a frenzy of conflict. The interlocking and spiralling form of the whole group is reflected in its constituent parts, in the fantastical armor of the soldiers and in the wildly

ABOVE: *Head of a Man Shouting*, c. 1505, red chalk, 9×7⅓ inches (22.7×18.6 cm), Budapest Museum of Fine Arts. Both of these drawings are studies for the *Battle of Anghiari*.

LEFT: *Head of a Man Shouting*, c. 1505, black and red chalk, 7½×7⅜ inches (19.2×18.8 cm), Budapest Museum of Fine Arts.

rippling manes of the horses. Struck through the center of this, bending beneath the tension, is the pole of the standard which has occasioned the débâcle. In fact the motif of the two central horses battling head-on was taken from a Roman sarcophagus in Florence, an allusion designed not

merely to demonstrate the artist's familiarity with classical precedents but also, perhaps, to stress Florence's long history and by implication the stability of the Republic. But perhaps the greatest triumph in the painting was the representation of expressive rage and anger in the soldiers' faces. About these

109

LEFT: *Madonna of the Yarnwinder*, c. 1501, oil on wood panel, 18¼×14¼ inches (46.4×36.2 cm). In the Collection of the Duke of Buccleuch and Queensberry, KT, Drumlanrig Castle, Dumfriesshire. Leonardo produced a painting of this subject for Florimond Robertet, Secretary of State to Louis XII of France, around 1501. Although the painting at Drumlanrig has long been assumed to be a studio copy, the high quality of some of the painting, especially the 'sfumato' of the Virgin's face (right), suggests that at least some of the painting is by Leonardo himself.

we can be reasonably confident as finished chalk drawings by Leonardo survive of two of the heads (pages 108 and 109). They reveal that he was practising what he preached in his treatise on painting, not only about there being a need to represent exactly the expressions on men's faces as these were a direct reflection of their emotions, but also, specifically, what he wrote about the appearance of soldiers' faces, with furrowed brows and teeth bared. The loss of this painting, perhaps even more than the decay of the *Last Supper*, represents the greatest tragedy of Leonardo's art.

Leonardo's unsettled life in the first years of the sixteenth century makes it especially difficult to work out exactly what he painted during these years, and in what order. One painting which we can assign with a reasonable degree of certainty to the first year or so of Leonardo's return to Florence is the *Madonna of the Yarnwinder*. This is known from a number of copies the best of which Leonardo may have had a hand in (page 110). This painting conforms closely to a description of a small painting in a letter from Fra Pietro da Novellara to Isabella d'Este in April 1501. Isabella d'Este had, since Leonardo had drawn her for a portrait, plagued Leonardo with requests for the completed portrait and for other paintings. Fra Pietro, leader of the Florentine Carmelites, was her contact in Florence and wrote to her about Leonardo's activities apparently in an effort to divert her attempts to secure paintings from him which were clearly doomed. He describes a little picture of a Madonna with a yarnwinder executed for Florimond Robertet, Secretary of State to Louis XII of France. He describes how the Virgin is intent upon spinning yarn, but the child, whose foot rests upon a basket of flax, takes hold of the yarnwinder and gazes intently at the four spokes which are in the form of a cross

and smiles as though he desires the cross and will not yield it to his mother, which she appears to wish him to do. The copy in the Buccleuch collection is so good that perhaps it is one of those copies Fra Pietro described as being made in Leonardo's studio to which he made additions himself. Certainly, although the background scenery lacks that vitality and subtlety which Leonardo himself had mastered as early as the portrait of Ginevra de' Benci (page 46), the accomplishment of the 'sfumato' modelling of the faces holds its own with those paintings confidently attributed to the master himself, such as the Louvre *Madonna of the Rocks* (page 71) the Mona Lisa (page 131).

This painting shares with the former the inclusion of a symbol of the Passion. Here, however, the artist has contrived a considerable advance from the painting of nearly twenty years earlier,

in that the symbol is so introduced that it serves its apparent function as part of a simple Virgin and Child picture, as effectively as it does its symbolic one. Moreover this successfully achieved duality extends to the interactions of the two figures. When we look at the painting we see a mother reacting to the determination of her child, as he grasps at a plaything; and we see the rapt gaze of Christ as he sees his crucifixion prefigured, which elicits an ambiguous gesture from the Virgin, torn between the conflicting interests of mother love and acquiescence to the will of God. If the copy is faithful in spirit to the original this is one of Leonardo's most humanly appealing paintings, and it may have been a conscious attempt to emulate the popular 'sweetness' of Pietro Perugino (page 11), who had established himself in Florence during Leonardo's absence in Milan.

LEFT: *Madonna of the Rocks*, c. 1506, oil on wood panel, 74⅝×47¼ inches (189.5×120 cm), Courtesy of the Trustees of the National Gallery, London.

RIGHT: *Bust of an Infant in Profile to the Left*, c. 1506, red chalk, 4×4 inches (10×10 cm), Windsor Castle, Royal Library 12519. © 1991 Her Majesty The Queen.

BELOW RIGHT: *Study for the Drapery of a Figure Kneeling to the Left*, c. 1506, 8⅜×6¼ inches (21.3×15.9 cm), Windsor Castle, Royal Library 12521. © 1991 Her Majesty The Queen. The drapery of the angel in the *Madonna of the Rocks* (left) is very similar in form to this study.

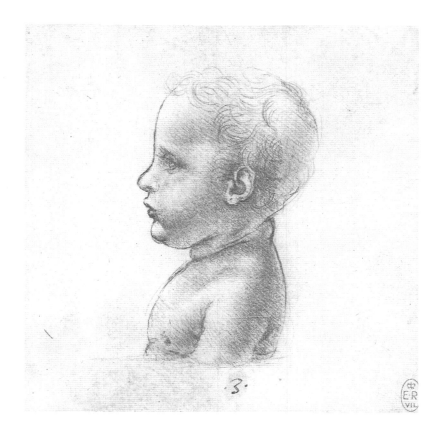

Florence, Milan, Rome, France, 1506-19

The reason for Leonardo abandoning his work on the *Battle of Anghiari* in April 1506 was that he was summoned back to Milan in that month to attend to some unfinished work. The Signoria had only authorized a three-month absence and it has been assumed that the unfinished business was the *Madonna of the Rocks*, which had still not, after 13 years, been delivered. As we have already seen, it is likely that the *Madonna of the Rocks* in the Louvre (page 71) was the original version of the 1480s, and that it was completed and then sold at that time when the Confraternity of the Immaculate Conception refused to pay Leonardo and Ambrogio da Predis a further fee. It is likely that the *Madonna of the Rocks* in the National Gallery in London was a second version begun in the 1490s and completed by Leonardo and perhaps Ambrogio da Predis or some other pupil by 1508. Such an arrangement would explain the variety of quality within the painting. Certain features represent a distinct step forward from the Louvre version. The painting has a greater sense of monumentality, in spite of its slightly smaller size, which is achieved by the greater scale of the figures within the painting and by their sculptural (one might almost but not quite say Michelangelesque) treatment. There is, moreover, a greater concentration in the interrelation of the figures brought about by the elimination of the angel's rather obvious pointing finger, and by the transfer of his gaze from the viewer to St John. The rather enamel-

RIGHT: Detail of the Christ child from the *Madonna of the Rocks* (page 112).

BELOW: These flowers, although a typical Leonardo subject, may be part of the *Madonna of the Rocks* produced by a member of Leonardo's studio.

LEFT: *Virgin and Child with St Anne and St John the Baptist*, c. 1505, 54¾×39¾ inches (139×101 cm), charcoal on brown paper, heightened with white, National Gallery, London.

BELOW: Study for the *Virgin and Child with St Anne*, c. 1500-05, pen, ink, and wash over black chalk, 10¼×7¾ inches (26×19.7 cm), Courtesy of the Trustees of the British Museum, London.

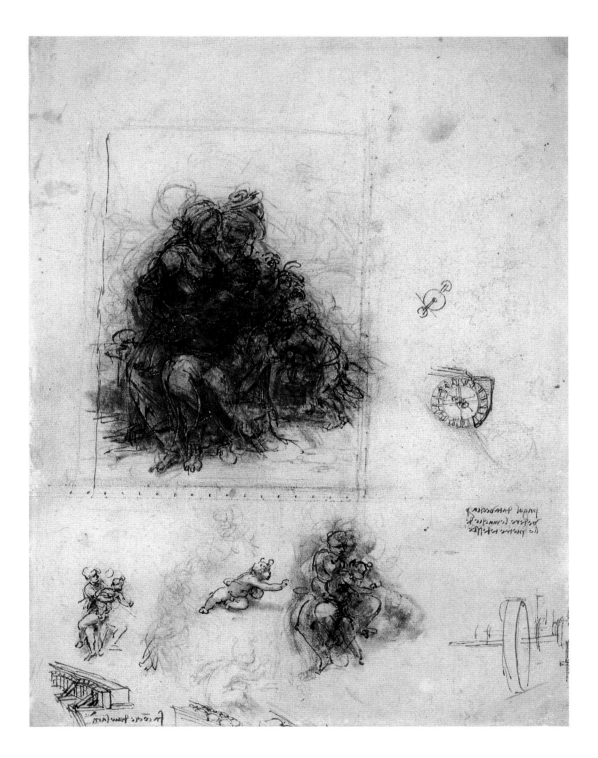

like quality of some of the flora and rocks, on the other hand, suggests that more assistance was involved in this painting than in the Louvre version.

The Florentines were once more fated to lose Leonardo to Milan. Not only did he clearly spend longer than three months completing the *Madonna of the Rocks*, but soon he had once more secured himself patronage from a source infinitely more wealthy and powerful than Ludovico Sforza. It had been at the behest of Charles d'Amboise, governor of Milan in the name of Louis XII of France, that Leonardo had returned to Milan in April 1506, but it was the King himself who by July 1507, on a visit to Milan, was referring to Leonardo as 'our dear and good friend Leonardo da Vinci, our painter and engineer in ordinary'; he was also paying him a salary. Leonardo's works from these early years of the sixteenth century are not easy to unravel, as reports of the time almost but do not quite fit with surviving works. One major work which was described in the same letters of Fra Pietro da Novellara to Isabella d'Este was a cartoon of a Virgin, Child, St Anne and a lamb. It depicts a Christ Child aged about one year, who half rises from his mother's arms and seizes a lamb which he draws to himself. The mother, half rising from St Anne's lap, takes the Child to draw it from the lamb, that sacrificial animal which signifies the Passion; Saint Anne, rising slightly from her seat, seems as if she would hold back her daughter, so that she would not separate the Child from the lamb, which perhaps signifies that the Church did not wish to prevent the Passion of Christ. These figures are life size, but they are in a small cartoon because all are seated or bent, and each one is placed before the other to the left. Many features of this description fit with the painting now in the Louvre (page 120), but certain crucial features such as the re-

LEFT, BELOW, AND BELOW RIGHT: Details of the heads of the Virgin, Christ, and St Anne from the *Virgin and Child with St Anne and St John the Baptist* (page 116).

straining action of Saint Anne and the distribution of the figures to the left (although Fra Pietro could mean *their* left) are missing. Matters are further complicated by the existence of a further version of the Virgin and Child with St Anne in a large-scale cartoon (page 116) and by Vasari's story of Leonardo at work on such as these as the basis for an altarpiece in Ss Annunziata in Florence. Vasari related in his *Life* of Leonardo first published in 1550:

When he returned he found that the Servite brothers had commissioned Filippino [Lippi] to paint the altarpiece of the high altar of the Annunziata; Leonardo said that he would gladly have undertaken such a work and when he heard this Filippino, like the good fellow he was, withdrew. The friars, in order that Leonardo might paint it, took him into their house and bore the expense of himself and all his household; and so things went on for some time, and he did not even make a beginning. But at last he made a cartoon wherein Our Lady and St Anne and a Christ, which not only filled all artists with wonder, but, when it was finished men and women, young and old, continued for two days to crowd into the room where it was exhibited, as if attending a solemn festival: and all were astonished at its excellence. For in Our Lady's face are to be seen all the simplicity and beauty and grace that can be ascribed to the mother of Christ, as Leonardo wished to show the humility and modesty appropriate to a depiction of the Virgin who overflows with joy at seeing the beauty of her Son. She holds him tenderly in her lap and lets her pure gaze fall on St John, who is shown as a little boy playing with a lamb; and this is not without a smile from St Anne, who is eminently joyful as she realizes the divinity of her earthly progeny.

Here Leonardo has hijacked a commission from the hapless Filippino who had had to paint a substitute *Adoration of the Magi* for the monks of San

LEFT: *Virgin and Child with St Anne and a Lamb*, c. 1508, oil on wood panel, 66⅛×44 inches (168×112 cm), Musée du Louvre, Paris.

BELOW: Study of the drapery of the Virgin in the *Virgin and Child with St Anne and a Lamb* (left), c. 1508, black chalk, Windsor Castle, Royal Library 12529. © 1991 Her Majesty The Queen.

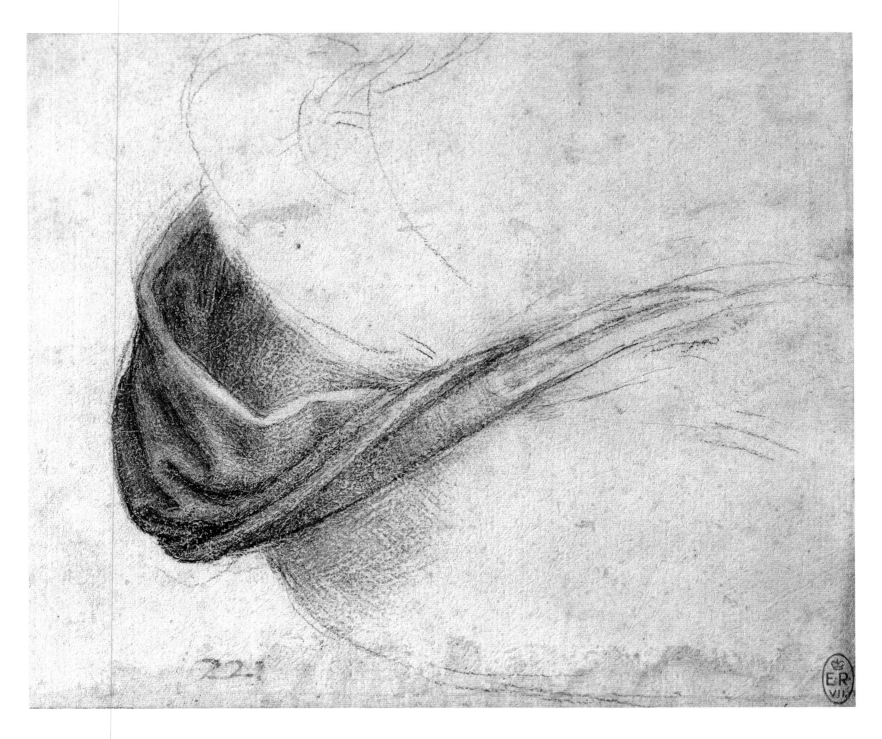

Donato a Scopeto after Leonardo had left his version unfinished in 1482. What this cartoon Vasari describes was intended for is hard to tell because it does not at all conform with the subject – a *Deposition of Christ* – that the Ss Annunziata commission required. In spite of the inclusion of St John in Vasari's account this could well be the same cartoon described by Fra Pietro to Isabella d'Este in April 1501, as Vasari, as we have already seen, was not always scrupulously accurate. On the other hand it could be that Vasari's account relates more to the other surviving cartoon of this subject (page 116) and its preparatory drawings. It seems unlikely, given that the London cartoon and the Louvre painting from their style date from at least five years later than Pietro's letter, that either was or

LEFT: Detail from the *Virgin and Child with St Anne and a Lamb* (page 120).

BELOW: *Head of a Woman Looking Down and to the Right*, c. 1508, black chalk, 7⅜×5⅛ inches (18.8×13 cm), Windsor Castle, Royal Library 12533. © 1991 Her Majesty The Queen. This finished drawing is a study for the head of St Anne in the Louvre *Virgin and Child with St Anne and a Lamb* (page 120).

arose directly from the works described; more likely they are reworkings of a theme that Leonardo clearly believed deserved further investigation; they might also relate to two 'Madonnas of different sizes' which he refers to in a manuscript of early 1508, and which he claimed were intended for his patron, Louis XII, who had also expressed interest in a portrait.

Given the similarity in content of the London cartoon of the *Madonna and Child and St John* and the Louvre painting of *Madonna, Child, St Anne and a Lamb*, it is difficult to discuss them entirely separately. And yet they are treated about as differently as it is possible for one artist to treat a similar subject. There exists a single preparatory drawing (page 117) for the London cartoon which reveals that Leonardo went through the same process of 'thinking on paper' as he had gone through thirty years earlier in his studies for a *Madonna and Child with a Cat* (page 55). The impression which emerged from this exercise was of a unified but essentially static group of four figures. This is the quality most notable from the cartoon itself, where a series of solid and static vertical and horizontal elements – the Virgin's and St Anne's knees, the right arm of the Virgin, for example – establish the tone of the composition. There is none of the ambiguity in the Virgin's attitude to Christ that we saw in the *Madonna of the Yarnwinder*: she smiles in acquiescence at Christ as he, equally unambiguously, reassures the infant St John with a gesture alluding to the will of God.

The painting in the Louvre, on the other hand, in content, and in the form which expresses this, reflects the dynamism of conflicting interests. The Virgin cannot restrain herself from reaching out towards Christ as he embraces the lamb, symbol of his Passion. Her look is tender, if a little wistful, leaving her gesture towards Christ open to interpretation. Is she restraining him mindful of his forthcoming death, or is she assisting him in the fulfilment of his destiny? Whichever connotation we put on this gesture, we can see that this is a much more animated representation of this scene than the London cartoon, and this is reflected in the composition of the figures. Where the London cartoon is all placid solidity here we have flowing movement. Gone is the rigidity of horizontals and verticals, replaced as they are by fluid and curving diagonal sweeps through the Virgin and Christ's arms, the Virgin's right leg and so on. Although apparently the Virgin is seated on St Anne's lap, this is not demonstrated explicitly. Rather it is the sense of movement, both physical and emotional, which is important to the painting's meaning, and this is emphasized not obscured by the spatial ambiguity of the figures.

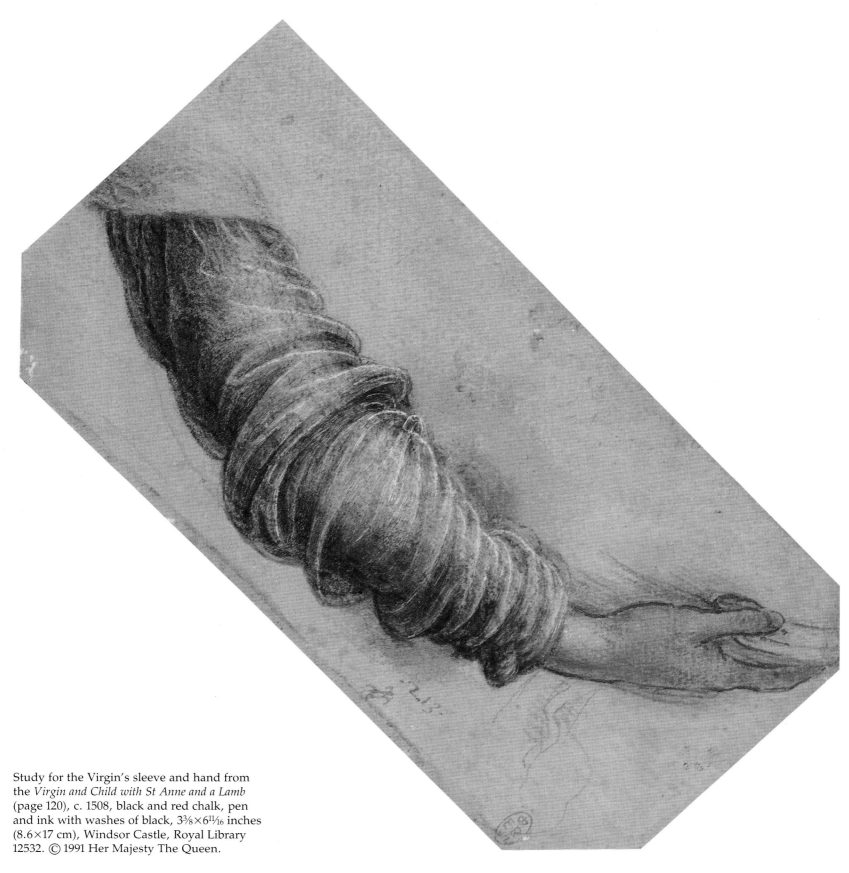

Study for the Virgin's sleeve and hand from
the *Virgin and Child with St Anne and a Lamb*
(page 120), c. 1508, black and red chalk, pen
and ink with washes of black, 3⅜×6¹¹⁄₁₆ inches
(8.6×17 cm), Windsor Castle, Royal Library
12532. © 1991 Her Majesty The Queen.

BELOW: Study for drapery for the Virgin in the *Virgin and Child with St Anne and a Lamb* (page 120), c. 1508, black chalk and black wash, heightened with white, 9×9⅝ inches (23×24.5 cm), Cabinet des Dessins, Musée du Louvre, Paris.

ABOVE: Studies for the Christ child in the
Virgin and Child with St Anne and a Lamb,
c. 1508, red chalk, 11×8⅝ inches (28×22 cm),
Galleria dell'Accademia, Venice.

RIGHT: Detail of the Christ child from the
Virgin and Child with St Anne and a Lamb (page
120).

BELOW AND BELOW RIGHT: Details from the
Virgin and Child with St Anne and a Lamb (page
120).

RIGHT: *Mona Lisa*, c. 1505-13, oil on wood panel, 30×20⅞ inches (77×53 cm), Musée du Louvre, Paris. Although it is now believed that there is no real evidence identifying the subject of this portrait with Mona Lisa, wife of the Florentine silk merchant Francesco del Giocondo, the picture has been known for so long and so widely as the *Mona Lisa* that it is an affectation to call it anything else.

BELOW: Detail of the hands of the *Mona Lisa* (right).

If all Leonardo's paintings after the *Battle of Anghiari* present difficulties of dating and interpretation, of none is this more true than the so-called *Mona Lisa* (right). The popular titles of this painting (*Mona Lisa, La Gioconda, La Joconde*) derive from Vasari who identified her as Madonna Lisa, wife of Francesco di Bartolomeo di Zanobi del Giocondo, a Florentine silk merchant. However, Vasari was describing a painting he had never seen, and it seems likely that his identification was based on a misinterpretation of the Anonimo Gaddiano who recorded that Leonardo had painted Francesco del Giocondo, not his wife. So who is she? Inconclusive references in documents of various dates, along with the prominent place the painting has in popular imagination and in the history of art, tempt us to identify her as some eminent or regal personage, perhaps Isabella d'Este or the Duchess of Burgundy, wife of Louis XII. Certainly, the latter is not improbable, as Louis XII was Leonardo's patron and had referred to the possibility of sitting himself for a portrait to Leonardo. However, it seems that the painting's history is as complex and darkly veiled as the lady herself.

Although it is more difficult to look with fresh eyes on this painting than on any other work of art, sustained contemplation of it reveals that the hold it has exercised is not solely based on some indefinable aura of mystery about her. The presentation and setting of the figure is highly original. Although the panel has been trimmed at the sides, we can see enough of the columns to recognize that the figure is seated on a balcony with a landscape vista behind her. Such a vision was almost totally

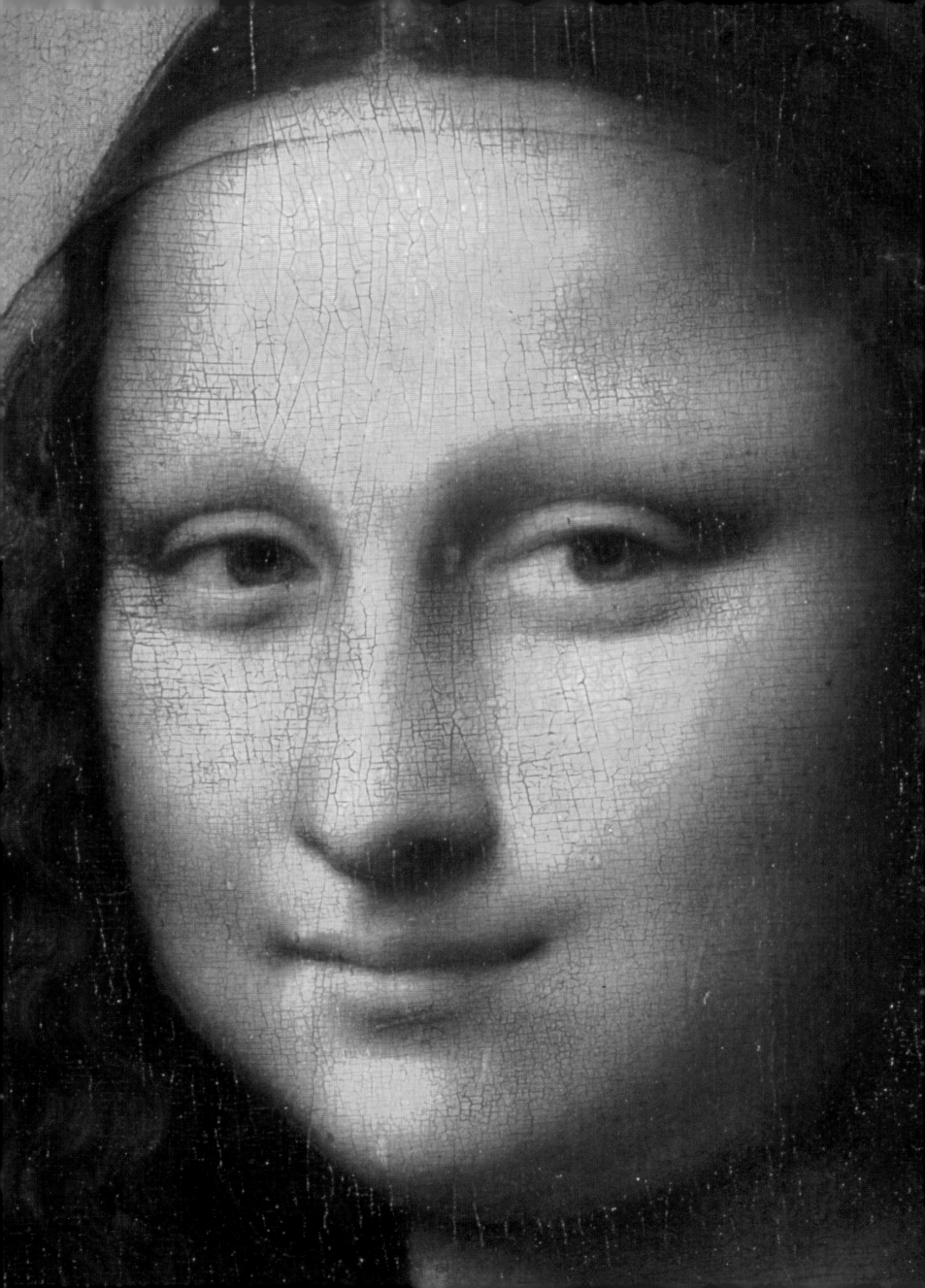

LEFT AND BELOW: Details from the *Mona Lisa* (page 131).

unprecedented in Florentine portraiture; even Leonardo's own previous exercises in female portraiture such as *Cecilia Gallerani* (page 76) or *Ginevra de' Benci* (page 46) had had no background, or only a glimpse, as through a small window, of such a scene. Here the figure and the landscape together constitute the painting, and the landscape is no longer merely a decorative backdrop. The way the treatment of the figure and of the landscape mirror one another is related to Leonardo's twin studies in the early years of the sixteenth century of the anatomy of the human body and its control of human action and expression, and of the movement and development of landscape through geological change and the actions on it of natural forces. This convergence of action and form is seen in the way the twisting flow of draperies and veils echoes the natural actions of the flowing river, and, most particularly in the reflexion of the curls of her hair with the spume of a waterfall. This demonstrates Leonardo's contention that opposing forces of curling and gravity in hair correspond in action and, therefore in form, to the opposing motions of the main current of a river and the force of deflected water.

But of course the reason for the *Mona Lisa*'s fame does not only rest on the fact of its establishment of a novel genre of portraiture, or its demonstration of one of the artist's abstruse theories. It does also have to do with the famous smile. The question immediately arises as to

whether or not she is smiling and this ambiguity is the key to the painting's effect. In the *Cecilia Gallerani* (page 76) and *Ginevra de' Benci* (page 46) portraits (and in *Le Belle Ferronière* [page 83], if you accept that as a work of Leonardo) great emphasis is placed on individual character and/or individual response to the viewer. In the *Cecilia Gallerani* portrait we sense very clearly the nature of the sitter's character and feel that we see her at a particular moment responding to some unseen presence. But her

gaze is directed away from us. With Ginevra de' Benci she stares at us with gaze open, as we have seen, to varied interpretation but which I would venture to suggest is rather general, whatever its meaning, and unfocussed. This is the central difference in nature from the *Mona Lisa*. Her gaze is directed at us as individuals, not as a collective and impersonal audience, and that particularity forces us to respond on a far more profound level than with any previous portrait. The question of whether or not

she is smiling is irrelevant. Leonardo had made great study as we have seen, on the particular response of the human face to particular emotions. He demonstrated these varieties in the *Last Supper* and in the *Battle of Anghiari*. We can, therefore, be certain that the variety of interpretations that can be put on the *Mona Lisa*'s expression is intentional; we are caught by her gaze and remain trapped by it, trying to ascertain its meaning which is so skillfully directed towards us.

LEFT: School of Leonardo *Leda*, oil on wood panel, 38×29 inches (96.5×73.7 cm), Collection of the Earl of Pembroke, Wilton House Trust, Salisbury, Wiltshire.

BELOW RIGHT: Study for the kneeling *Leda*, c. 1504, pen, bister, and wash over black chalk, 6¼×5½ inches (16×13.9 cm), Devonshire Collection, Chatsworth House, Derbyshire. Reproduced by permission of the Trustees of the Chatsworth Settlement. Several drawings for a lost painting of *Leda* survive, of which the earliest show Leda kneeling. Because most of the sixteenth-century copies show Leda standing (pages 136 and 140), it is usually assumed that Leonardo's settled on this formula in his painting.

Many of the uncertainties surrounding the *Mona Lisa* are due to the lack of preparatory drawings of any kind which would help us date it and understand something of its genesis. Similar problems surround another major project which must have been roughly contemporary with the *Mona Lisa* (certainly if we assign it as wide a span of dates as 1506 and 1516). This is the *Leda*, although with this work it is the final painting we lack, not the preparatory drawings. The earliest of these date from around 1504 when Leonardo was hard at work on the *Battle of Anghiari*. These and subsequent drawings up to around 1506 developed a scheme of a Leda kneeling on one knee, with one arm around the swan. (The story of Leda and the swan tells how Jupiter, disguised as a swan, fathered by Leda four children, Castor, Pollux, Clytemnestra and Helen, who were hatched from eggs.) This kneeling Leda has classical precedent in a type of kneeling Venus. From a drawing at Chatsworth House (right) we can see that Leonardo's conception of the picture at this time was of a relentless sense of movement and undulation. This is expressed not only by the various swirling forms of the plants, Leda's pose, the eggs, etc, but also by his drawing style: the lines of the pen now parallel and follow the contours he is describing.

Some time around 1507-08 Leonardo transformed Leda into a standing figure. We may assume that it was this version he used as the basis for his painting, because of these later drawings, and because the most convincing copies show this form, with some variations (pages 136 and 140). This type of figure also had classical precedents, but the reason for the change may have been to temper somewhat the frantic sense of spiralling form and movement suggested by the kneeling Leda drawing. The standing Leda has a more gentle contemplative curve through

her head, neck, torso and hips; the many subtle variations on this figure we can find in the drawings reveal that the decision to choose the standing figure was carefully calculated. Certainly the sense of teeming life is still there in the burgeoning forms of plant life and, in the hatching babies, animal life, making *Leda* something of a hymn to fecundity.

Both *Leda* and the *Mona Lisa* repre-

sent ideas that were formulated in Florence at a time when Leonardo was deeply involved in anatomical and geological studies, and then worked on over a number of years up to and perhaps beyond the time he left for France in 1516. A project which occupied him for a much shorter period of time was the Trivulzio monument. Giovanni Giacomo Trivulzio was a Milanese condottiere who in 1504 had assigned 4000

LEFT: School of Leonardo *Leda*, c. 1510-15, oil on wood panel, 44×37⅞ inches (112×86 cm), Galleria Borghese, Rome.

BELOW RIGHT: Andrea del Verrocchio (c. 1435-88) *Lady with the Primroses*, c. 1475, marble, height 24 inches (61 cm), Bargello, Florence. The similarity in conception between this and several of Leonardo's female portraits, especially the *Lady with an Ermine (Cecilia Gallerani)* (page 76) has prompted the suggestion that Leonardo may have assisted his master with this work. Otherwise, no sculpture by Leonardo is known to survive.

ducats to pay for a monument to himself. Leonardo presented detailed drawings and estimates for an equestrian monument, perhaps anxious to revive some of the ideas he had been prevented from realizing in the Sforza monument. Certainly, he seems to have toyed again with the idea of a rearing horse, but the scheme that he seems to have fixed upon was for a walking horse mounted on a canopy over an effigy of Trivulzio on a coffin. The version which he favored seems to have had its head turned to one side, somewhat in the manner of his master Verrocchio's Colleoni monument (page 7) in Venice. But, once again, Leonardo was foiled in his attempt to create a grand equestrian monument. Trivulzio had fled to Naples and was not on good terms with Charles d'Amboise, governor of Milan. After Charles's death in 1511 when Trivulzio returned to Milan, Leonardo's drawings suggest he hoped the scheme might be realized, but presumably the funds were put to some other use.

Over the years attempts have been made to assign various pieces of sculpture to Leonardo. This is, on the face of it, unsurprising, as he was trained in the studio of Verrocchio whose finest surviving works are sculpture. And yet, when we understand Leonardo's own views on the relative merits of painting and sculpture it seems more of a wonder that he even contemplated undertaking work in three dimensions. The question of the relative merits of the arts, not just the visual arts, greatly exercised Leonardo's mind, as it did many of his contemporaries. In his notes for a treatise on painting, Leonardo has this to say about painting and sculpture:

The painter has ten considerations with which he is concerned in finishing his works, namely light, shade, color, body, shape, position, distance, nearness, motion and rest; the sculptor has only to consider body, shape position, motion and rest. . . . Therefore sculpture has fewer considerations and consequently is less demanding of talent than painting. (Translated by Martin Kemp, © 1981.)

Perhaps for the very reason that he considered sculpture inferior to painting as a means of artistic expression, relief, whose expression could, on the face of it, more easily be achieved in sculpture, was always of central importance in his painting. We have already seen its use in the London *Madonna of the Rocks*, but nowhere is it

LEFT: *St John*, c. 1509, oil on wood panel, 27⅛×22½ inches (69×57 cm), Musée du Louvre, Paris.

used with such singular conviction as in the *St John the Baptist* in the Louvre. This is the only surviving Leonardo painting which seems, on the strength of a drawing relating to it which can be dated, to belong wholly to the period after he left Florence in 1508. The effect of age must play a part in the darkness of this painting in its present form, but this is merely an exaggeration of the original effect. It is a purist demonstration of the effect of relief achieved by bringing a figure brightly lit out of a dark background. This chiaroscuro effect is present to a lesser or greater extent in all of Leonardo's paintings, but here it is used uncompromisingly to underline St John's uncompromising message, with the crucifix and the gesture of the raised finger found so

ABOVE: Study for the *Trivulzio Monument*, c. 1511, pen, ink, and red chalk, 8½×6⅝ inches (21.7×16.9 cm), Windsor Castle, Royal Library 12356r. © 1991 Her Majesty The Queen.

LEFT: Study for parts of a garment for the lost *Salvator Mundi* painting, c. 1510-15, red chalk and white on pink prepared surface, 6½×6¼ inches (16.4×15.8 cm), Windsor Castle, Royal Library 12525. © 1990 Her Majesty The Queen.

often in Leonardo's paintings from the *Adoration of the Magi* onwards. Yet the effect of such contrast is prevented from being too jarring by the use of 'sfumato,' the meltingly subtle modulations of tone which contribute so much to the mystery of the Mona Lisa's smile.

It is very difficult to determine what paintings Leonardo was working on after 1510, apart from continuing to rework the *Mona Lisa* and, presumably, *Leda*. Some red chalk drawings (pages 143 and 144) certainly date from 1510 or after and may be studies for a 'Christ à demi corps' recorded at Fontainebleau in 1642. Several versions of a *Salvator Mundi*, a hieratic figure of Christ with a globe in one hand, the other hand raised, must be copies of the painting for which these drawings are studies. More convincing as a work at least partly by Leonardo is the strange *St John-Bacchus* in the Louvre (page 145). This is largely by a pupil of Leonardo, but was based quite closely on a very fine red chalk drawing by Leonardo formerly in a mountain monastery at Varese. The drawing is certainly of a seated St John figure, and the transformation, the reason for which we can only speculate on, to Bacchus was achieved merely by adding a crown of vine leaves and a leopard skin.

There is something inherently very frustrating about the increasing difficulty we experience in trying to piece together Leonardo's activities as a painter in the last years of his life. Given the longstanding veneration he had, by then, enjoyed, it is puzzling that we should know so much more about his activities 10, 20 or even 30 years earlier. However, it cannot be forgotten that his activities as a painter occupied only a proportion, varying at different times of his life, of his interest. To understand the diversity of his activity we must study his drawings and manuscripts, to which we shall now turn.

The Drawings and Manuscripts

MARIA COSTANTINO

WHEN Leonardo dictated his last will and testament in France on 23 April 1519, he bequeathed all the books he had with him to his friend and student Francesco Melzi. Throughout his life Leonardo had carried with him his notebooks in which he would write down his ideas or sketch impressions. Manuscripts survive containing drafts of letters, rough copies of his treatises on painting and anatomy, as well as shopping lists, accounts and lists of his books.

After Melzi's death around 1570, the collection which included a great many of Leonardo's drawings, notes and anatomical studies passed to Melzi's son Orazio, who later sold the majority to a sculptor Pompeo Leoni (c. 1533-1608) in 1590. Leoni sorted and arranged the works into a number of volumes, grouping together studies with related subjects such as botanical and mechanical studies. In order to accomplish this, Leoni cut up many of the original sheets and placed them in different albums.

When Leoni went to Madrid where he was court sculptor until his death, he took with him the main part of his collection. The remainder (the Codex Atlanticus) was left in Milan and was bought after Leoni's death by Galeazzo Arconati. In 1637 along with ten further notebooks, the Codex Atlanticus was given to the Biblioteca Ambrosiana.

Leoni's Spanish volumes appear to have been bought by agents on behalf of the collector and antiquarian Thomas Howard, Earl of Arundel, and brought to England in the late 1620s. By 1690 they formed part of the Royal Collection, where they remain at the Royal Library, Windsor Castle. In addition to the Windsor-Leoni volume, Arundel also had the Codex Arundel, now in the British Museum, London. Whereas the 1700 sheets of the Codex Atlanticus are contained in album form, each of the 600 or so Windsor drawings is mounted individually.

In addition to the Windsor drawings and the Codex Atlanticus, there exists a series of manuscripts – some still in the form of Leonardo's original notebooks – in the Library of the Institut de France in Paris, and are named Manuscripts A through to M. Additionally, there are the Codex Forster in the Victoria and Albert Museum, London; the Codex Hammer (formerly the Codex Leicester) in the Los Angeles County Museum; the Codex Trivulziana in Milan and two re-discovered notebooks in the Biblioteca Nacional in Madrid – the Codices Madrid I and II.

In the early eighteenth century, the two Madrid codices were kept in the palace library of Philip V of Spain where they remained until 1830. At this time they were moved to the National Library. Erroneously catalogued, the notebooks were recorded as 'missing' until 1965, when they were rediscovered.

Despite the number of drawings and notes made by Leonardo that have survived, they are only a proportion of what must at one time have existed; the list of items in his possession when he left Florence in 1482 says that Leonardo had drawings of many flowers, angels, old men and women, nudes and studies of sections of the human body. The use of the word 'many' reminds us of the great quantity of works, particularly from his early years, that have been lost.

In those that have survived, however, we are not only able to see the wide variety of types of drawings – diagrams, maps, studies from life and nature, preparatory drawings for paintings, architectural and engineering works – but the range of drawing media used by Leonardo throughout the different periods in his lifetime – pen-and-ink drawings, metalpoint, washes, colored chalks and pastels.

RIGHT: *Human Figure in a Circle, Illustrating Proportion*, 1485-90, pen and ink, 13½×9⅝ inches (34.3×24.5 cm), Accademia, Venice. This drawing is related to Leonardo's studies of human and animal proportions.

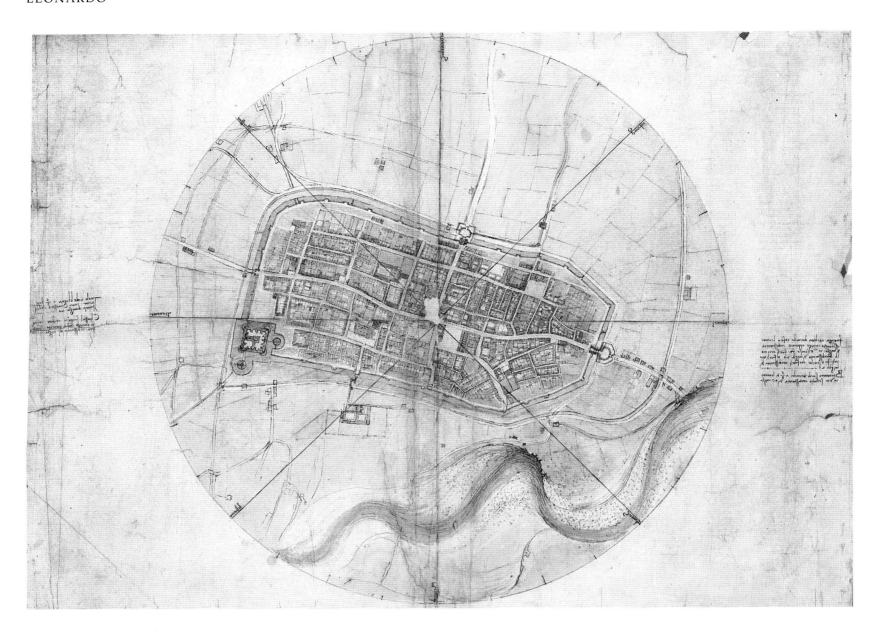

Weapons, Machines and Engineering

When Leonardo wrote to Ludovico Sforza, Duke of Milan, offering him his services and writing of his many talents, in the list of skills which the artist offered, thirty were of a technical nature and six were artistic. As a designer of machines and weapons in an age of transition from the crossbow to the cannon, Leonardo left us a wealth of drawings. Ironically, Leonardo despised war and called it a 'madness.' But living as he did at the beginning of the sixteenth century he was exposed to the conflicts that arose between the great powers of France, Naples, Milan, Venice and the Papal States which gave rise to an increased demand for the technical means of warfare, of military engineering and of defensive architecture.

The mid 1400s had already seen capable and experienced fortress builders like Filippo Brunelleschi. Later years saw the rise in importance and esteem of military architects like Francesco di Giorgio (1439-1501) who, although he was a painter and sculptor, achieved the position of chief director of buildings and waterworks in his native city of Siena, where he was entirely respon-

sible for the architectural defenses of the city; he was later appointed architect and military engineer to the Duke of Urbino.

Leonardo, who between 1490 and 1505 served no less than five different masters as a military architect and engineer, was no stranger to Francesco di Giorgio: in 1490 he and Leonardo were in Pavia to consult on the construction of the cathedral. Leonardo also had a copy of Francesco di Giorgio's *Treatise of Architecture, Engineering and the Military Arts*, which contained drawings for weapons and fortifications, and from which Leonardo freely borrowed ideas and designs. From his readings of the works of Archimedes, Pliny and Vitruvius, Leonardo also became familiar with the military methods of the Roman period.

At the fall of Ludovico Sforza in the summer of 1499, all we know of Leonardo's work was that he was the 'ducal painter and engineer' – we have no exact description as to the nature of his engineering works except that he acted as an adviser for the duke's fortifications at Pavia, Vigevano and Milan.

When the French arrived in triumph in Milan, Leonardo was already out of the city, stopping en route to Florence

at Venice in March 1500 where he suggested to the government of the Serenissima the flooding of the Isonzo valley as a defensive measure against a possible land-borne invasion by the Turks. By Easter of 1500 Leonardo was back in Florence, where it seems he was regarded principally as a painter. Just over a year later, however, he entered the service of Cesare Borgia as an architect and general engineer. Borgia, as Duke of Romagna, was seen by Florence as a possible threat. In order to secure a peaceful relationship, Florence bought an alliance with Borgia by making him a condottiere of the Republic with an annual income of 30,000 gold ducats. As chargé d'affaires at his court, Borgia appointed Niccolò Machiavelli, whose task it was as political observer to report on the general situation.

In the summer of 1502 Leonardo accompanied Cesare on his conquering expedition through Emilia and the Marches, operating as the chief inspector of military buildings. The Manuscript L in Paris is Leonardo's diary of this journey and records the stops in the region between Imola, Cesena, Rimini, Urbino and Pesaro. But apart from some sketches outlining improve-

LEFT: *Plan of Imola*, c. 1502, pen, ink, and watercolor, 17⅓×23⅔ inches (44×60.2 cm), Windsor Castle, Royal Library 12284. © 1991 Her Majesty The Queen.

RIGHT: Leonardo made this map of Milan during the 1490s. Below the circular plan of the city is a perspective view of it, with the Cathedral near the center. Biblioteca Ambrosiana, Milan.

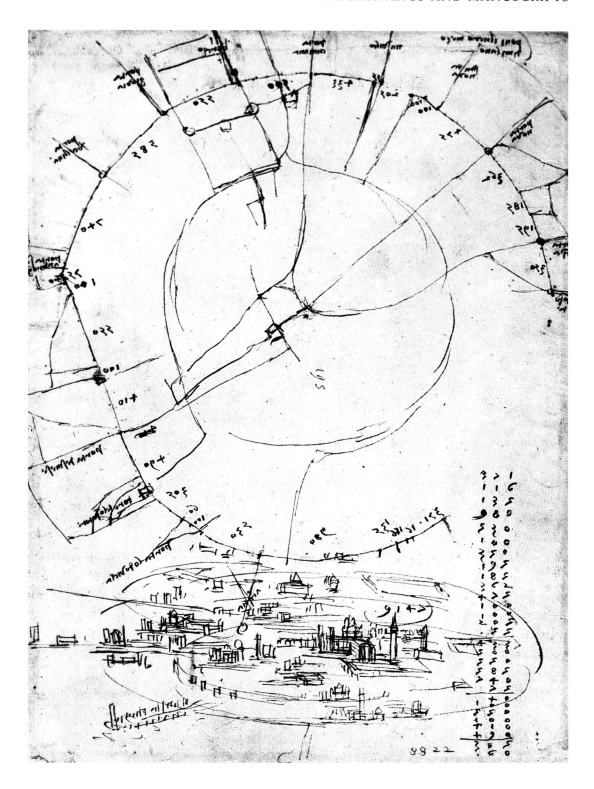

ments for the docks at Porto Cesenatico, we do not have any further insight into Leonardo's official activities.

Leonardo did, however, draw up the areas of Borgia's military operations: part of a map of Tuscany and Romagna was made for Borgia as was the magnificent *Plan of Imola*.

Imola was under the leadership of Borgia after 27 November 1499 and was an important strategic center. The map is normally dated around 1502, at the time when Cesare was planning a new campaign against the condottieri and some members of the nobility. Around the same time Machiavelli was in Imola and must certainly have met with Leonardo. For the circular map of the city, Leonardo used a horizontally mounted and graduated surveying disk – an astrolabe or some related instrument – in order to record the radial angles of the important features viewed from a high central vantage point. From the center of the circular plan are 64 equally spaced radiating lines, eight of which are drawn more boldly and labelled according to the tradition of the 'wind-rose,' a circle enclosing a double cross signifying the four cardinal points and four intermediate directions. The eight points are thus labeled: *septantrione* (north), *grecho* (north east), *levante* (east), *sirocho* (south east), *mezzodi* (south), *libecco (south west), ponente* (west) and *maesto* (north west). The distance on the ground between features was measured by 'pacing out'; the linear and angular measurements were then correlated to produce the developed version of the map. (In the Windsor Royal Collection there is a study sheet on which individual sections have been surveyed and the fortifications and town gates sketched in).

The end product is an immensely accurate and beautiful map where every detail is pin-pointed and color-coded: houses are tinted pink, public squares a dark yellow and the streets in white. Imola, with its castle at the lower left, is surrounded by a moat colored blue. The notes to either side of the circular plan, written very neatly but nevertheless in mirror writing (from right to left with the letters in reverse form) refer to the geography, distance and bearings of Bologna and other cities of military importance or interest to Cesare Borgia. During the 1490s in Milan, Leonardo had also sketched maps. On the map of Milan Leonardo drew the circular groundplan with the city gates named on the circumference. Below this he sketched in perspective a view of the city showing the main buildings – the cathedral in the middle and the Castello Sforzesco at the left.

From the remarks Leonardo made in Ms L, we are able to see that he also visited the area of Piombino, part of Cesare's dominion at the northern end of the Tyrrhenian Sea. The city of Piombino itself was of economic importance for it was in its fortified harbor that iron ore from the island of Elba was unloaded, and was of political importance as it occupied a central point between the bordering territories of the Papal States in the south, Lombardy and Genoa to the north and Florence to the east.

Following a protracted siege in 1501, Borgia succeeded in wresting Piombino from its ruler Jacopo IV Appinani. Pope Alexander cemented his son's victory by assigning all ruling rights to Cesare Borgia who was now able to add 'Signore di Piombino' to his long list of titles.

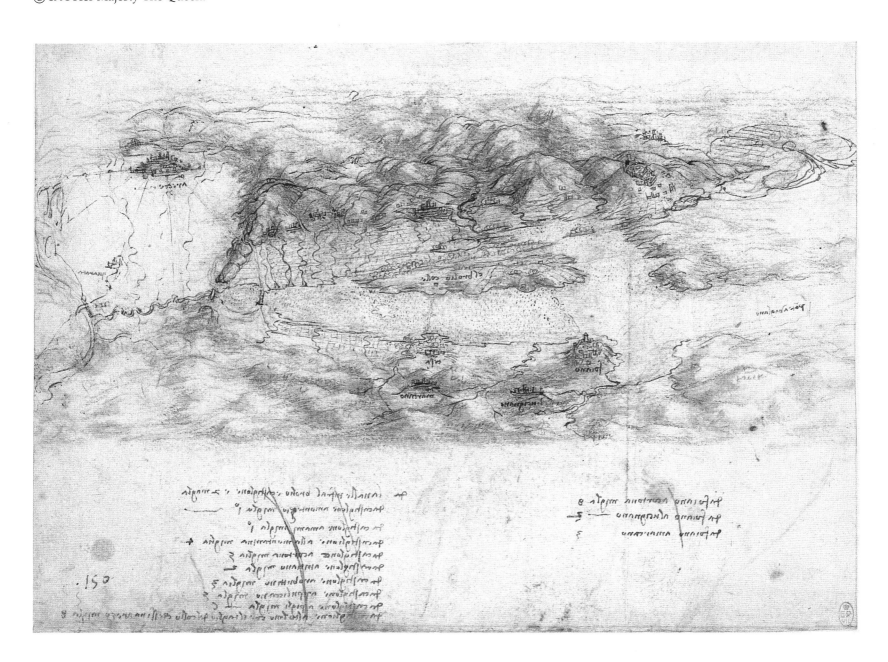

In 1502 Leonardo possibly made a map showing Arezzo and the valley of Chiana for Borgia. The map appears as though it has been drawn from the air but was in fact created by using an imaginary perspective and views and studies Leonardo had earlier made of the region.

By the spring of 1503 Leonardo had given up his post with Borgia and returned to Florence which at the time was engaged in a lengthy war against Pisa. In the new campaign against its old rivals, there emerged in the Florentine camp a plan to divert the course of the river Arno, to cut the Pisans off from their access to the sea and thus starve the city into submission.

One of the chief promoters of the scheme to the leader of the Florentine Republic, Piero Soderini, was Niccolò Machiavelli who was at this time the war minister. Leonardo must have had knowledge of the plan but whether he was actively involved in its organization is uncertain. In July 1503, by order of the council, Leonardo set off for the Florentine camp to inspect the trench digging. For over a year the Arno scheme was in action. Two canals were finally decided upon: one in the estuary area was for diverting the Arno waters off to the river Serchio; the second canal was to run from Vico Pisano to the Stagno Livorno. In terms of the manpower required to dig the canals, which

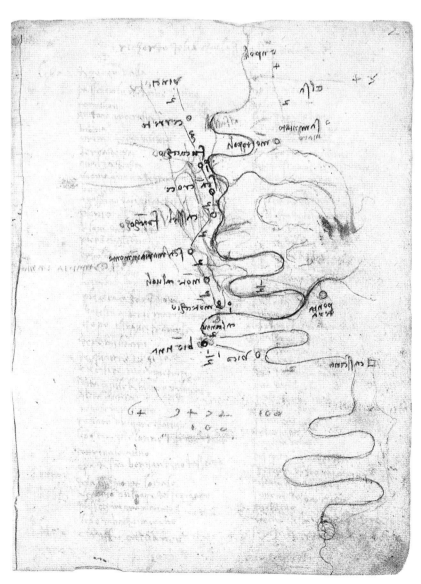

were to be some 40-60 feet wide, the Signoria calculated on 2000 men completing the work in 200 days. In fact, they had underestimated the workforce by some 8000 workers. Furthermore, frequently overdue with payments to the workforce, they had made it difficult if not impossible to secure the labor and when a section of canal wall collapsed after flooding, dissention for the project started to mount. Machiavelli continued to push for the scheme in letters and reports, but in October 1504 the scheme was finally abandoned.

Leonardo himself had for some years a strong interest in diverting the Arno – not to isolate Pisa but to make the river navigable from Florence to Pisa and thereby increase trade in Tuscany as a whole. In another study of the canal system for the Arno, exact about distances, Leonardo stated that a canal would make the waterway twelve miles shorter and that 'Prato, Pistoia and Pisa as well as Florence will gain 200,000 ducats a year and will lend a hand and money to this useful work.'

The diversion into a canal system of the Arno with its sharp bends and variations of level had been suggested one hundred years before Leonardo's birth: in 1347 and again in 1458 Florence set about canalizing the river. In 1487 the

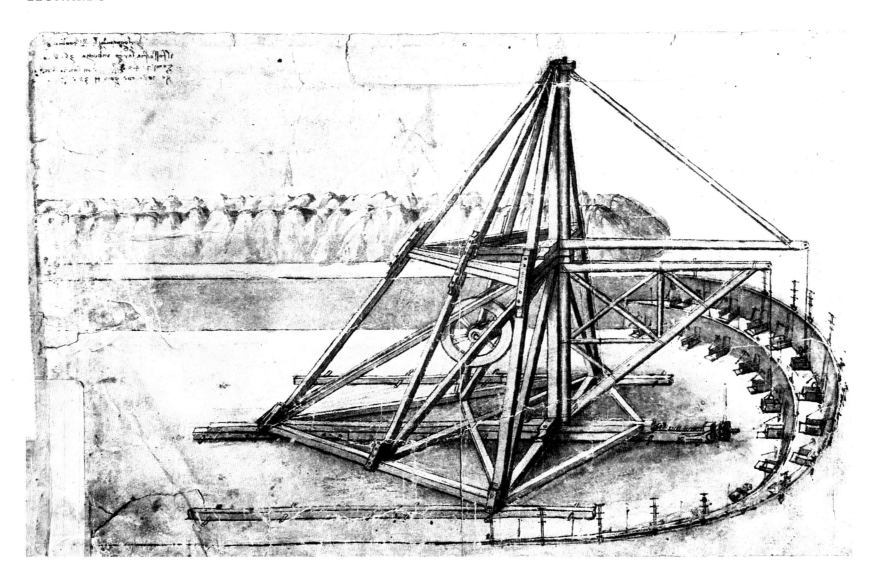

Milanese architect Luca Francelli, reminded his patron Lorenzo de Medici that Piero de Medici had also had a similar plan in mind.

In Leonardo's map he traced the course of the river from Pisa (at the bottom) to Empoli, near Florence and between the towns on the river he noted their distances. Also, aware of the inefficiencies of men working with shovels, Leonardo designed a treadmill-powered digging machine which could do the work of many men.

Despite such marvellous designs, Leonardo's exact position in the Arno scheme is difficult to determine. He was certainly aware of the plan, possibly entrusted with putting the scheme into operation, but remained critical of it. He did produce a map, drawn over a double page, of the military operations around Pisa. In this map the topographical names stated such as Serchio, Arno, Torre di Foce, Verrucola and Vico correspond with the center of operations cited by Machiavelli's letters. Furthermore, 'fossi' or canal courses have been plotted. The place names are written neatly in Leonardo's ordinary hand and not in mirror writing suggesting that this map was destined for his employers, but it is still doubtful whether the map was intended as a proposal or plan of execution. On the double page of the

Codex Madrid II f 22v-23v, Leonardo drew, in color, the course of the Arno from Florence to the estuary behind Pisa and to the sea. The river can be seen meandering across the two pages from Florence at the lower right, to Pisa at the extreme left. The two lines that curve north from Florence are the two possible routes that Leonardo studied between Florence and Pistoia: one goes

east through Prato, the other via Poggio a Caiano. At Pistoia the canal would then skirt Monte Albano, run through a pass or tunnel at Serra Alse and run south to rejoin the river at Vico Pisano. Although never constructed, 400 years later engineers would more or less follow a similar route when constructing the autostrada linking Florence to the sea.

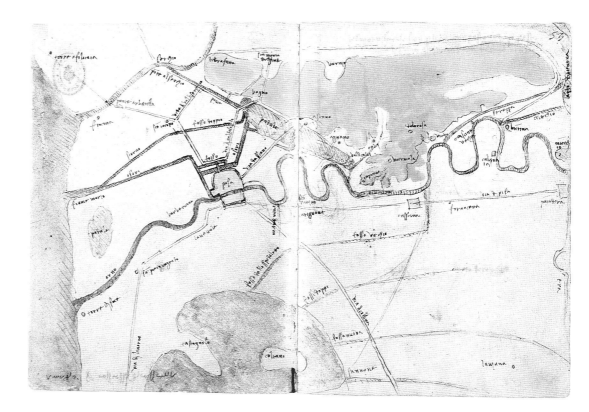

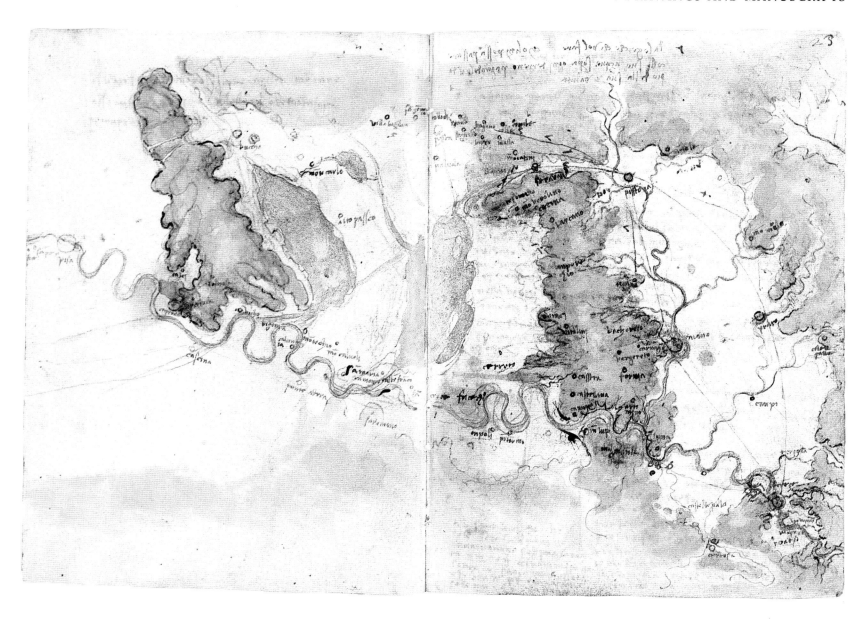

ABOVE LEFT: Many of Leonardo's inventions were designed specifically to aid other of his grandiose schemes. This is a design for an excavating machine. Biblioteca Ambrosiana, Milan.

ABOVE: Here Leonardo has drawn the course of the Arno from Florence to the estuary near Pisa. Biblioteca Nacional, Madrid.

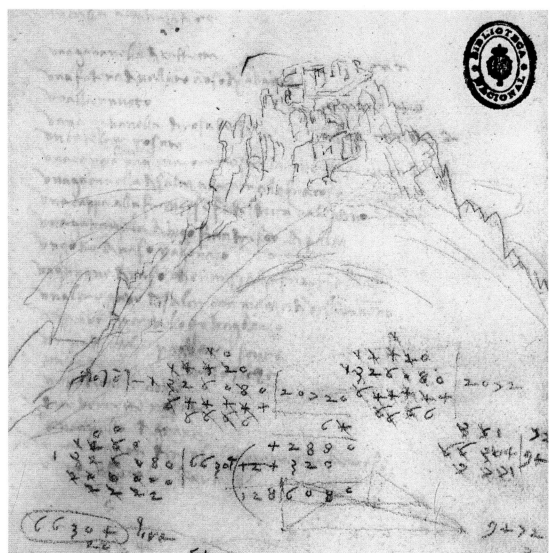

BELOW LEFT: Leonardo's scheme for canalizing the Arno. Biblioteca Nacional Madrid.

RIGHT: Leonardo calculated how to guarantee that two tunnels started on opposite sides of a mountain would meet in the middle. Biblioteca Nacional, Madrid.

When the plan to cut Pisa off from the sea collapsed (along with the canal itself) military activities were halted, albeit temporarily. The Signoria, recalling the Florentine troops, now planned to isolate Pisa through political channels.

In April 1504 Machiavelli went to Piombino: his mission was to make a treaty on behalf of Florence with Jacopo IV Appiani who had returned to the city after Cesare Borgia's fall from power. It was a delicate mission since Jacopo had been passed over for the position of a highly paid condottiere in favor of Borgia in 1499. Machiavelli now had the task of trying to win back the confidence of Jacopo and to ensure his neutrality in the arguments and hostilities between Florence and Pisa and Florence and Siena. The neutrality to Pisa was easy enough – Jacopo still bore a grudge against the city for having forced the Appiani family out of Pisa four generations earlier. In order to woo him to neutrality towards Siena, in the fall of 1504 it is not surprising that we find Leonardo in Piombino advising Jacopo on the fortifications of the city. Ironically, the defense of Piombino had been a project originally devised by Jacopo's arch-enemy, Cesare Borgia, before his demise.

ABOVE: *Bird's-eye View of the Coast of Italy, North of Terracina*, c. 1515, pen, ink, and watercolor, 10⅞×15¾ inches (27.7×40 cm), Windsor Castle, Royal Library. © 1991 Her Majesty The Queen.

BELOW: Leonardo designed this breakwater for the harbor of Piombino. It may owe something to the ideas of Francesco di Giorgio (right). Biblioteca Nacional, Madrid.

Although no-one knows whether any actual construction was carried out, the tower of the main gate at Piombino is still known today as 'Leonardo's tower.'

That Leonardo advised Jacopo Appiani on the fortifications of Piombino is relatively new information made available by the 're-discovery' of the Madrid Codex II. In this codex Leonardo also drew plans for a reconstructed harbor (Porta Falesia) with a breakwater which had by this time fallen into ruin. In his new plan Leonardo added a fortification to guard the breakwater from sea-borne assaults. Such a breakwater had already been devised by Franceso di Giorgio in his *Treatise of Architecture, Engineering and Military Art*, a copy of which Leonardo owned.

BELOW: Francesco di Giorgio (1439-1502) *Design for a Harbor with a Semi-circular Breakwater*. Biblioteca Nazionale Centrale, Florence.

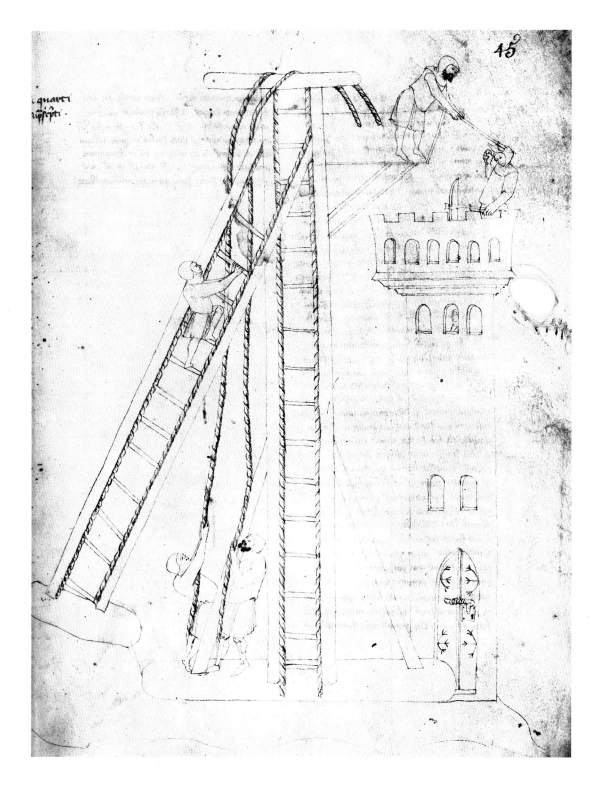

From him, Leonardo also borrowed a sketch for a citadel with rounded towers. The increasing power of firearms at the end of the fifteenth century made it necessary to rethink the principles of fortress building. Until the 1470s, most fortified buildings had square turretted towers and high walls. To counter the effects of bombardments, architects were now building forts with rounded towers with thick inclined walls that were better suited to deflecting and withstanding heavy artillery fire. In his plans for Piombino, Leonardo paid particular attention to the need for an efficiently organized firepower: in place of hot tar dumped on soldiers who tried to scale the fortress walls with ladders, Leonardo placed a cannon – one of the first military architects to do so. In the Codex Madrid II, Leonardo shows in one sketch his cannon in the tower, and in another sketch he plots the cannon's line of fire.

ABOVE: This fourteenth-century military treatise illustrates a mobile tower for attacking ramparts; Leonardo was to make use of a similar idea.

RIGHT: With increasing use of artillery, castle design changed rapidly, from the use of square towers with high walls, to round towers and much squatter walls, Leonardo borrowed the idea for this castle design from Francesco di Giorgio's treatise on military architecture, a copy of which he owned. Biblioteca Nacional, Madrid.

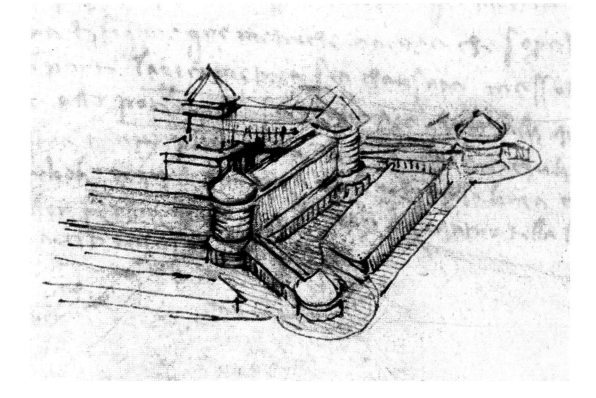

156

BELOW: As part of plans for Piombino, Leonardo designed this cannon to be used in a tower. Biblioteca Nacional, Madrid.

BELOW: The trajectory of a cannon ball was traditionally reckoned to be two straight lines joined by a short curve. Although this view prevailed into the seventeenth century, Leonardo had recognized the true parabolic nature of the cannon ball's trajectory. Biblioteca Nacional, Madrid.

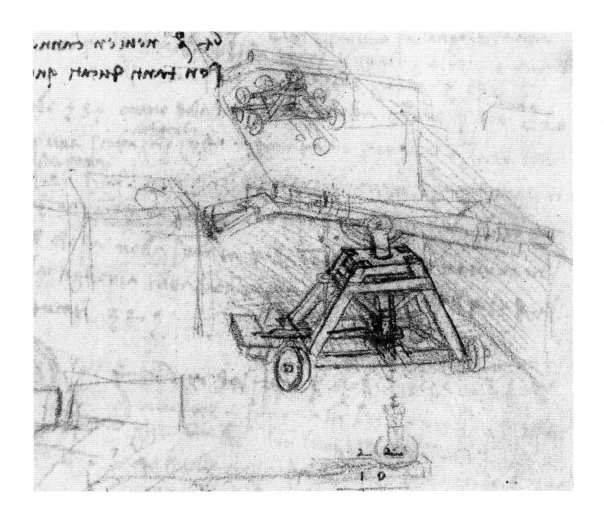

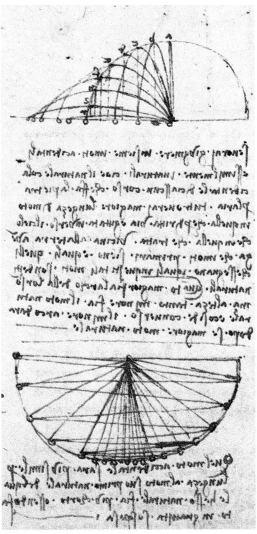

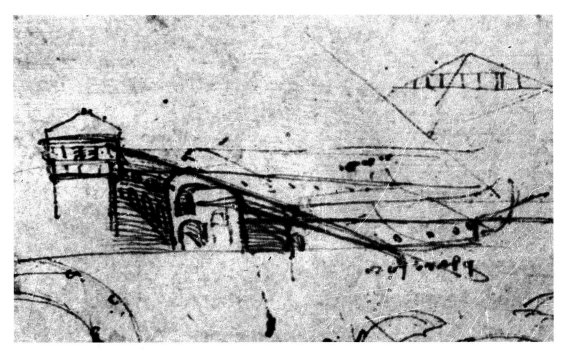

LEFT: In his military engineering and architecture, Leonardo produced both offensive and defensive designs.

In his letter to Ludovico Sforza, Leonardo claimed that he could make canon and mortars that were both beautiful and different from those already in use. Renaissance firearms had several limitations, the chief being their inaccuracy and slow rate of fire. One of Leonardo's solutions was to organize a series of light cannon or 'scoppietti' in a fan pattern as shown in his design for a *Gun with an Array of Horizontal Barrels* dated c. 1481. The 10-barreled gun, whose aim could be altered by means of a screw jack, would be most effective against ranks of infantrymen as the machine would saturate the enemy with its fire. At the top of this sheet also appears a design for a gun that would also heavily bombard the enemy, but has the added advantage with its arrangement of three ranks of 11 barrels, that while one rank was being fired, a second rank could be being loaded. This design, arranged 'a organi' (in the manner of organs) that could also be arranged in a fan pattern, as seen in the drawing at the foot of the folio.

Leonardo seems to have had a particular interest in designs that multiplied a single force: almost a year after he arrived in Milan he made the sketch depicting a mounted warrior carrying not one but three lances, two of which are attached to the riders' saddle.

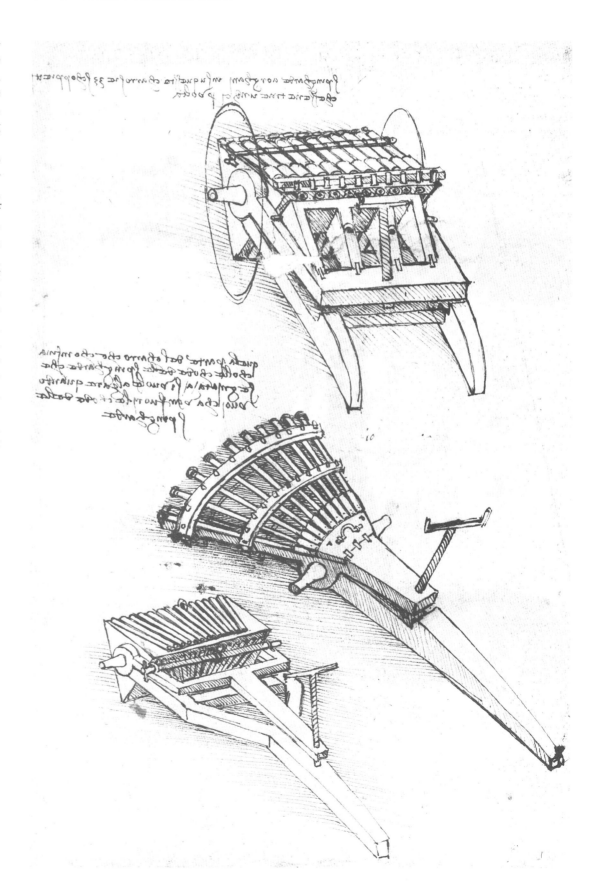

ABOVE: *A Scythed Chariot, Armored Vehicle, and a Partisan*, c. 1485-88, pen, ink, and wash, 6⅞×9⅝ inches (17.3×24.6 cm). Courtesy of the Trustees of the British Museum, London.

One of Leonardo's most famous war designs is that of *A Scythed Chariot, Armored Vehicle and Partisan*, c. 1487, in the British Museum. The scythed chariot was most likely inspired by descriptions of antique machines: history students will no doubt recall a similar chariot driven by Queen Boudicca. Beneath the chariot Leonardo explains that when the chariot moves through the ranks of one's own army, by raising the shafts of the scythes, no one will be injured. Two views of the armored

vehicle or tank are given by Leonardo. Like a turtle rolled on its back, the upside down view of the tank without its roof, shows the arrangement inside the car which he designed to carry eight men. As it moved along, the tank created a cloud of dirt, useful for breaking up the ranks. With its roof on, the tank backs up Leonardo's claim that he could provide Sforza with safe covered vehicles capable of penetrating the enemy ranks and clearing a path for the following infantrymen.

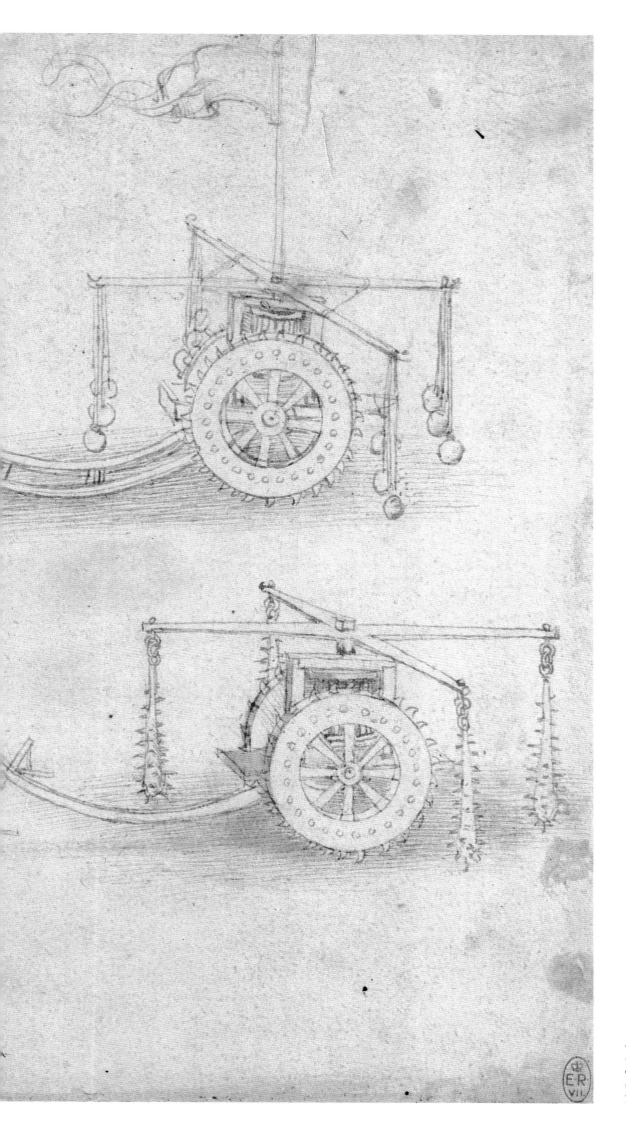

A Chariot Armed with Flails, an Archer with a Shield, and a Horseman with Three Lances,
c. 1485-88, pen, ink, and wash, 7⅞×11 inches
(20×20.7 cm), Windsor Castle, Royal Library
12563. © 1991 Her Majesty The Queen.

RIGHT: *Studies of Mortars, One Firing from a Boat, and of Cannon*, c. 1485-88, pen and ink, 11⅛×8⅝ inches (28.2×20.5 cm), Windsor Castle, Royal Library 12652r. © Her Majesty The Queen.

BELOW: *A Giant Crossbow on Wheels*, c. 1485-88, pen, ink, and wash, 7⅞×10⅝ inches. Biblioteca Ambrosiana, Milan.

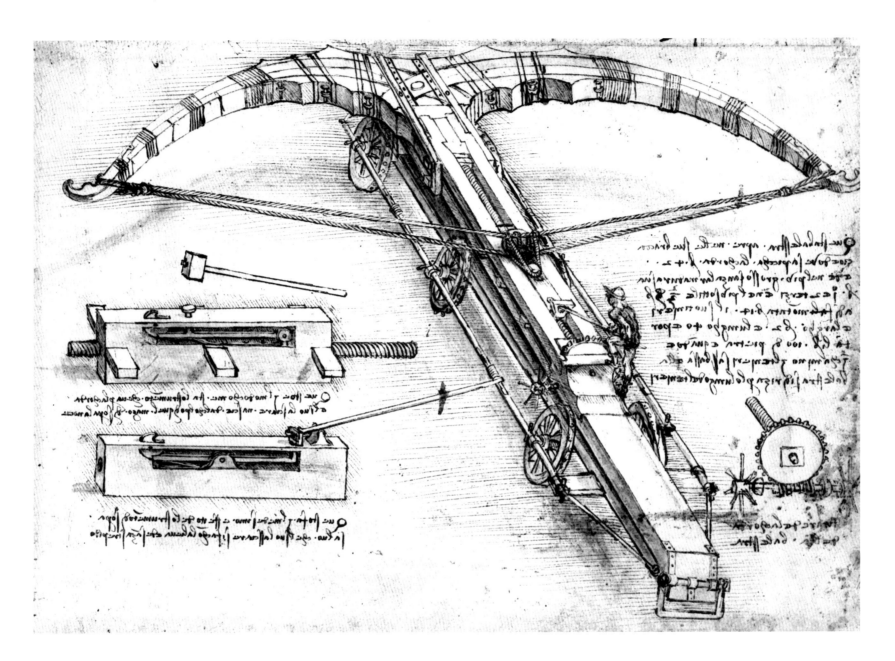

Like the project for the armored car, Leonardo's designs for *Marine and other Weaponry*, c. 1483-84 (WRL 12652) supports the claims he made to Sforza for both offensive and defensive vessels for war at sea. The device at the top of the page, a cannon, was intended to hurl small stones like a hail storm or to shoot salvos of Greek Fire (incendiary shells) causing terror and confusion to the enemy. The cannon is shown mounted on the boat at the foot of the page but from the design it is difficult to see whether the cannon was supposed to shoot forwards. On the same folio there appears a design for an ignition method – possibly for the boat-mounted gun; a design for an upright motor and a double-barreled gun which is mounted on a pivot so that it could be swung around to face the enemy and fired while the other barrel

was being loaded. At the very top of the page appears the words: 'If ever the men of Milan did anything which was beyond the requirements or never?' which are generally interpreted as a sign of Leonardo's impatience with his Milanese employers over their unwillingness to put any of his ideas into action.

Leonardo's designs for weapons can be divided into three broad categories: catapults (ballista), cannon and muskets (arquebus). Until the refinement of the cannon the principal artillery weapon was the catapult (or ballista, as the larger models were called) which had been used by the Romans who called their machine 'scorpio.' Leonardo's drawing of an enormous ballista features some advanced designs: the bow is laminated for extra flexibility while the bow string is drawn back by a

worm-and-gear mechanism depicted in the lower right-hand corner. The two drawings to the left of the ballista are designs for the release mechanisms: the upper one is a spring device released by a blow from a hammer while the lower drawing shows a lever-action release mechanism.

The demand for increased fire power led to grander schemes like the *Design for a Treadmill-powered Crossbow*, a sort of huge machine gun where the archer is perched inside a big treadmill and releases in turn four crossbow arrows. The treadmill is turned by the foot-power of soldiers placed on the outer rim of the wheel for greater leverage, but who are protected, it was hoped, from any enemy fire by a pivoted shield of planks. On the right of the main drawing is a preliminary sketch of the crossbow as if it were in action.

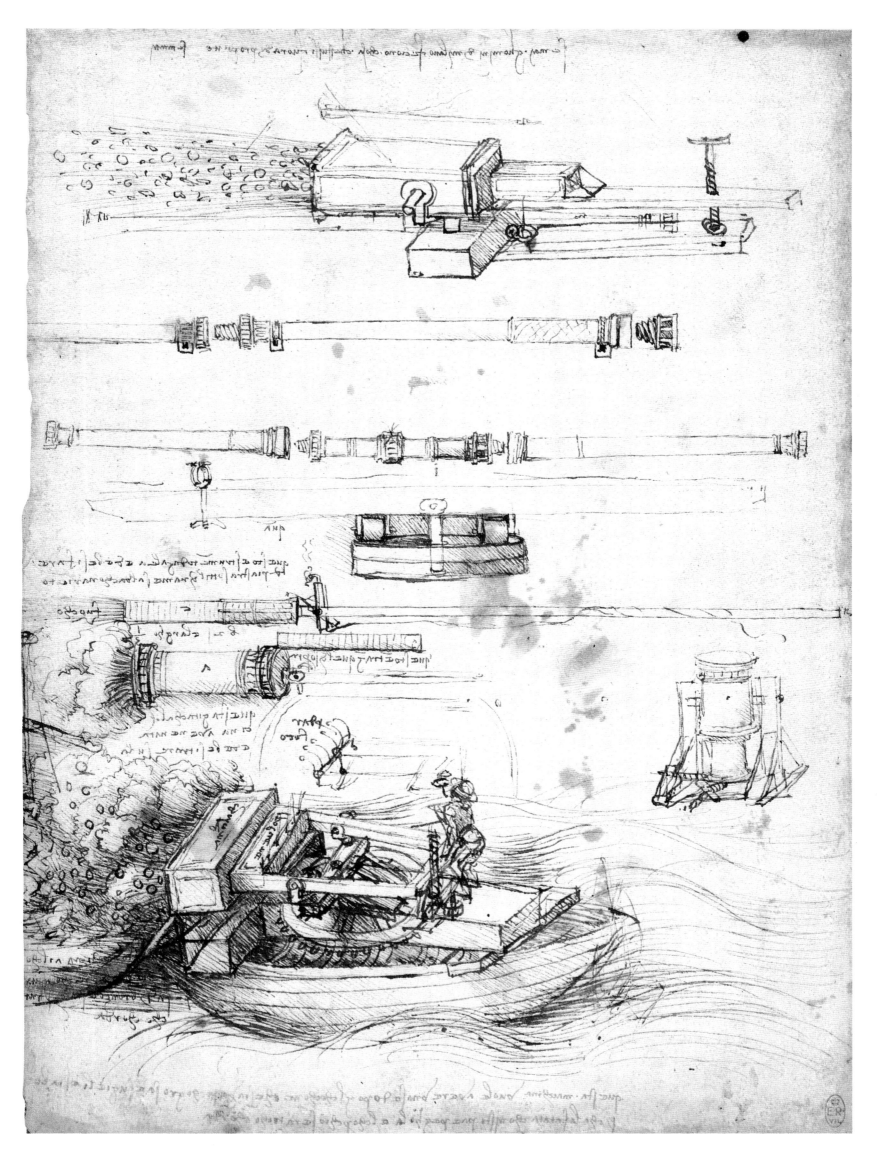

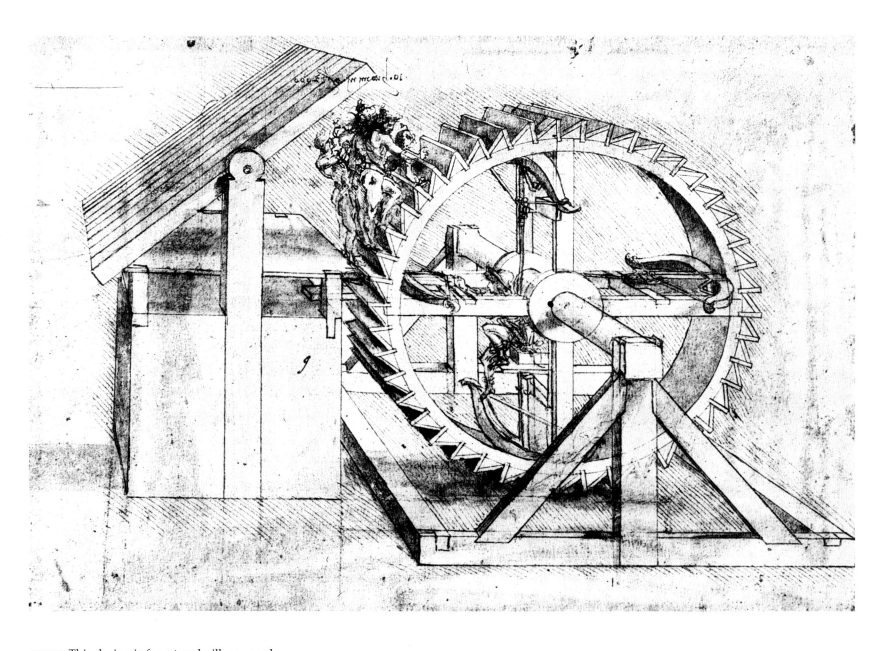

ABOVE: This design is for a treadmill-powered
crossbow: it allowed the archer – suspended in
the middle – to maintain a rapid rate of fire.
Biblioteca Ambrosiana, Milan.

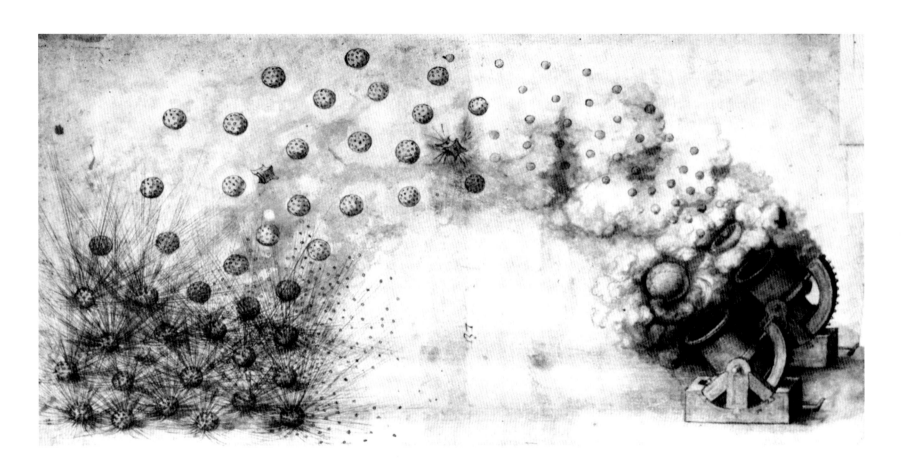

ABOVE: *Mortars with Explosive Projectiles*, pen,
ink, and sepia wash, 7½×14⅝ inches
(19.3×37.2 cm). Biblioteca Ambrosiana, Milan.

Guns and artillery and their fire-power were a constant area of study for Leonardo. Since the Battle of Crécy in 1346, when two cannons were used to fire shots propelled by gunpowder, the use of long-range firearms had advanced little. Leonardo was, however, in many respects well in advance in his studies. He was concerned with designs for breech-loading guns rather than muzzle-loading ones, multiple-fire capabilities and advanced gunmaking techniques as well as what he called the most deadly machine – a huge mortar firing shrapnel shells that exploded on impact, scattering their fragments.

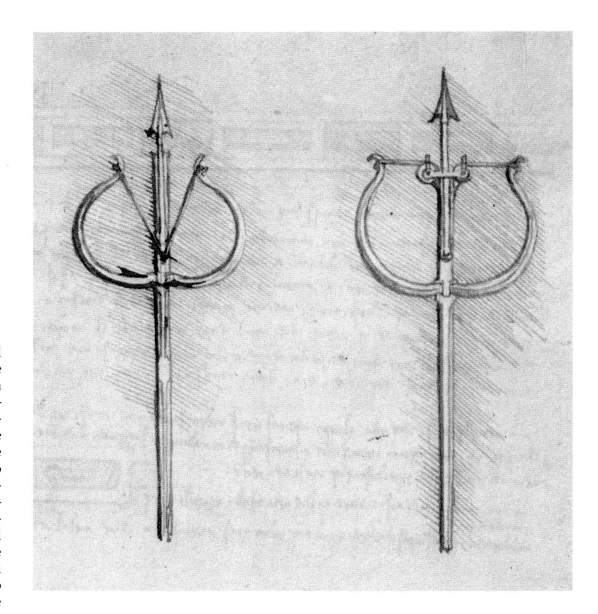

The sketches of crossbows and arrows in the Codex Madrid I are the records of a series of ballistic tests. In a note over one sketch Leonardo cautions 'test it first and state the rule afterwards' and in a margin of a page he notes one of his rules: 'The length of the arrows' descent will be in proportion to the weight used in spanning the crossbow.' In other tests Leonardo introduced feathers to help or hinder missiles' distance and direction. He noted also that the firing of a gun would be louder in foggy air, over water and against a wall. Furthermore, Leonardo did not subscribe to the belief that the trajectory of a cannon ball could be traced by two straight lines – the second line being vertical joined to the first by a short curve. Up until the late seventeenth century, military treatises still depicted the trajectory of a cannon ball in this manner. Leonardo however saw the actual parabolic curve produced by studying jets of water, but it would not be until 1632 that Galileo's mathematical reasoning proved it. Galileo, unlike Leonardo, did not see the role played by air resistance. To overcome it, Leonardo proposed streamlined and directional finned missiles.

The effectiveness of hand-held guns was recognized in the mid fifteenth century and from 1495 from a number of drawings for matchlock mechanisms. The matchlock, which fired a handgun by igniting gunpowder with a slow match, was still something of a novelty when Leonardo set about improving its design. In Codex Madrid I (f 18v) Leonardo sketched three devices for simultaneously opening the powder chamber and igniting the charge by a match in the form of a slow burning wick soaked in niter. Five years later in 1500, Leonardo would further refine his designs into a prototype wheel-lock mechanism – the same principle that we can find at work today in a wheel and flint cigarette lighter.

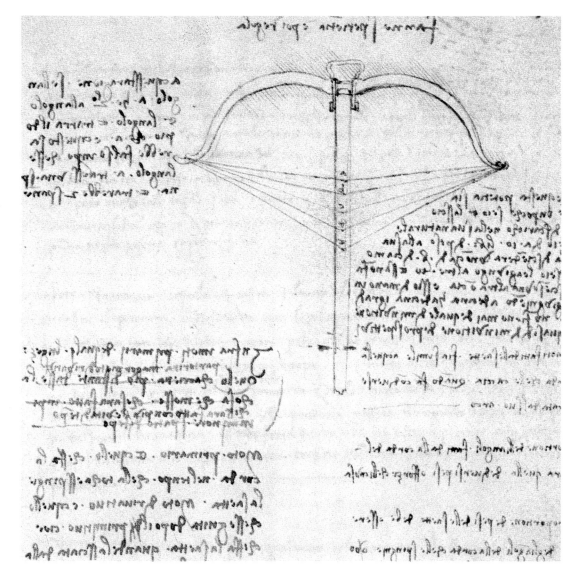

BELOW: This drawing reveals that Leonardo had devised a wheel-lock mechanism, the invention of which is usually attributed to a German watchmaker fifteen years later. To the left is the steel wheel and helical mainspring, next to which is the holder for the pyrite material used as a flint. At top right is the trigger mechanism, which forces the wheel to rub against the flint and produce a spark. Biblioteca Ambrosiana, Milan.

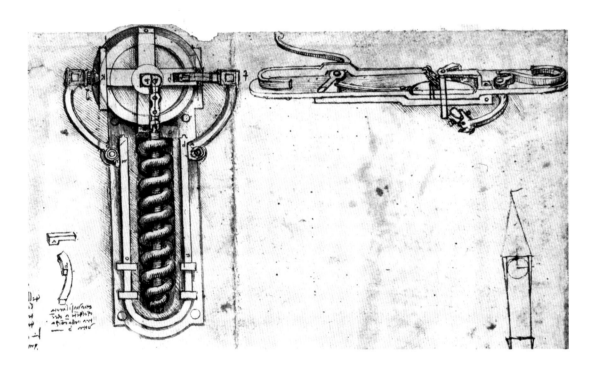

BELOW: This drawing shows Leonardo's ideas for improving the matchlock firing mechanism of a gun. The three mechanisms shown simultaneously open the powder charge and set fire to the touch-hole. Biblioteca Nacional, Madrid.

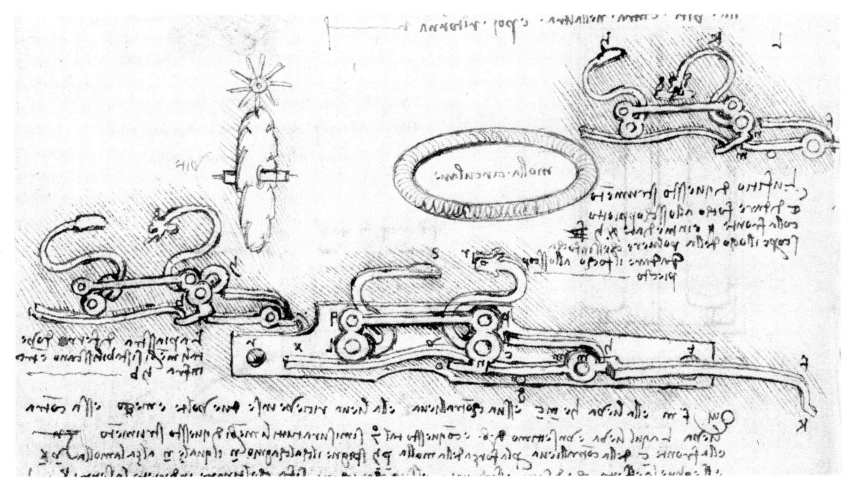

BELOW: The mechanism of this file-maker is so designed that the hammer falls at a regular rate to make the file evenly ridged. Biblioteca Ambrosiana, Milan.

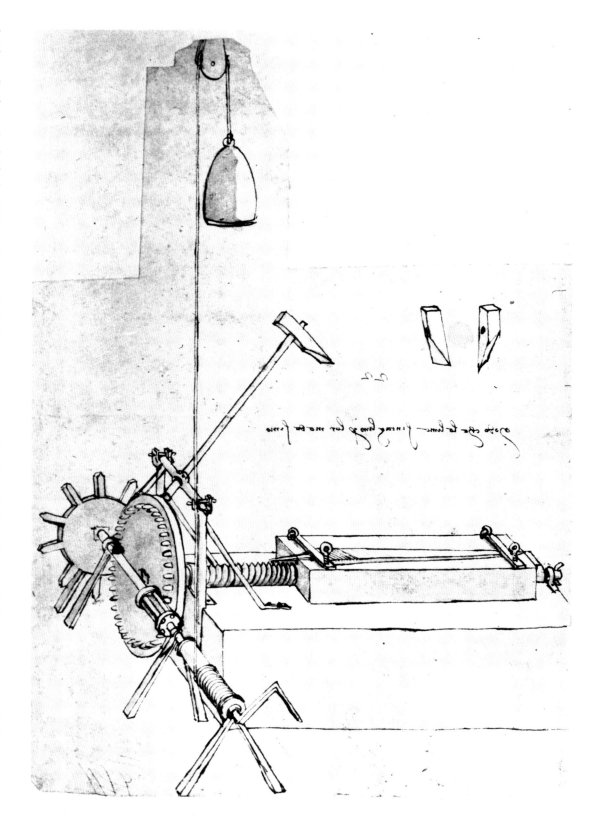

Whereas designs such as these were in advance of their time as they reduced the number of human actions required, in other of Leonardo's drawings he draws upon the need for sheer human force. From his early days in Milan, around 1487, comes *An Artillery Park*, a fusion of imagination and fact. Shown in the drawing, are teams of naked men struggling to raise an enormous cannon barrel by means of ropes, pulleys and wheels and in the foreground there is a cradle of rollers, a method of transporting large objects in use since Roman times. When this drawing was made, Leonardo was also studying the problems involved in casting his huge bronze equestrian monument. Ironically, the bronze earmarked for that project eventually found itself used in gun barrels.

An unusual piece of artillery that Leonardo devised was the 'architronito,' a steam-powered cannon. The breach of the cannon was to be placed in a basket-like brazier which contained burning coals. After the shot was rammed in and the breach sufficiently heated, water would be placed in the chamber that would normally hold the gunpowder. The explosion of steam was evidently enough to drive a cannon ball weighing '1 talent 6 stadia.' In this design the rate of fire is less important than the novelty of steam power, but steam-powered cannons were also practical weapons and were used effectively during the US Civil War and even in World War II when they were known as Holman Projectors. Not all of Leonardo's design were for machines of destruction. There are designs that were intended to be applied to general use in industry for hammering, shaping and boring, for raising weights and casting metals, for weaving, grinding and digging. Leonardo's own inventory divides these into the major categories of those for improving mechanical work, and thus

BELOW: This drawing of a windlass is
remarkable not just for the concept, but for the
modern way the device is presented in
composite (left) and exploded (right) view.
Biblioteca Ambrosiana, Milan.

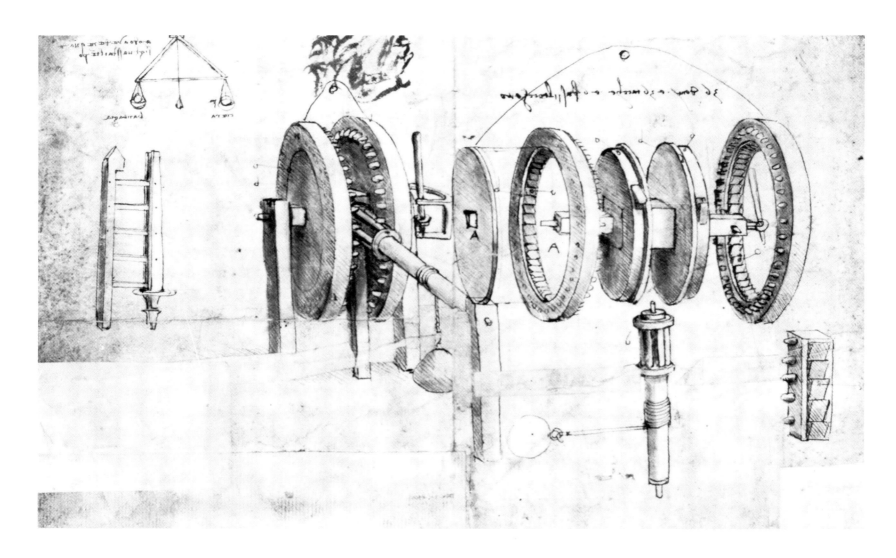

productive, and those with a military
use, and thus destructive.

One of Leonardo's earliest designs is
for a file- or rasp-maker. The machine
was designed to strike the teeth of the
file evenly on the face of a metal blank.
Once started, the machine would not
require any further human intervention except for re-cranking the weight
to its start position. The machine could
thus produce a larger number of files of
greater uniformity at a lower price.

There are also a number drawings of
devices which aimed at solving the
problem of translating rotary motion
into a reciprocating or piston-like action
(and vice versa). One design that deals
with this is the *Design for a Windlass* to

be used for hoisting heavy loads. Leonardo offers us two views of his device:
on the left we see the assembled windlass and on the right an exploded view
of the mechanism. Action begins when
the operator moves the vertical lever
(set in the square shaft in the assembled
version of the drawing forwards and
backwards. The teeth on the two inner
discs engage ratchets that line the two
outer rings (as seen in the exploded
drawing). The gear teeth on the outer
rings engage with the lantern gear at
the end of the shaft holding the weight.
Whether the lever is moved forward or
backwards, the lantern gear is always
moved counterclockwise, thus lifting
the weight.

So clear are Leonardo's designs that
it would be possible for those of us who
are unfamiliar with these types of
machines or drawings to mistake them
for modern machines. One drawing
that always appears as remarkably
modern is the *Design for Boring Holes in
Logs*. Up to the late seventeenth
century, when cast-iron piping was
used for water mains, logs with holes
bored through their centers completed
this function. What is particularly in-
ventive about Leonardo's device is the
set of adjustable chucks which are
shown clamping the log. These chucks
would ensure that the axis of the log remained in the center of the machine
whatever the diameter of the log.

RIGHT: This device, although it superficially resembles a modern lathe, is for drilling wooden water-pipes. A set of adjustable wooden chucks, shown clamping the log, ensure that the drill always operates at the center of the wood being drilled, no matter what diameter it is. Biblioteca Ambrosiana, Milan.

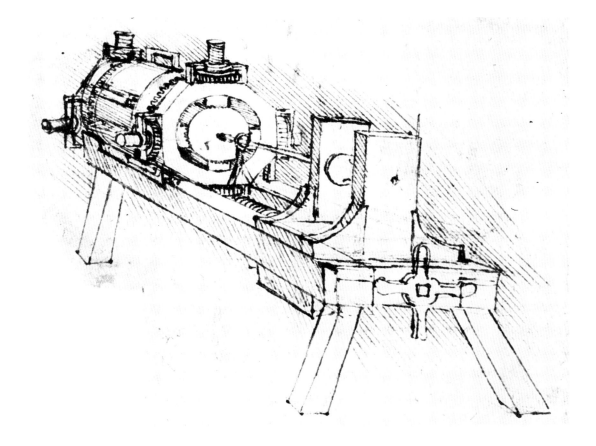

No matter how mundane an occupation might have been, it did not escape Leonardo's keen observation. The tedious job of cutting with hand-held shears the excess hair from the surface of newly woven cloth could have been replaced altogether by his design for a *Napping Machine* from the 1490s. As well as saving time, the machine would have reproduced a constant level of nap. The woolen cloth was to be stretched over a traveling frame and, as the strips of fabric were moved across the frame, the shears cut the nap.

BELOW: *Design for a Napping Machine*, c. 1497, pen and ink. Biblioteca Ambrosiana, Milan.

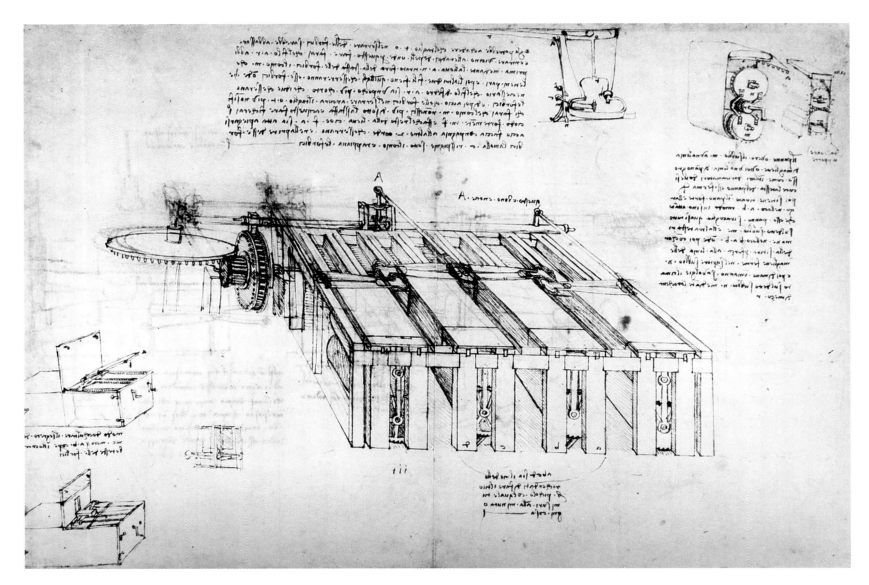

BELOW: Leonardo devised this ball-bearing race, 250 years before it was reinvented for use in vehicle wheels. Biblioteca Nacional, Madrid.

In the Codex Madrid I (f 20v) Leonardo sketched a ball-bearing race. Although roller and ball bearings had been used by the ancient Greeks, Leonardo realized that if the balls or rollers made contact with each other, the resulting friction would impede the movement. His solution was to place the bearings in a ring-shaped race which allowed them to rotate freely and independently. It would not be until 1772 that the ball-bearing race appeared – re-invented and used in road vehicles.

On the whole, it appears that it was the more modest modifications of already existing machines and mechanisms that Leonardo found favor with in his time, but later applications of some of his designs and thoughts have proved to be most successful. A method of bending beams first thought of by Leonardo would be successfully used in later centuries for wooden bridges, particularly in Switzerland.

Although the most grandiose schemes and designs never left Leonardo's notebooks he did, however, understand the impact that new machines and technology would have on society and his feelings are expressed in some of his 'Prophecies.' The prophecies were riddles that were recited at court gatherings to be solved by the assembled guest. In the disguise of clever word-games Leonardo not only pointed out the problems of his own age but also commented on humanity in general, comments that are regrettably holding true today:

Creatures will be seen upon the earth who will always be fighting one another ... there will be no bounds to their Malice, by their fierce limbs a great number of the trees of the immense forest of the world shall be laid level to the ground...

Codex Atlanticus 370r

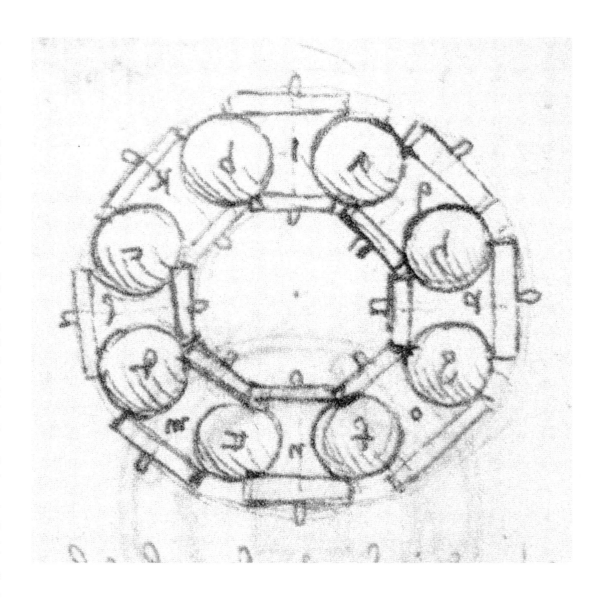

BELOW: Leonardo devised this ball-bearing race, 250 years before it was reinvented for use in vehicle wheels. Biblioteca Nacional, Madrid.

BELOW: In the 1480s, when Leonardo executed all the drawings on this folio of manuscript, he may have visited Egypt and Turkey and advised on military architecture. Biblioteca Ambrosiana, Milan.

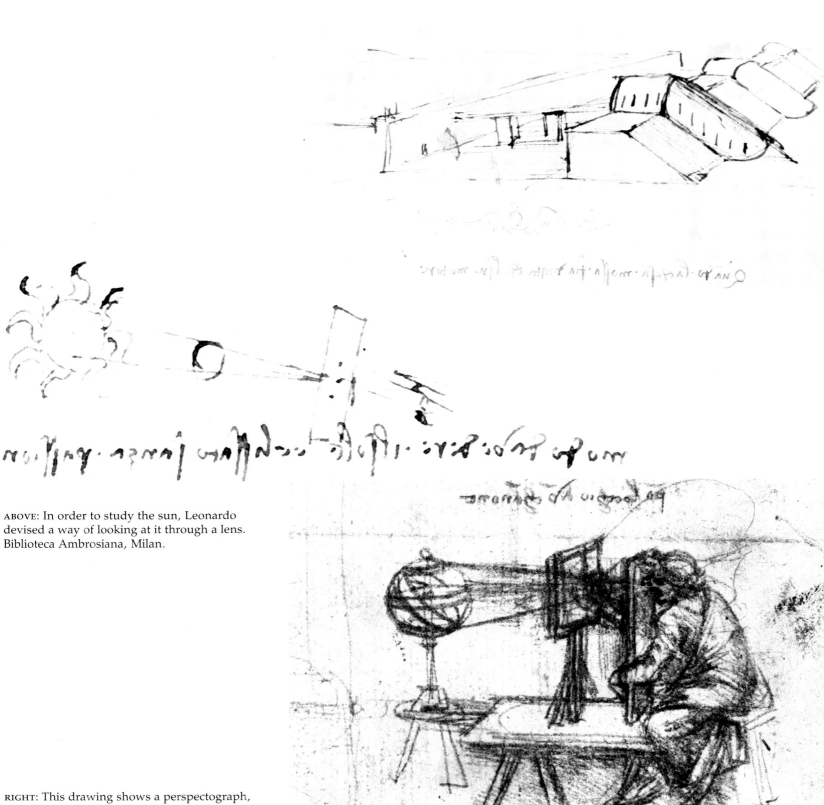

ABOVE: In order to study the sun, Leonardo devised a way of looking at it through a lens. Biblioteca Ambrosiana, Milan.

RIGHT: This drawing shows a perspectograph, whereby, with one eye closed, an artist could trace the outline of what he saw on to plain glass. In this way he could reproduce linear perspective. Biblioteca Ambrosiana, Milan.

City Planning, Churches and Villas

In addition to his designs for fortified buildings, Leonardo also made sketches of a variety of centrally planned domed cathedrals in his manuscripts. In these manuscripts Leonardo dealt with the structural problems of church building both theoretically, such as what form of church would have the best acoustics, and from an artistic point of view.

Manuscript B in the Institut de France contains a series of drawings of churches or 'temples' which appear to have been made around the year 1488 when Leonardo was involved with the project for a domed crossing for Milan cathedral. Such centralized church designs were particularly favored by Renaissance architects and theorists such as Alberti, who was himself inspired by the Roman treatises of Vitruvius.

The majority of Leonardo's designs are variations on centralized plans – squares, polygons, circles or combinations of these – with the side chapels forming a subsidiary geometric element. His studies are presented using solid exterior views in perspective, plans, and sections. The method is similar in fact to the manner in which Leonardo presented his studies of human skulls, since he was aware of the proportional and structural similarities between the dome of the skull and the dome of a temple.

Whether Leonardo's temple designs were made for specific projects is uncertain: some are believed to be ideas for a Sforza mausoleum. Such a mausoleum was, in fact, built but by Bramante at Santa Maria della Grazie in Milan, home of the *Last Supper*. The thirty schemes drawn by Leonardo, however, represent his most sustained exploration of an architectural theme.

The outbreak of plague in Milan in 1483 may have inspired Leonardo to draw up plans for the remodeling of the city. His plan called for the streets to be on two levels. The lower streets were set aside for use by carts, animals and the lower classes of citizen, with storage areas in houses, while the upper level would be a promenade for the nobility, with hanging gardens for their pleasure. Archways and unobstructed views of the sky would provide light and ventilation to the lower levels and, at every hundred meters or so, a staircase would link the two levels. Leonardo had noticed that the city dwellers tended to leave their garbage in corners and to overcome this he planned his staircases as spirals.

Built entirely of stone and laid out with mathematical precision, the city houses would, he explained, have their backs facing each other creating a space that could be used as a garden area. Provisions such as wood and wine were to be carried into the storage spaces through doors while an underground drainage system emptied the privies and stables. Furthermore, nothing was to be thrown into the canals and every barge would be re-

RIGHT: *Stuidy for the Triburio of Milan Cathedral*, c. 1487, pen and ink. Biblioteca Ambrosiana, Milan.

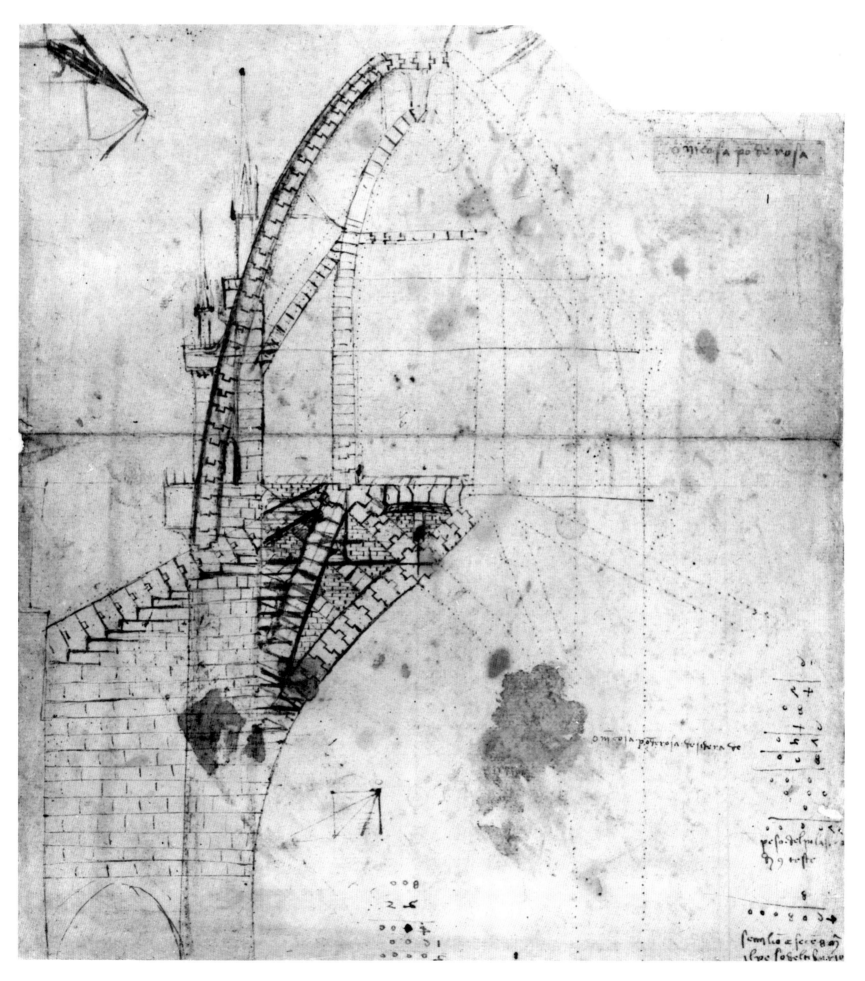

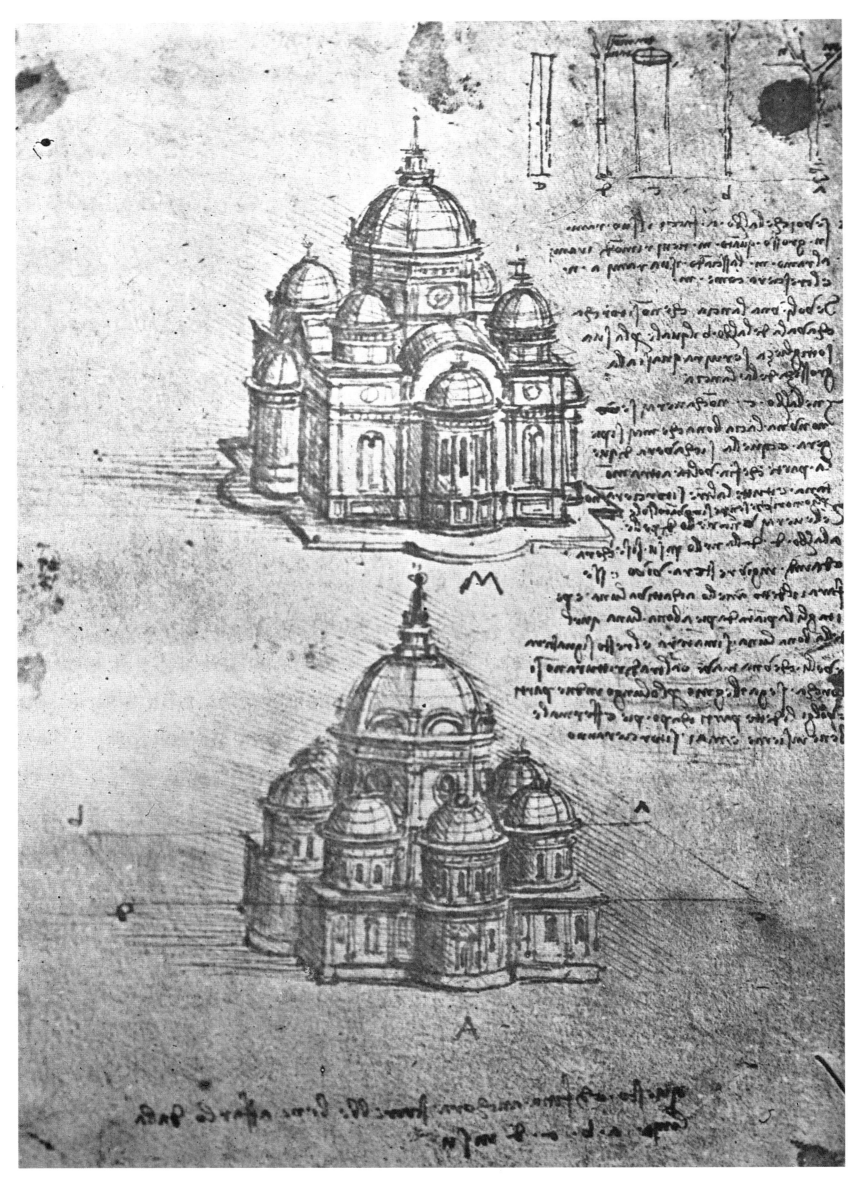

LEFT: *Two Designs for a Domed Churched with Surrounding Cupolas*, c. 1488-89, pen and ink, 9×6¼ inches (23×16 cm). Bibliothèque de l'Institut de France, Paris.

BELOW: *Design for a Multi-leveled Town*, c. 1488, pen and ink. Bibliothèque de l'Institut de France, Paris.

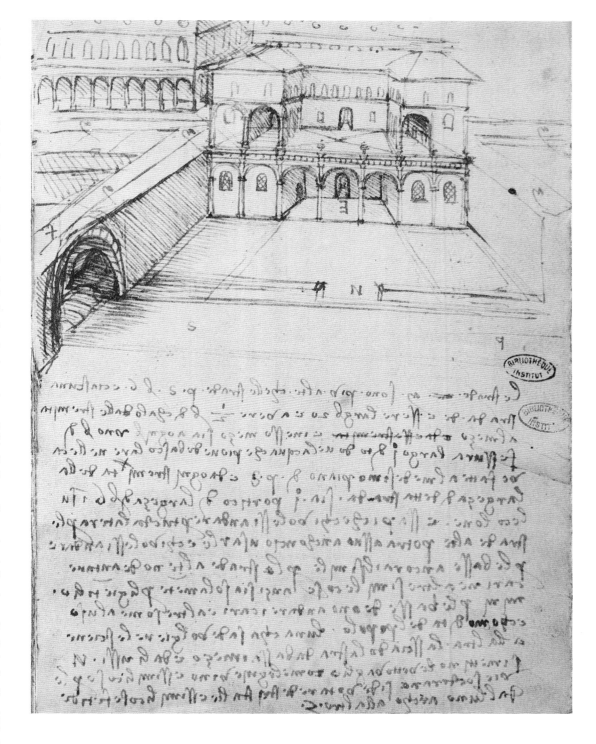

sponsible for carrying away a certain amount of dredged mud to deposit at certain points on the canal bank. The city would be enlarged by a ring of ten sections outside of the city gates.

Gardens, both terraced and hanging, intrigued Leonardo. By the beginning of the fourteenth century, the political climate had changed enough to allow the wealthier classes to spend a period of time in the summer in the country away from the heat and smells of the city. Consequently, the rich families began to build themselves summer residences of villas and gardens. The first of these began to appear around Pisa, Mantua, Murano and Milan, the most important courts in Italy. The ideal garden was to be laid out on a hillside, enclosed by high walls. Within the walls were geometrically arranged paths with trellises, trees and hedges, while the central feature of the garden was to be a fountain.

In 1477 Leonardo appears to have been working under the patronage of Lorenzo 'Il Magnifico' de Medici in the gardens of the Piazza San Marco where Lorenzo was establishing his academy. In order to establish his academy for the study of classical art and antiquity, Lorenzo appropriated the land adjacent to the monastery of San Marco and had marbles from Greece and Rome brought in order that his students could contemplate the ideal beauty of art.

Leonardo had just returned to Florence from Mantua and Venice in 1500 when he was commissioned by Francesco Gonzaga of Mantua to draw the Villa Tovaglia, so that a copy of the villa and gardens could be constructed in Mantua. The Villa Tovaglia, near Val d'Ema, south of Florence, had been designed by Lorenzo da Montaguto and built between 1480 and 1490 for Agnolo de Lepo del Tovaglia. Around the end of the century Francesco Gonzaga had been a guest at the villa where the architecture and gardens pleased him so

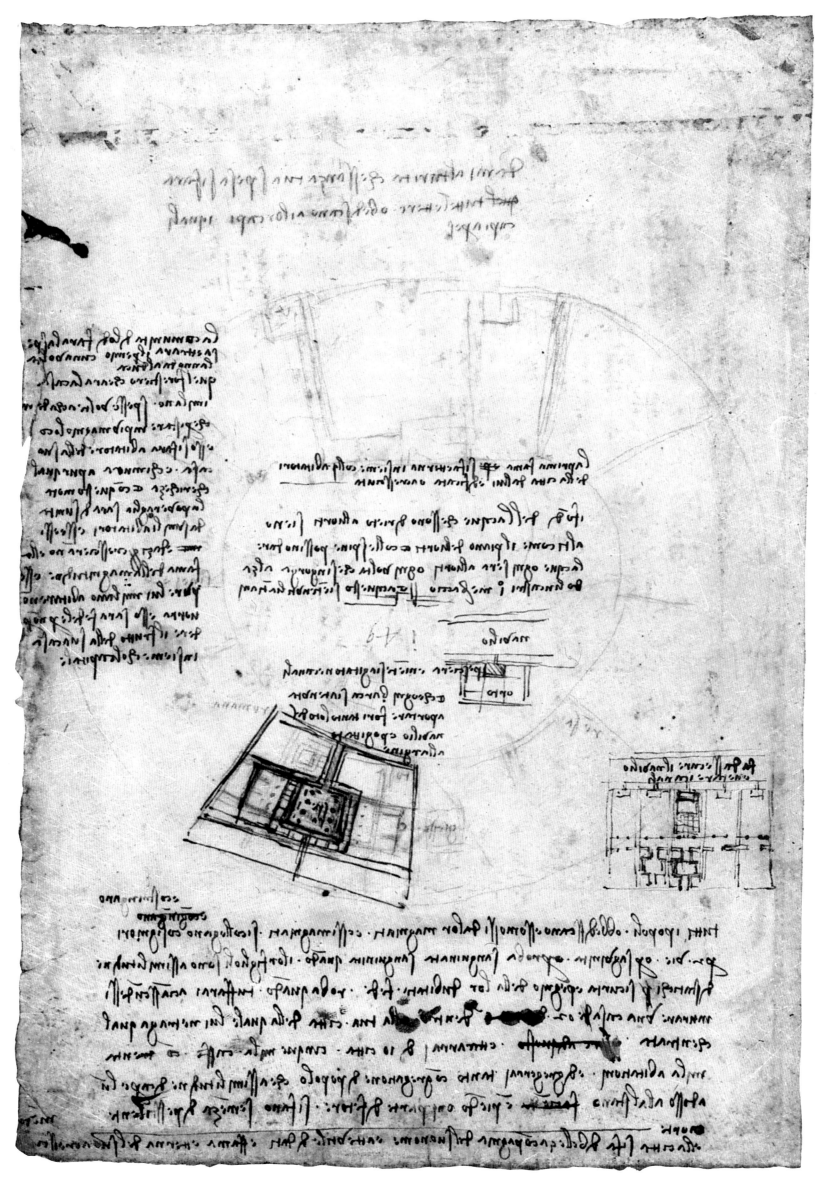

LEFT: Leonardo designed a scheme for the enlargement of Milan around 1493. Outside the old confines of the city he proposed to build ten new sections.

BELOW: These studies form part of Leonardo's scheme for a new Medici palace. Details of the garden and portico walls show foliated, interweaving, spiraling branches as applied

decoration, which may allude to the Medici emblem of new branches growing from a tree-stump. Biblioteca Ambrosiana, Milan.

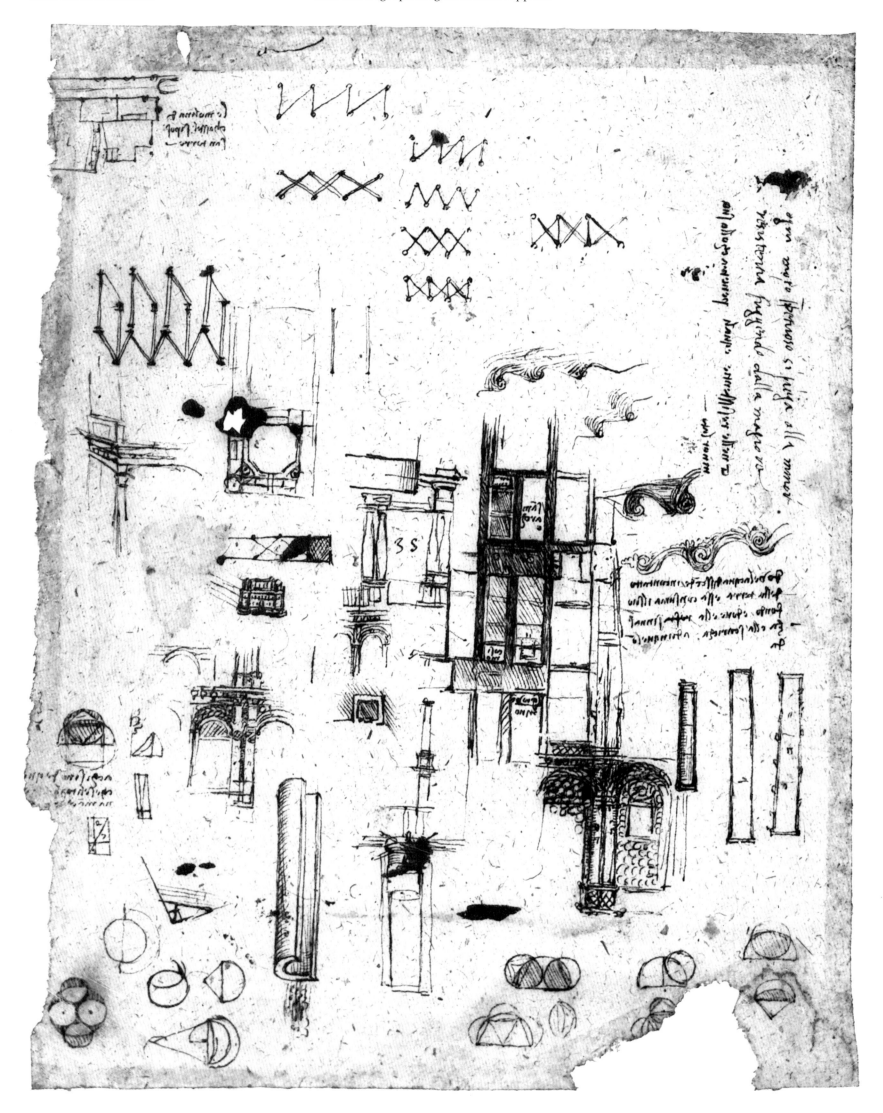

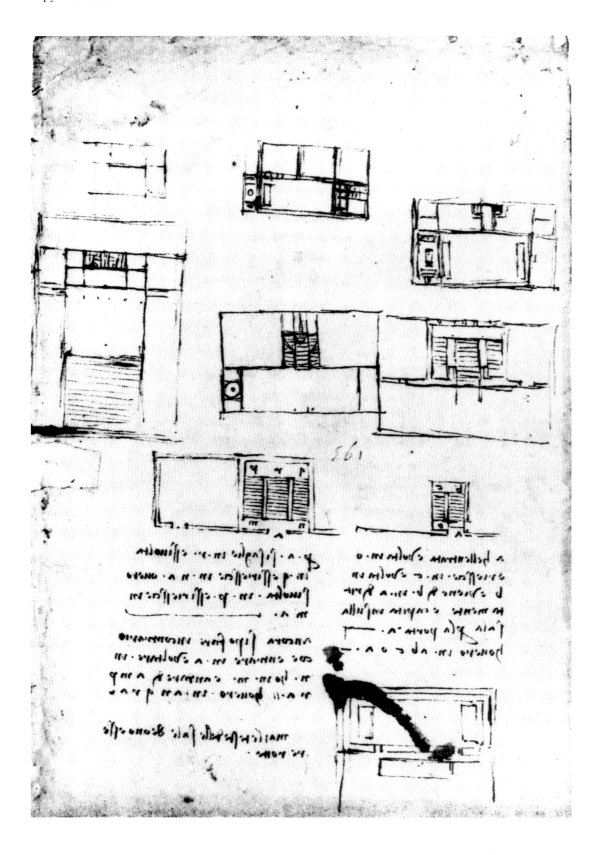

much that he intended to duplicate it for himself in Mantua.

Between 1505 and 1508 Leonardo was planning a villa outside the city for the French governor of Milan, Charles d'Amboise. In addition to a theater and a sprinkler system that could be turned on to give guests a brief shower from the outlets hidden alongside the pavements, the gardens also had an orangery. In a second manuscript of around 1508, Leonardo described how citrus trees could be grown without the usual recourse to lighting fires for heating the trees in winter. Rather than growing the trees in large terracotta pots which allowed them to be moved indoors in cold weather, Leonardo suggested that the trees could be grown permanently in a covered area watered by a natural spring. In summer the spring would water the trees and in winter, by means of a hydraulic mill, Leonardo would produce a current of warm air to protect the covered-over trees and prevent them from freezing.

For Charles's villa, Leonardo also made provision for a series of rivulets running through the garden; a table with running water to cool wine and for fish to be visible when swimming in a central stream. Recognizing the need for the cleanliness of the water, Leonardo decided that only plants such as watercress should be left on the shingly banks of the streams as it served as food for the fish. In the same way he also cautioned against introducing tench, eel and pike to the streams as they devoured other fish.

The concept of a total garden for Leonardo involved pleasant music: in addition to the songs of exotic birds contained in the garden by means of an overhead copper net, a sort of organ was devised, powered by the stream's water. Thus Leonardo's conception of a garden was a combination of elements to please the senses: it diverted the eyes by providing views with architectural

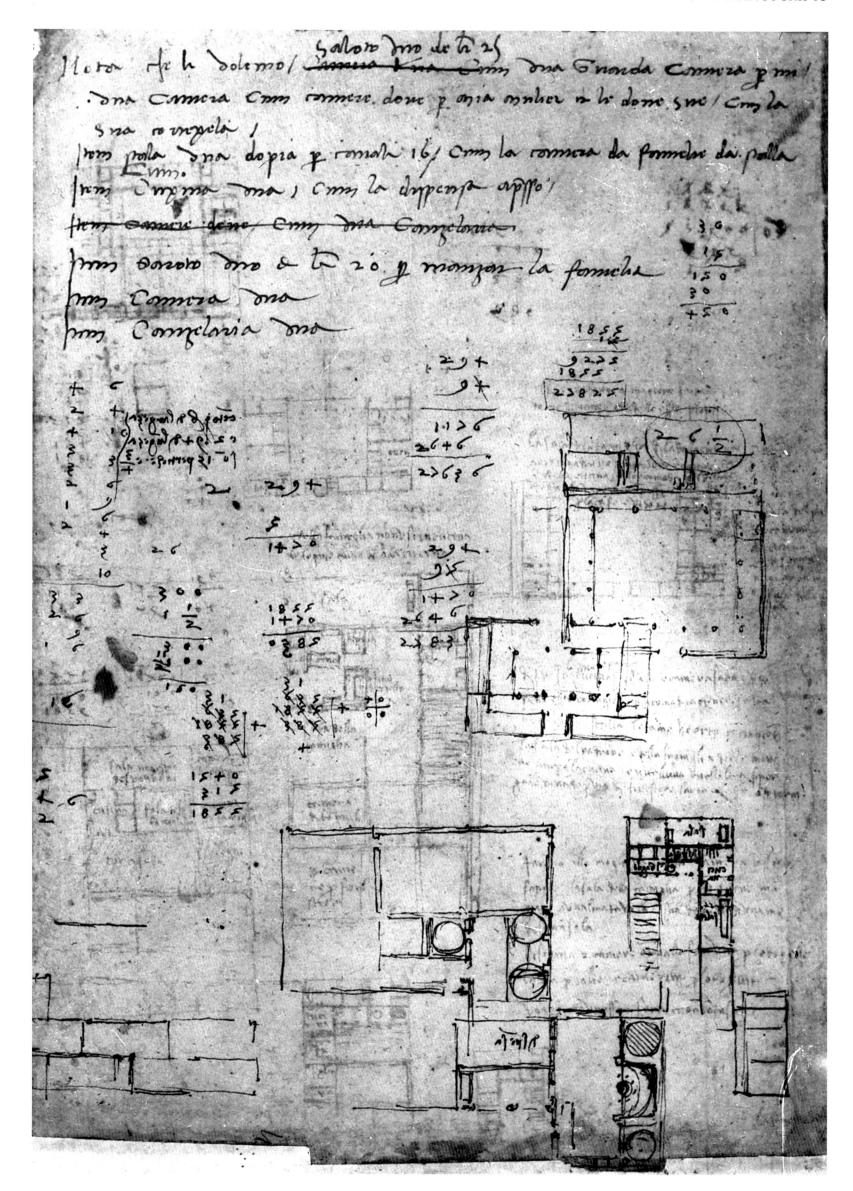

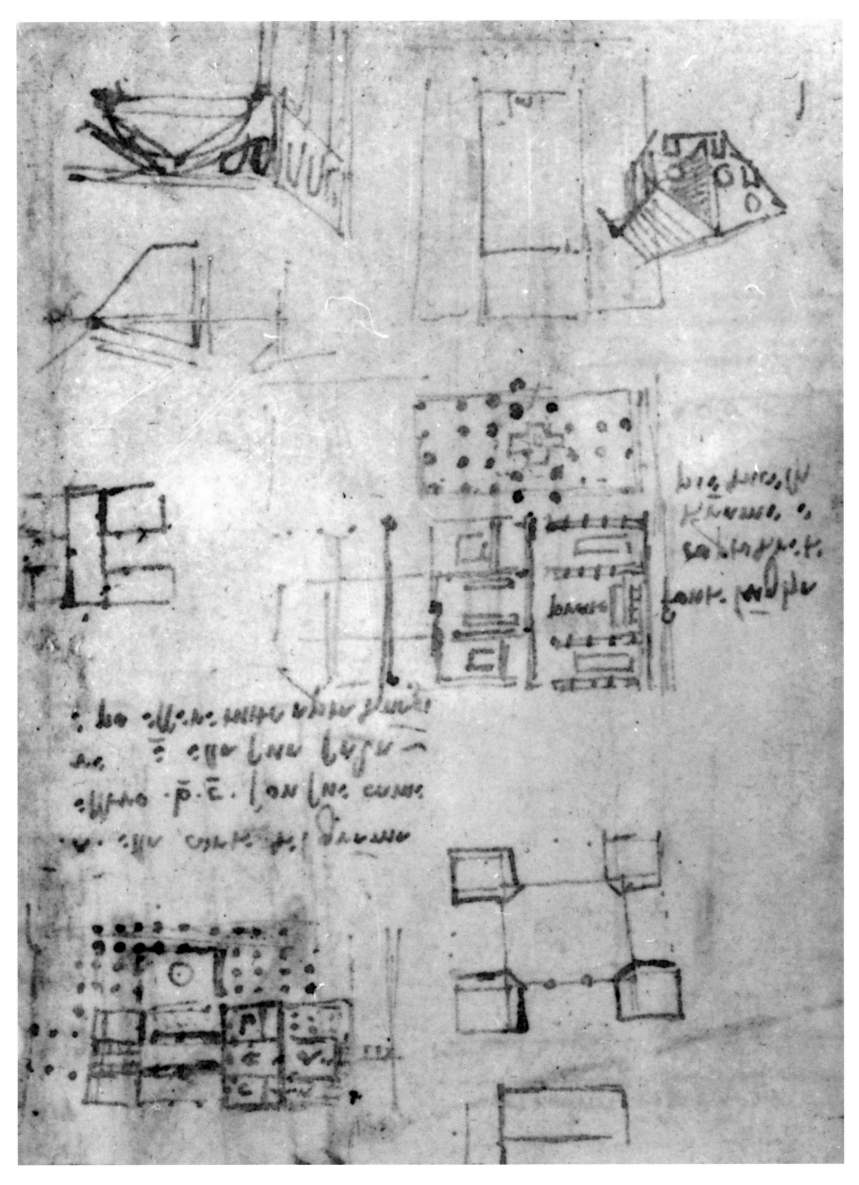

and sculptural elements, the ear with bird songs and hydraulically produced music and splashing fountains and the nose by the scented flowers and trees.

Between 1511 and 1513 Leonardo lived and worked at the villa of his friend and lifelong companion Francesco Melzi at Vaprio d'Adda. Leonardo was already familiar with the area from 1508 due to his earlier studies for the canalization of the Adda river to provide a navigable waterway between Milan and Lake Como. Furthermore, the Villa Melzi was quite accessible from Milan, being only twenty miles from the city. As a guest of the Melzi family, Leonardo was to be involved in the projected enlargement of the villa. The ground plan of the building shows part of the interior and exterior of the villa and notes indicate that the garden was to be reached from the ground floor of the house or from the cellar. The gardens, with terraced slopes, facing the River Adda would provide a pleasant view,

while the building itself was to have corner rooms topped by cupolas. The terraces and the stairs were eventually to be built but the wings, pavilion and the gardens were never constructed. We can only imagine how the scheme might have looked and sounded with its statuary and waterfalls.

As Leonardo's life drew to a close, he continued to produce plans and sketches. Between 1516 and 1518 he drew up plans for the Queen Mother's palace at Romorantin. Although never carried out, the plans are interesting in that they prefigure French architecture of the seventeenth century.

Although Leonardo intended to write a treatise on architecture, and proposed section-titles in his notebooks, the project was not realized. What we find instead are definitions:

What is an arch? An arch is nothing else than a force originated by two weaknesses, for the arch in a building is composed of two segments of a circle, each of which being very weak in itself tends to fall, but as each opposes this tendency in the other, the two weaknesses combine to form one strength.

According to Antonina Vallentin, Leonardo also approached François I of France about making practical improvements to the castle at Amboise in conjunction with Jacques Sourdeau, the architect in charge of the improvements at Blois. Vallentin points out that although there are no notes or sketches to provide evidence of a Leonardo design, there is an odd spiral staircase at Blois which winds from left to right. Vallentin suggests that the staircase could have been designed by a left-handed architect – or by one who had lost the use of his right hand, as Leonardo had. It would be ironic that the only completed architectural masterpiece is not even associated with Leonardo's name.

LEFT: Around 1506-08 Leonardo designed this villa for Charles d'Amboise. Its garden, replete with 'oranges and citrons,' was to have an automated watering system, a water organ and an aviary. Biblioteca Ambrosiana, Milan.

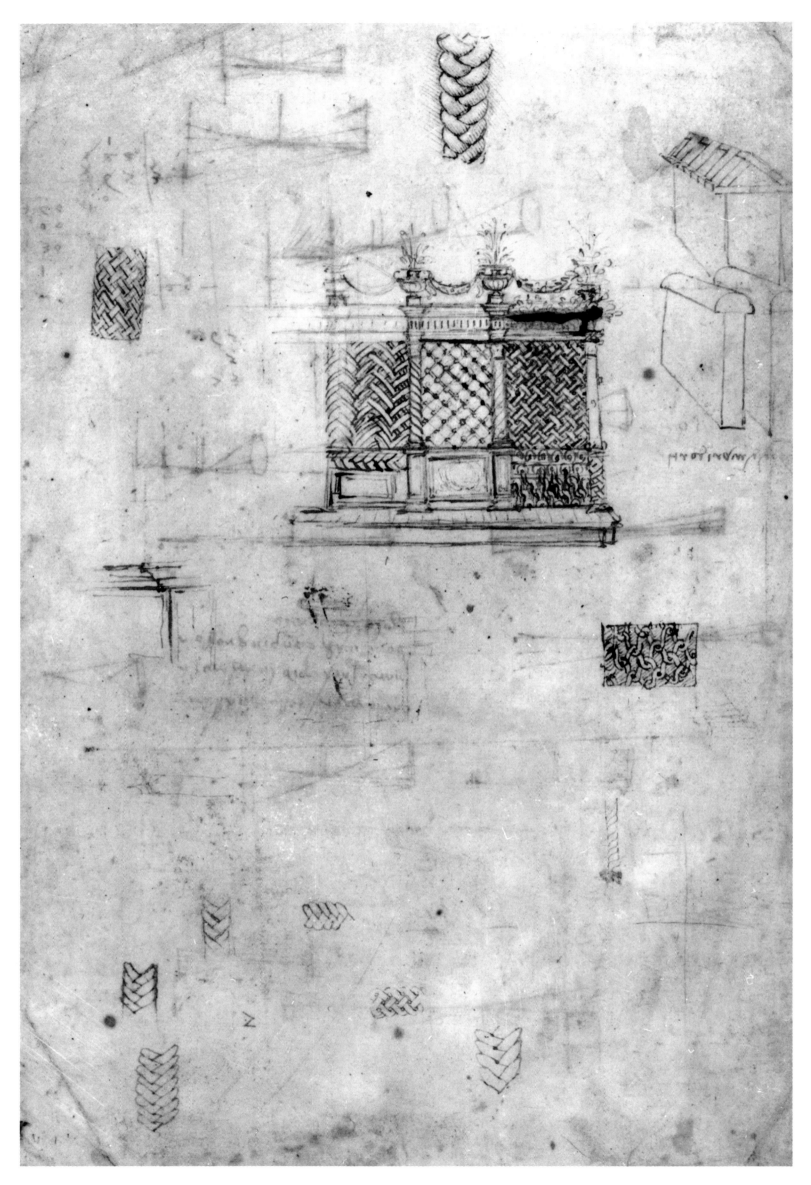

BELOW: Leonardo sketched this projected façade for the Villa Melzi, Vaprio d'Adda, around 1513. Biblioteca Ambrosiana, Milan.

LEFT: Leonardo designed these interwoven garden walls for his new Medici palace scheme in 1488. Biblioteca Ambrosiana, Milan.

ABOVE: While staying with Francesco Melzi at Vaprio d'Adda, Leonardo designed enlargements for the villa. Biblioteca Ambrosiana, Milan.

BELOW: One of Leonardo's last projects was for a palace at Romorantin, France, 1516-18. Biblioteca Ambrosiana, Milan.

Anatomical Drawings

'On the second day of April 1489 book entitled *Of the Human Figure.*'

This is the first date that occurs in Leonardo's notebooks on the subject of anatomy but the majority of his anatomical drawings, including the famous studies of hearts and embryos, were carried out during the second period in Milan between 1506 and 1513.

The anatomical studies did, however, gain impetus from a dissection that took place in the winter of 1507-08 in Florence of an old man, the 'centenarian.' Leonardo believed that the old man's death was brought about by the failure of the blood to maintain a supply of life-giving humors to the parts of the body. In an analogy with the earth and landscapes, the old man's channels were seen to have been silted up, no longer capable of irrigating the body.

In his study of *Principal Organs and Vascular and Urino-Genital Systems of a Woman* c. 1507 (page 189) Leonardo produced one of his greatest attempts at synthesizing his investigations of the 'irrigation' system of the human body. The whole drawing had been planned with utmost care: the sheet was folded vertically to transfer, by pricking holes around the outline, the image from the left to the right side of the paper. The whole drawing was then pricked all over again to transfer it to a second sheet. On the verso Leonardo has drawn the outlines of the body and the main organs.

RIGHT: Although the draftsmanship in this thirteenth-century treatise on anatomy is primitive, some of the ideas about the constitution and workings of the human body are basically the same as Leonardo's. The Bodleian Library, Oxford.

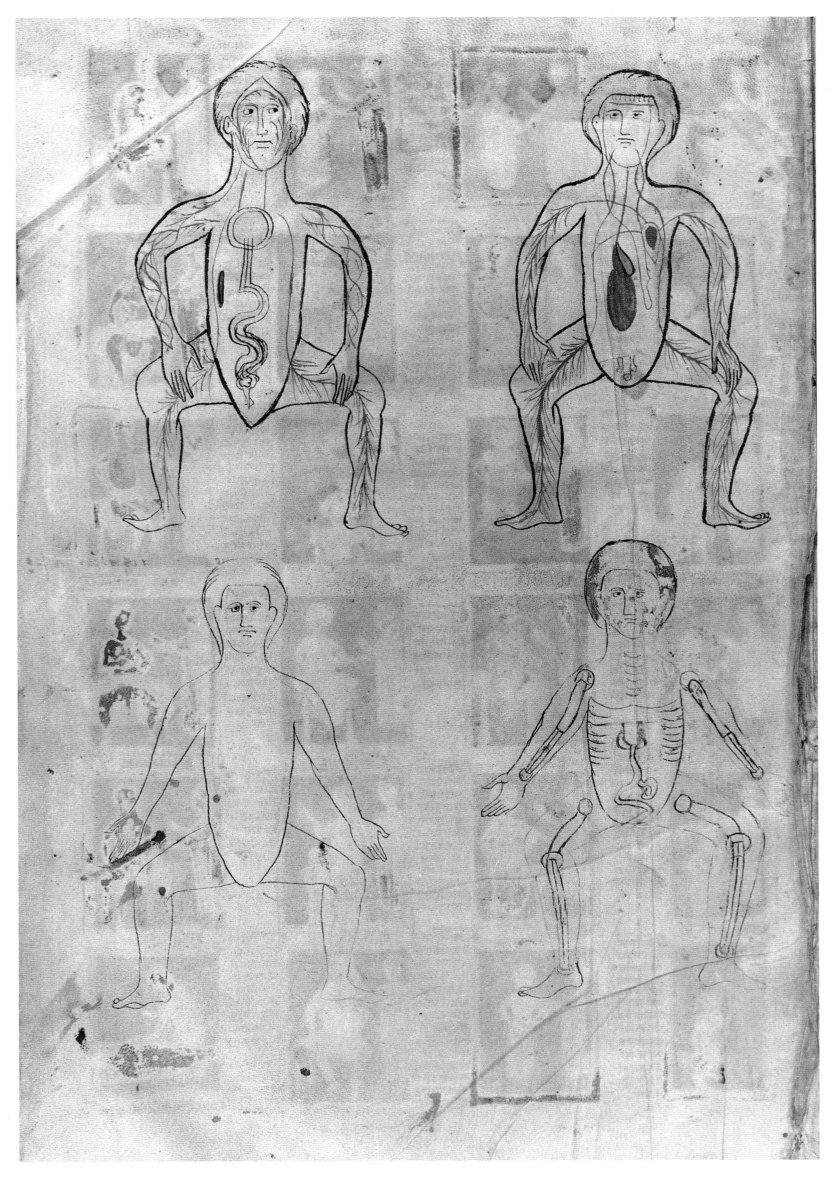

In his drawing, some of the forms appear in section, some are transparent while others are shown three-dimensionally. While some of the organs – the liver, spleen, kidneys and bronchial tubes demonstrate Leonardo's knowledge gleaned from dissections, other organs are conceptualized, such as the heart, as it lacks atria, and the spherical womb with its horn-like tubes. What Leonardo has done is fuse together ancient inherited beliefs with a functional design.

In the accompanying notes Leonardo writes of his intention for a series of works that begins with the formation of the child in the womb, a discussion of digestion, reproduction and the blood vessels, as well as the cycles of life and death within the human body.

RIGHT: *Dissection of the Principal Organs of a Woman*, c. 1510, pen, ink, and wash over black chalk, 18½×13 inches (47×32.8 cm). Windsor Castle, Royal Library 12281r. © 1991 Her Majesty The Queen.

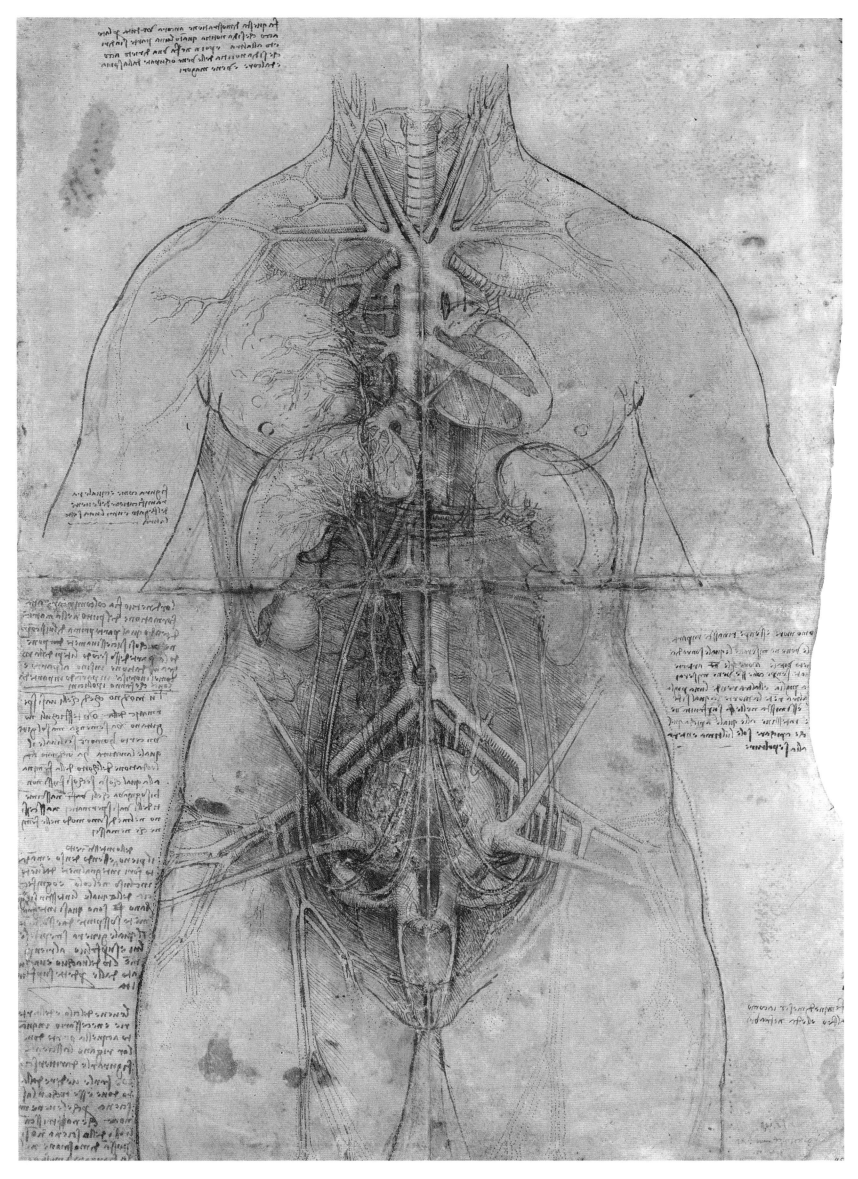

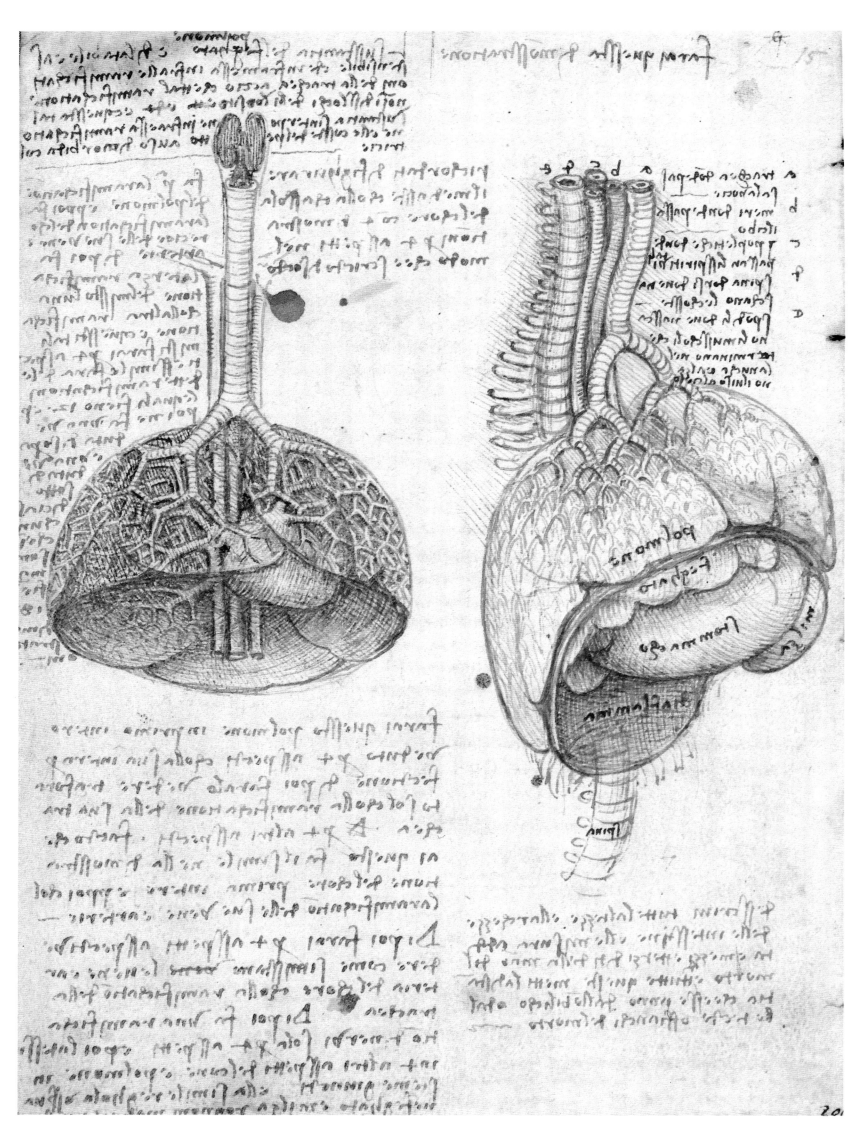

Whether the drawing *Lungs and the Upper Abdominal Organs (Possibly of a Pig)* c. 1508-09 (page 190) is the result of the dissection of the centenarian or is related to the experiment with a pig's lung is uncertain. In his notes Leonardo mentions an experiment to inflate a pig's lung in order to observe whether the lungs increase in width and in length or whether they increased in width while diminishing in length.

On this sheet, the conduits at the top of the right-hand drawing are labeled:

a – trachea, whence the voice passes
b – esophagus, whence the food passes
c – apoplectic [i.e carotid] vessels where pass the vital spirits
d – dorsal spine whence the ribs arise
e – vertibrae, whence the muscles arise which end in the neck and raise the face to the sky

The organs below are labeled: lungs, liver, stomach, diaphragm, and spine. The diagrammatic technique that Leonardo used in his attempt to show both the exterior and interior appearance and the inner workings of the organs caused him some problems. His solution was to show the lung complete and what he called 'fenestrated' – showing the substance of the lung as transparent. One commentator likened the approach to looking through a window at a tree without its leaves.

LEFT: *The Upper Abdominal Organs (Possibly of a Pig)*, pen and ink, Windsor Castle, Royal Library 19054. © 1991 Her Majesty The Queen.

RIGHT: *Study of the Foot and Lower Leg*, pen and ink, Windsor Castle, Royal Library. © 1991 Her Majesty The Queen.

In the winter of 1510 it appears from a note accompanying a drawing of a foot and lower leg (page 193) that Leonardo was hoping to complete all his studies of the human anatomy. Leonardo was convinced that his true task as an investigator was to explain each detail of the human body on the basis of its function. Thus the bones and muscles of the human body are conceived as perfect mechanical designs – small and economic yet capable of an infinite number of complex movements.

From a series of skeletal and myological studies drawn during Leonardo's second period in Milan comes the *Superficial Anatomy of the Foot and Lower Leg* c. 1510. This drawing is believed not to have been made from direct observation of a dissection but composed of earlier studies and combined in a finished drawing. Seeing the bones of the body as levers, the muscles as ropes and the brain as a motor, Leonardo pointed out:

Remember that to be certain of the point of origin of any muscle, you must pull the sinew from which the muscle springs in such a way as to see that muscle move.

The drawing of four sequential studies of *The Muscles of the Right Arm, Shoulder and Chest*, c. 1515 is in fact linked to a second sheet which shows four further related views. The first sheet shows a sequence of views rather like a film strip and Leonardo explains the system behind this in a note and in the star-shaped diagram at the bottom right:

I turn the arm into eight aspects, of which three are from the outside; three from the inside and one from behind and one from the front.

The effect is the same whether it is the object that is turned or if the eye of the viewer moves around the chosen object.

At the top of this page are three drawings of the musculature of the upper spine and neck and are labeled 'the first, second and third demonstrations of the muscles of the cervical spine.' Leonardo often depicted the muscles of the neck and cervical walls as ropelike structures in order to show how the play of 'antagonistic' muscles hold the head upright. His investigations were not simply used for the accurate rendering of the human body in paintings, the structure and weight-bearing activities of the human body were of interest in the way that they related to his architectural schemes.

RIGHT: *The Muscles of the Right Arm, Shoulder, and Chest*, pen and ink, Windsor Castle, Royal Library 19008v. © 1991 Her Majesty The Queen.

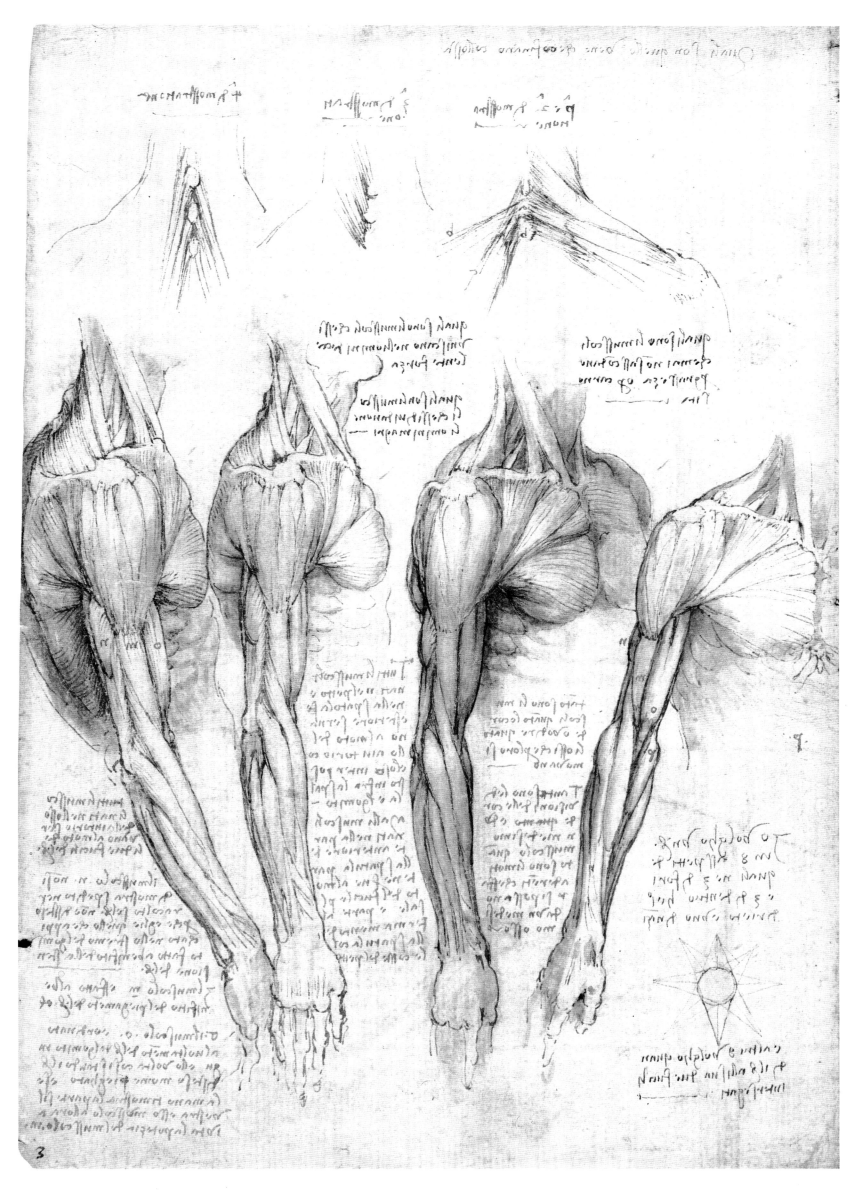

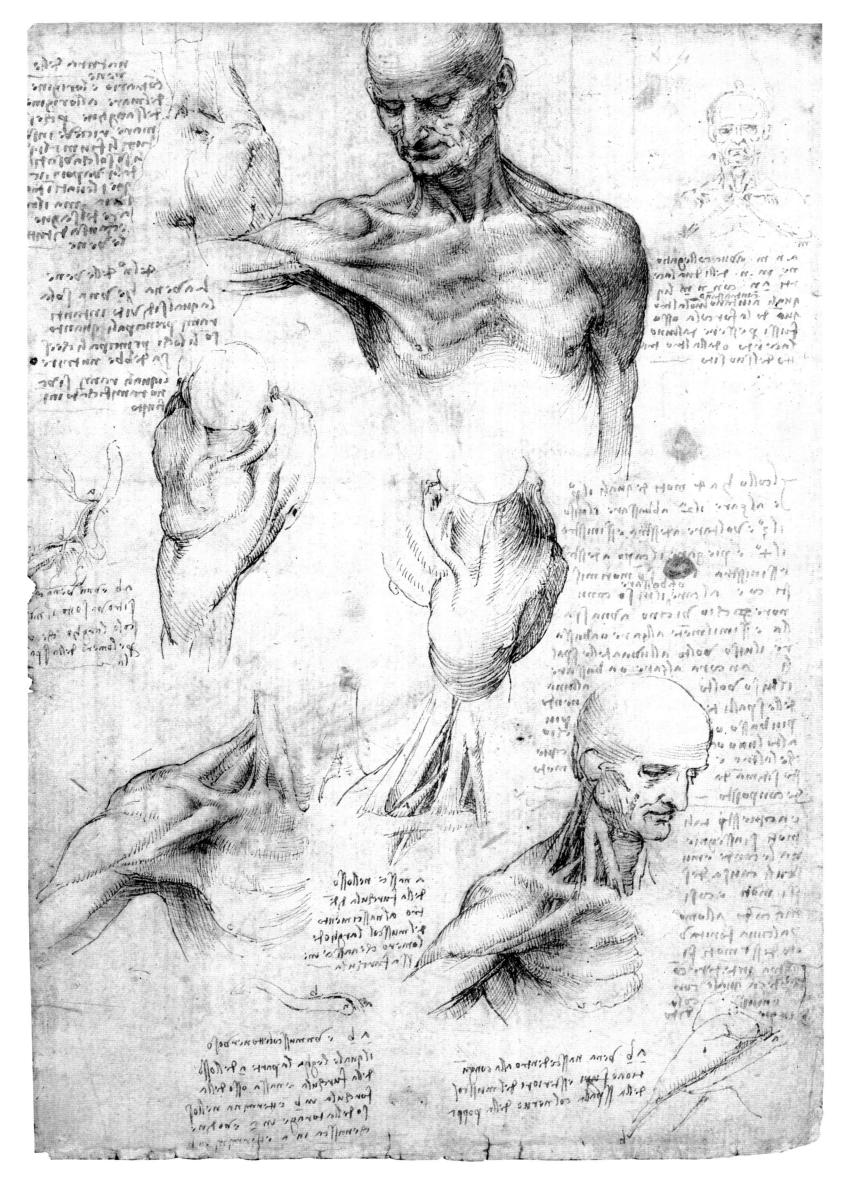

RIGHT: *Study of the Back View of a Skeleton*, c. 1513, pen and ink on blue paper, 10¾×8 inches (27.4×20.4 cm), Windsor Castle, Royal Library 19075v. © 1991 Her Majesty The Queen. Leonardo had a somewhat schematic and mechanistic idea of the workings of the neck and shoulders.

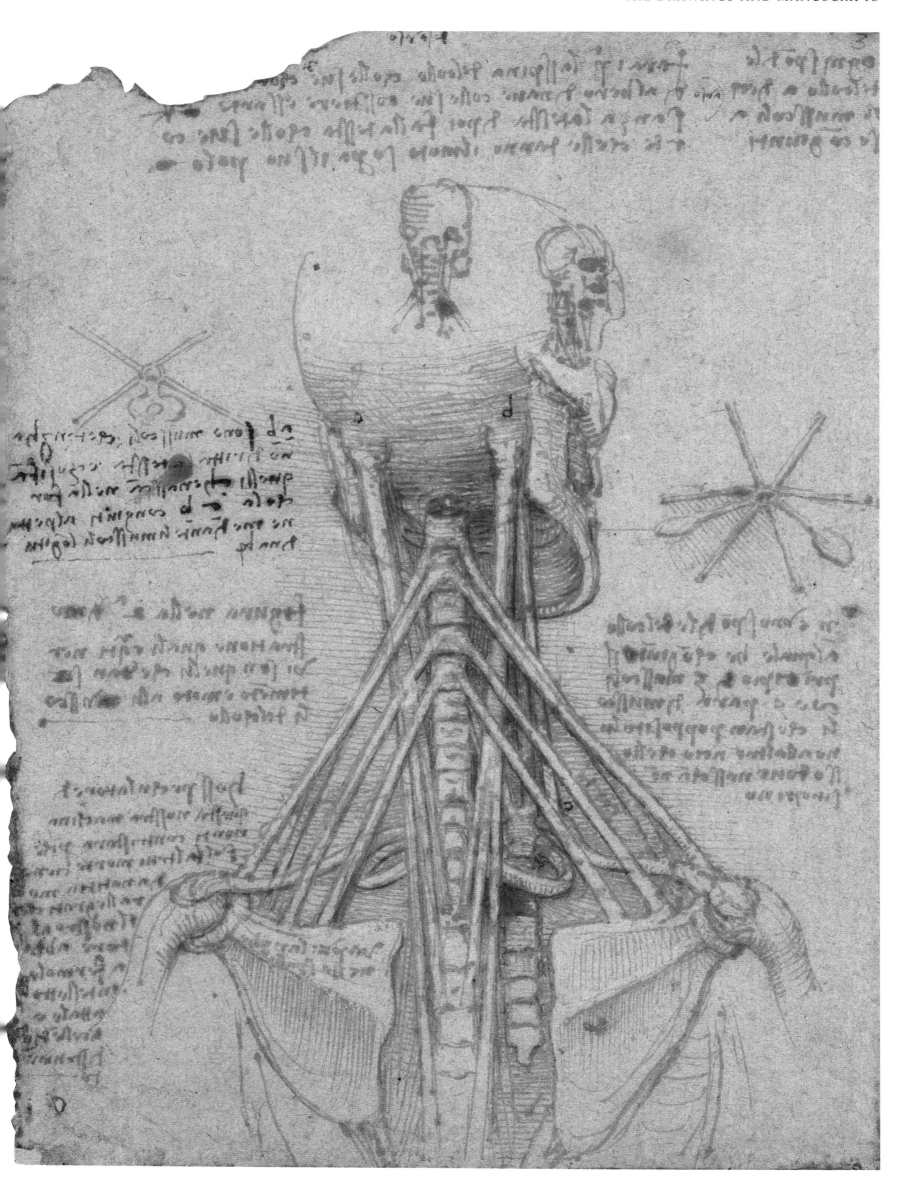

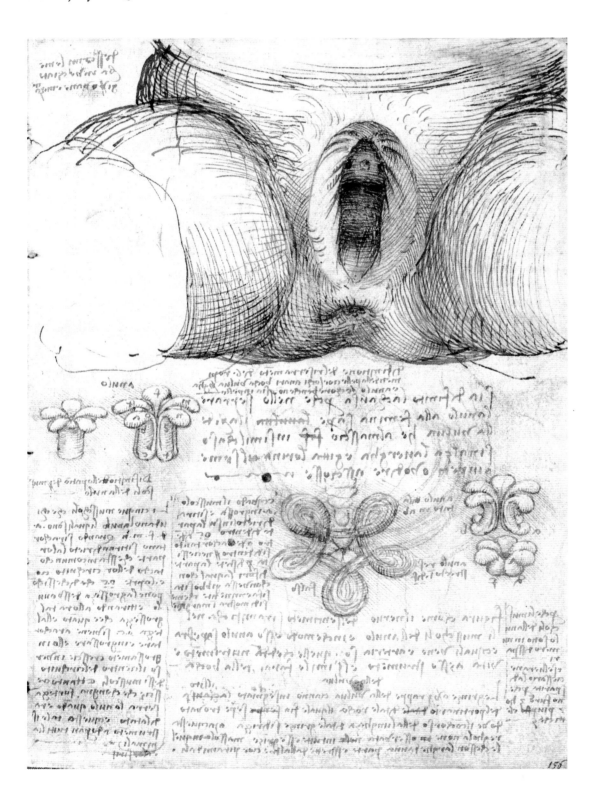

In the last decade of his life, Leonardo concentrated his anatomical studies in two fundamental areas: the heart and embryology. He was the first to draw the uterine artery and the vascular system of the cervix and vagina as well as the single-chambered uterus at a time when it was generally believed that it was made up of several compartments. For this was the explanation normally given for the mysteries of twin births and litters in animals.

Furthermore, Leonardo was the first to describe the fetus *in utero*, correctly tethered by the umbilical cord – although he was in error when he suggested that the cord was equal in length to the baby at each stage of its development and that the child did not respire since it was in 'water.' In Leonardo's world, human beings could not breathe underwater without drowning.

Although Leonardo noted that the fetus used in this study was almost four months old, it appears to be more developed. The womb and placenta moreover, are compiled once again from studies of animal anatomy and not from direct dissection. Thus the drawing is rich in emotionally potent images, scientific content and imaginative diagramatic techniques. Rather like the outer layers of a seed having been pulled away, the fetus has been revealed. In an accompanying note Leonardo has written:

The same soul governs the two bodies and the desires and fears and sorrows are common to this creature as to all the other animal parts, and from this it arises that something desired by the mother is often found imprinted on the limbs of the infant ... and a sudden terror kills the mother and child.

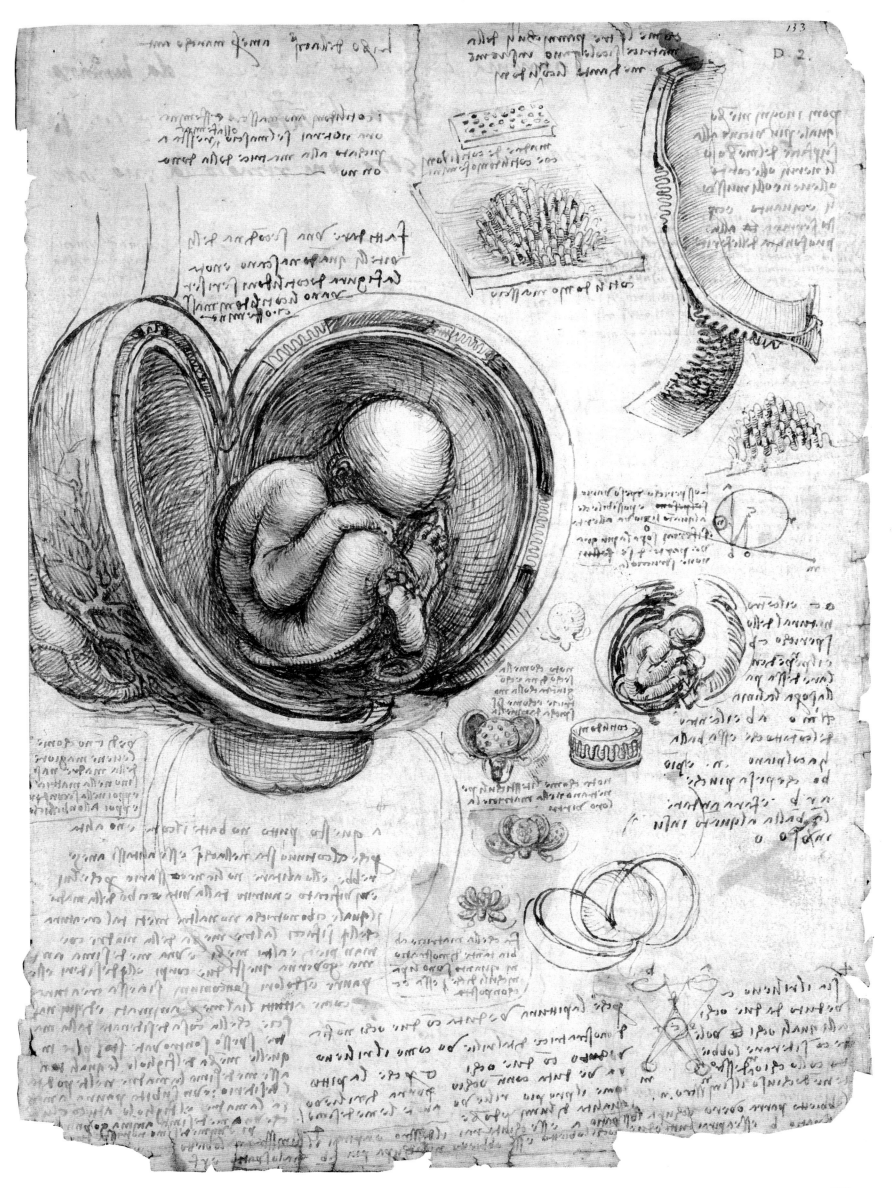

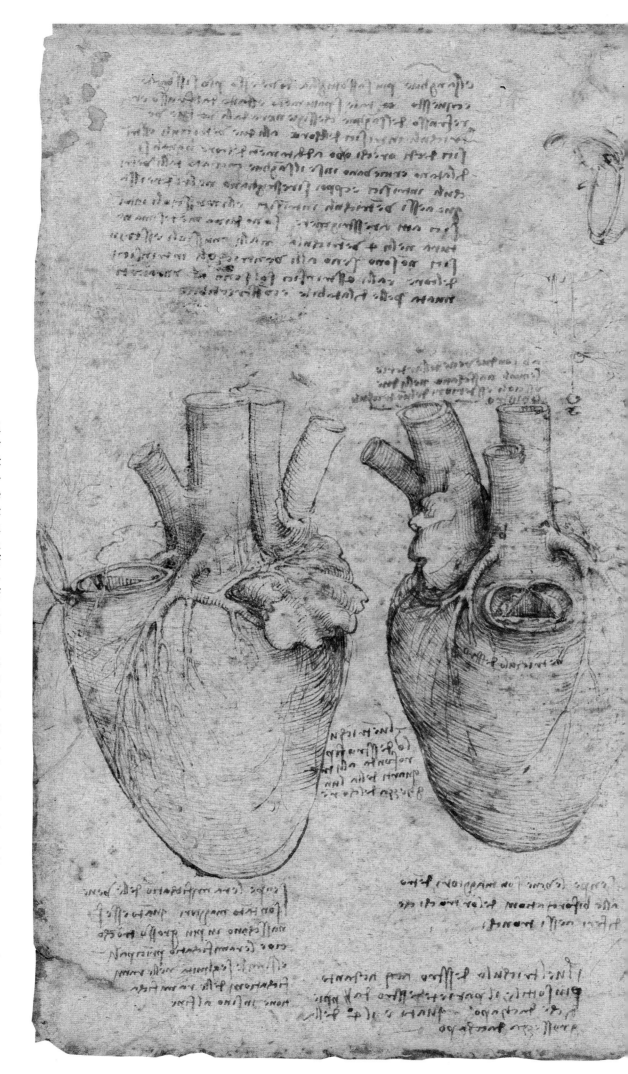

The circulatory system was described in detail, often lavishly, in over fifty drawings of the heart. The earliest drawings of the heart show two ventricles while in the later ones we see the four chambers in minute detail. But Leonardo did not grasp the connection between the pumping, driving action of the heart and the circulation of blood, since he was reasoning by analogy. For Leonardo, the circulation of water in the heart, the flow of sap in plants and the movement of blood in animals were all analogous processes.

To a series of drawings in pen and ink on blue paper from around 1513 comes the study of *The Heart of an Ox*. This page is twice the usual size of paper Leonardo used for his drawings, but it indicates the original sheet size and until recently was kept folded, hence the two inventory numbers.

Here the heart of an ox is shown from various viewpoints. On the left-hand page, the heart is shown with the pulmonary artery severed (on the left in the left-hand drawing and at the front in the right-hand diagram). Also shown are diagrams of the septum, which was important since in the Galenical system, the septum was believed to be where the blood distributed the vital spirits to the rest of the body.

On the right-hand sheet, the ox-heart is shown from other viewpoints with other vessels severed, while in the center of the margin Leonardo shows the ring of blood vessels surrounding the top of the heart like a crown (hence the name coronary arteries). At the foot of the margin are drawings of two aortic valves, the one on the right captioned 'ap[er]ta' (open), and on the left 'serrata' (closed).

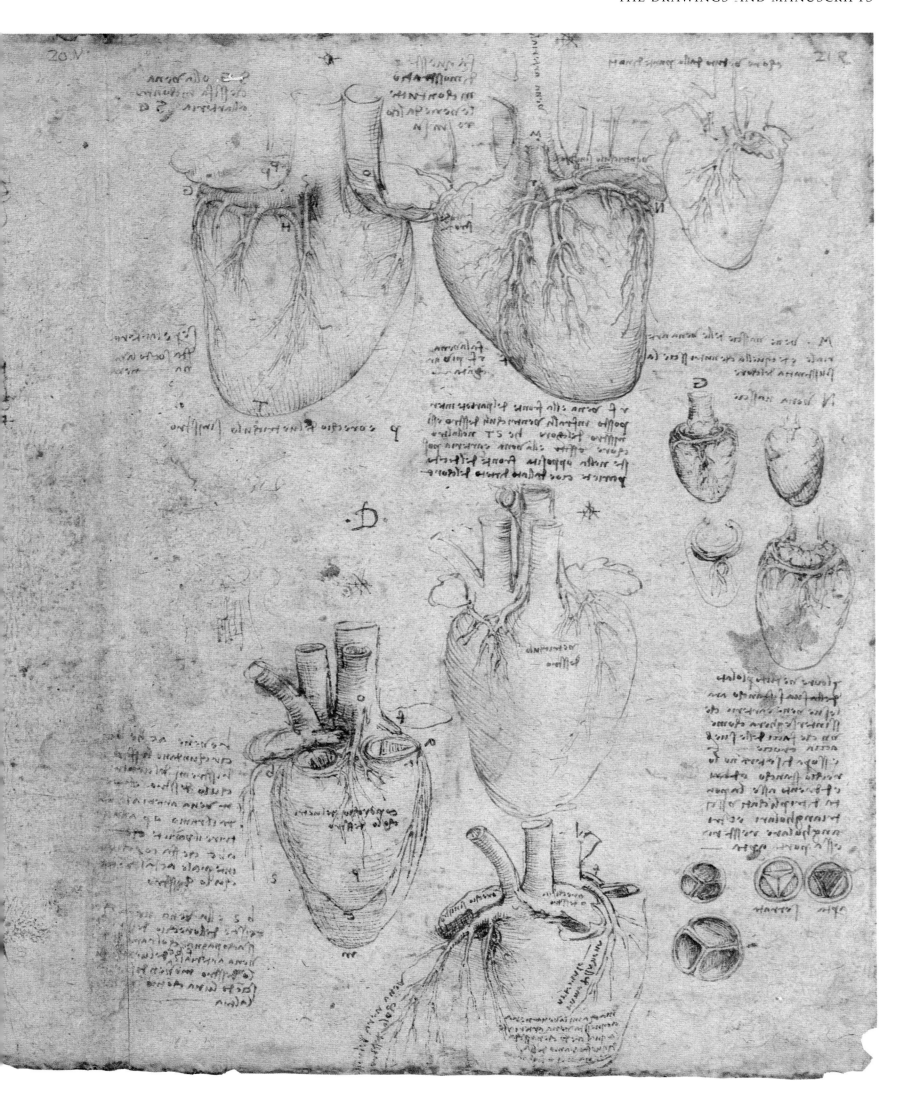

Leonardo's *Treatise on Anatomy*, like so many of his treatises, was never finished and although he observed the body with an anatomist's eye, he was neither a physician nor a surgeon, but a painter. Leonardo's observations of the movement and anatomy of man and beasts served to further his skills as a painter. In his advice to the artist in his *Treatise on Painting*, Leonardo wrote:

Remember to be careful in giving figures limbs that appear to agree with the size of the body and likewise the age. Thus a youth has limbs that are not very muscular, not strongly veined and the surface is delicate and round and tender in color. In a man the limbs are sinewy and muscular while in an old man the surface is wrinkled, ragged and knotty and the sinews are very prominent.

For Leonardo, the knowledge of anatomy was not enough. The artist must penetrate deeper in order to express the spirit. In Leonardo's eyes, the human body was the visible expression of the spirit and, as a painter, by understanding and 'reconstructing' the body, only then could he give expression to this spirit.

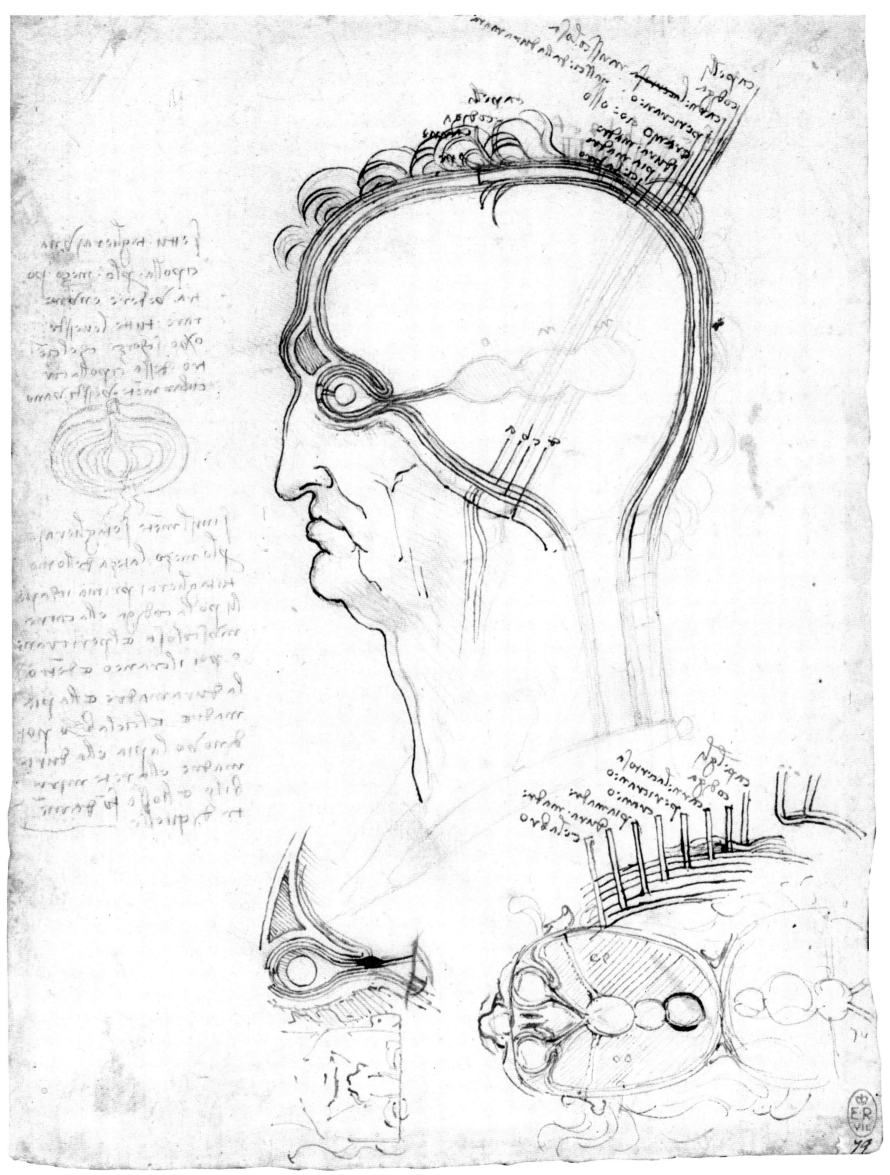

205

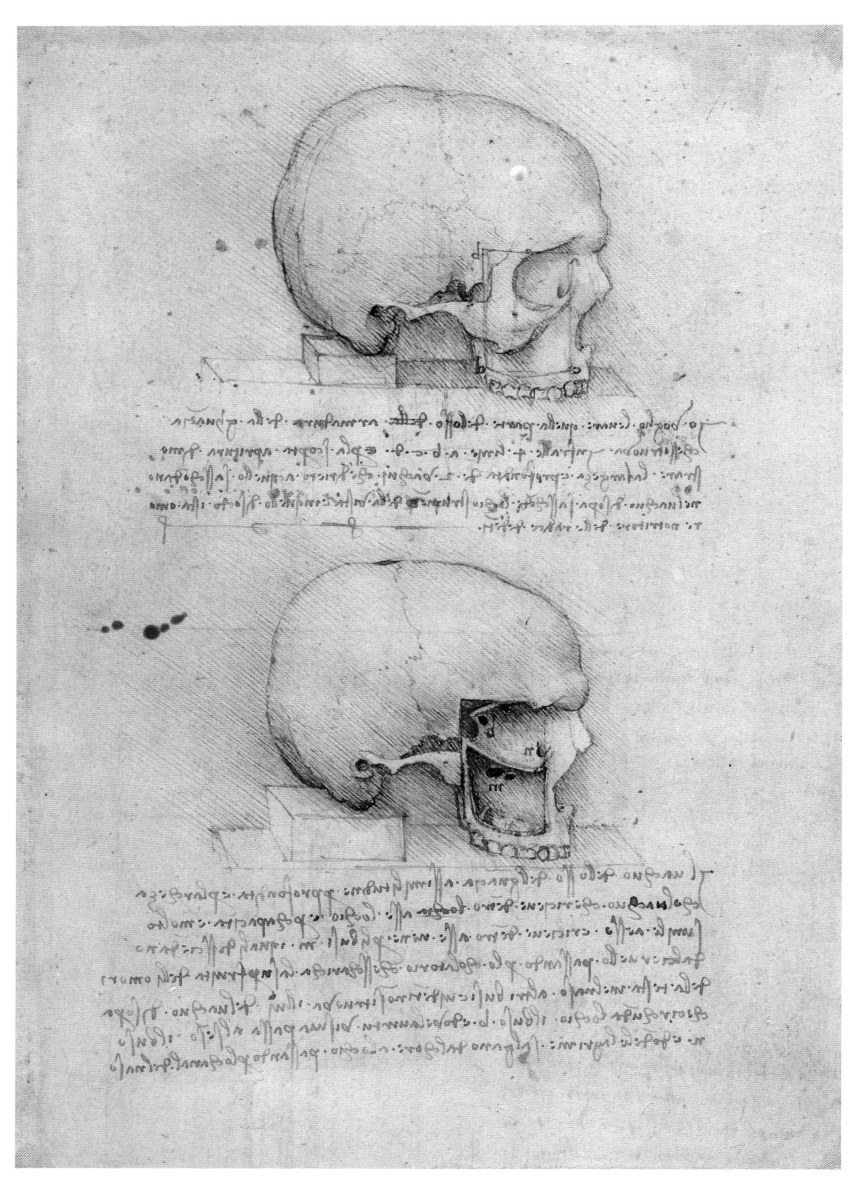

LEFT: *Two Skulls in Profile to the Right*, 1489, pen
and ink, 7×5 inches (18.1×12.9 cm), Windsor
Castle, Royal Library 19057v. © 1991 Her
Majesty The Queen.

Landscapes, Plants and Animals

Leonardo's ability to practice several arts led him to compare what they had in common and what differed between them. He challenged the prevailing classification of human knowledge in which the seven Liberal arts represented the highest forms of human effort. Included in the seven were Poetry and Music, but painting was relegated to the Mechanical Arts or crafts since it involved manual work which was considered inferior. In an attempt to show that the painter was superior to the poet, Leonardo argued for the primacy of sight over the other senses by claiming that it was sight alone that compelled men to seek the pleasures and beauty of nature and the countryside.

Leonardo was particularly interested in translating the landscape into his pictures. The sheer number of drawings testifies to the passionate interest with which he observed nature. In addition to recording the slight variations within families of trees, Leonardo laid the basis for a theory of landscape in his *Trattato della Pittura*. For Leonardo, the purpose of a landscape as an art work was not merely a decoration but had to correspond to something actual and true.

It is not surprising therefore that Leonardo's first dated drawing from 1473 is

ABOVE: *Study of a Copse of Birches*, c. 1498, red chalk, 7½×6 inches (19.1×15.3 cm), Windsor Castle, Royal Library 12431r. © 1991 Her Majesty The Queen.

of a landscape, the *Val d'Arno*. The building at the top left of the drawing is probably the castle of Montelupo and this view of the Arno valley reappears in several Florentine paintings, notably by Antonio Pollaiuolo, while the rocky structure to the right recalls the background of Verrocchio's *Madonna and Child with Angels* in the National Gallery, London. Leonardo's technique of using parallel lines in depicting is conventionalized, but he was already beginning to notice the ways that the foliage appears in different lights and at different distances, something that he would explore in greater depth later in his career.

A Copse of Diverse Trees, c. 1500, is one of many references to trees in Leonardo's manuscripts that reveals his interest in their changing appearance under different lighting conditions as well as in their growth patterns. On the reverse of this drawing is a study of a single tree with the accompanying note:

The part of the tree which has shadow for background is all one tone, and wherever the tree or branches are thickest they will be darkest, because there are no little intervals of air. But where the boughs lie against a background of other boughs, the brighter parts are seen lightest and the leaves lustrous from the sunlight falling on them.

ABOVE: *Study of a Tree*, c. 1498, red chalk, 7½×6 inches (19.1×15.3 cm), Windsor Castle, Royal Library 12431v. © 1991 Her Majesty The Queen.

The two drawings may well have been made as possible illustrations for the *Treatise on Painting*. Although Leonardo had first used red chalk in the 1480s, these two drawings have been dated from anywhere between c. 1495 and 1510: the earlier date because of the similar technique used in *Landscape with Storm over the Alps* and the later date because the handwriting and arrangement of the text is closer to that for drawings related to the Trivulzio Monument project.

Leonardo excelled in modeling by gradations of light and dark and was a promoter of the chiaroscuro and sfumato techniques. His interest in reflections, contrasts, neutralizations of color and his observations of atmospheric effects in many ways make Leonardo a forerunner of the Impressionists. In his modeling of mountainous landscapes, Leonardo's skills as an artist, engineer and geologist are fused to produce the magical results seen in the backgrounds of the *Mona Lisa* (page 131) and *The Virgin and Saint Anne* (page 120). In the drawing *Study of Mountains* Leonardo demonstrates his own advice that the bases of mountains be represented paler than their summits.

Around 1506 and 1508, the formation of clouds and rainfall captured Leonardo's attention as he sought to understand the dynamics of the cyclical movements of fluids above, within and on the earth. The optical effects of rainfall were also of great interest and he noted that the rain, as it fell from the clouds, was the same color as the clouds themselves. By observing carefully the appearance of nature, Leonardo wrote that painters can 'depict mist through which the shape of things can only be discerned with difficulty, rain with cloud-capped mountains and valleys shining through; clouds of dust whirling about combators' (Trat. 40).

RIGHT: *A Storm*, c. 1511, red chalk, Windsor Castle, Royal Library 12409. © 1991 Her Majesty The Queen.

·137·

BELOW: *Study of Mountain Ranges*, 1511, red
chalk on red prepared surface, heightened
with white, 4⅛×6¼ inches (10.5×16 cm),
Windsor Castle, Royal Library 12410. © 1991
Her Majesty The Queen.

A Riover, a Canal, and a Castle on a Hill, c. 1503,
pen and ink, 4×5¾ inches (10×14.7 cm),
Windsor Castle, Royal Library 12399. © 1991
Her Majesty The Queen.

An extraordinary group of studies, those known as the *Deluge Drawings*, are among the most original and fascinating of Leonardo's works. The ten studies illustrate the destruction of the earth and the gradual annihilation of all plant and animal life, over towns and whole mountains. Each of the finished chalk drawings appears to have been made as a work of art in its own right, although their true purpose has never been explained. Dating from the time Leonardo was in Rome (around 1514), it is possible that these drawings were designed as illustrations for the *Treatise on Painting*, but they may also be a record of a natural disaster that occurred in the Alps near Bellizona in 1513 and again in 1515, when a major landslip led to the destruction of villages in the area. An earlier violent storm in 1505 is also noted by Leonardo as it damaged his cartoon for the painting of the *Battle of Anghiari*. Whatever their origin or purpose, the *Deluge Drawings* allowed Leonardo to demonstrate his knowledge of the structure and movement of natural forms.

LEFT: *Studies of Water Formations*, c. 1507-09,
pen and ink, 11½×8 inches (29×20.2 cm),
Windsor Castle, Royal Library 12660v. © 1991
Her Majesty The Queen.

ABOVE: *Deluge*, c. 1513, black chalk, 6½×8¼
inches (16.3×21 cm), Windsor Castle, Royal
Library 12378. © 1991 Her Majesty The Queen.

The inventory of items in his possession that Leonardo made around 1482 when he left Florence for Milan stated that he had drawings of 'many flowers from nature' and reminds us of the volume of work that has been lost, for the earliest surviving plant study is the drawing of the *Madonna Lily* from around 1472-5. The drawing cannot be identified as the direct model for the lily held by the angel in the *Uffizi Anunciation* since it differs in the arrangement of flowers, buds and leaves as well as inclining in a different direction. Because of the size of the drawing and the outline having been pricked for transfer to a panel and the different medium Leonardo used, it is likely though that this drawing was used as in the preparation of a painting now lost. The faint and incomplete geometrical drawing that appears at the foot of the page may also relate to a perspective projection like that for the *Adoration of the Magi*.

RIGHT: *A Lily*, c. 1475, pen, ink, and brown wash over black wash, heightened with white, the outlines pricked for transfer, 12⅜×7 inches (31.4×17.7 cm), Windsor Castle, Royal Library 12418. © 1991 Her Majesty The Queen.

The majority of Leonardo's extant botanical studies are related to the years 1508 and after: around this time he seems to have been working on variations of the theme of Leda and the Swan, depicting a standing Leda and a kneeling Leda. The painting of Leda is known only from drawings and from sixteenth-century copies of the work: the Rotterdam *Leda* includes the drawing of a plant, *Sparganum erectum*. As well as this elegant marsh plant, in the Chatsworth *Leda*, a highly finished drawing of the kneeling Leda, Leonardo also included a spiraling plant *Ornithogalum umbrellatum* at Leda's feet. The study of this plant in red chalk, pen and ink is probably Leonardo's best-known botanical drawing, as well as being one of the most spectacular – there are in fact three different species of plants depicted on this page of studies – even though it has been suggested by botanical authorities that the Star of Bethlehem in its leaf formation does not have such a pronounced spiral arrangement. This appearance is probably due to Leonardo's method of observation and analysis, which, as in some of his anatomical studies, tended to result in an emphasis being placed on the underlying structure of things and the patterns that the structures produced.

Aware of the iconography of plants and flowers in paintings, Leonardo nevertheless ensured that any plant life that appeared, did so in its proper 'ecological' setting. Thus, at the same time that the plants in his works carry symbolic meaning, they are true to nature.

The spiraling form that is apparent in the drawing of the *Star of Bethlehem*, and the energies embodied in the spiral form were an area of interest to which Leonardo often returned: we can see the spiral form in his studies of water and in the *Deluge Drawings*.

In a similar way, some of the plant studies are related to architectural forms such as arches and vaults. The study of the grass *Coix Lachryma-Jobi* was a relatively new plant to Europe when Leonardo made his study of it and, as well as reminding us of his definition of an arch, we see the similar shape in his studies for churches and in the Triburio for Milan Cathedral. At the same time, this drawing also explores the theme of reproduction that can be seen in an earlier series of flowering and seeding plants and the studies of the human reproductive system and embryos.

It comes as no surprise then to find the human body compared with plant life on the same page of studies. In it Leonardo makes a comparison between the vascularization of the heart and a germinating peach seed, while in WRL 12603, analogous to the layers of an onion are the overlying sections of the human skull with its dermal and bone layers.

Other drawings that at first sight appear to be purely botanical studies are also related to motifs that appear in paintings: *Oak and Dyers Greenweed* WRL 12422, comes from a group of studies in the Royal Collection related to the lost *Leda and the Swan*. Furthermore, the oak also appears as a motif in the lunette garlands of the *Last Supper* and in *Bacchus-St. John*, and the generative potential seeds and nuts is expressed in Leonardo's *Fables*.

In both its presentation and botanical notation the drawing of two aquatic plants WRL 12427 *Scirpus lacustris and Cyperus monti* reinforces the belief that Leonardo was planning a book on plants. He had produced one, it would have been the first of its kind for in the notes accompanying the drawings, Leonardo makes no mention of any medical properties the plants have. It is likely that instead of producing a 'Herbal', Leonardo would have continued to study and draw plants in the manner of the true botanist; revealing the qualities of each plant for no other reason except for understanding their structure, growth, flowering and seeding patterns.

RIGHT: *Flowering Rushes*, red chalk on pink surface, 7⅞×5⅝ inches (20.1×14.3 cm), Windsor Castle, Royal Library 12430r. © 1991 Her Majesty The Queen.

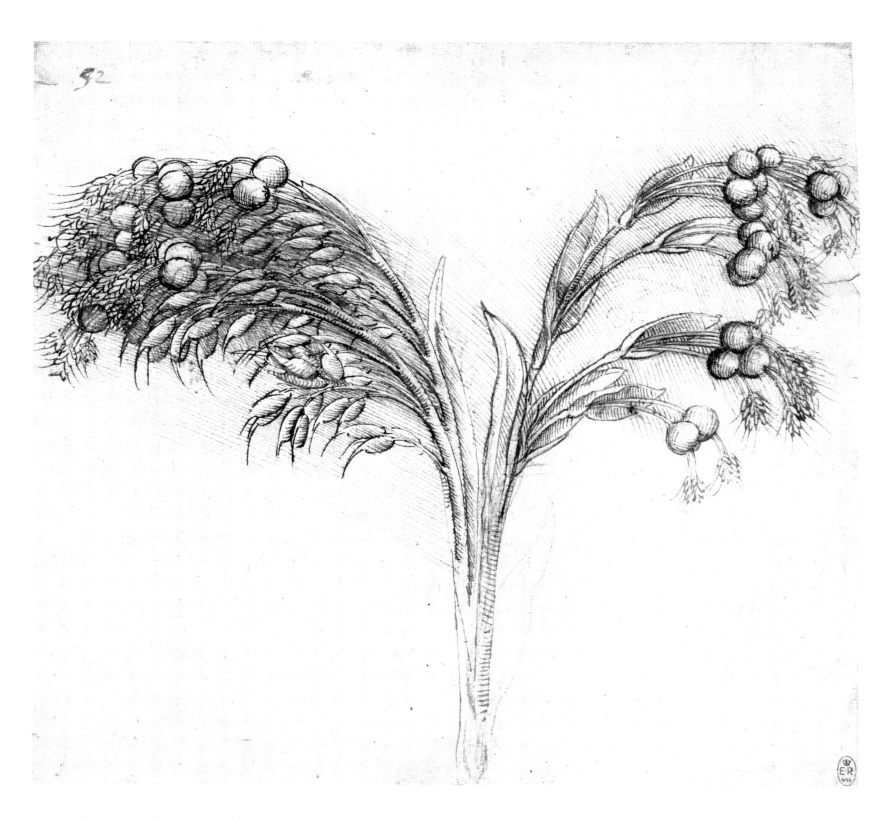

ABOVE: *A Long-stemmed Plant*, c. 1505-08, pen
and ink over black chalk, 8⅝×9 inches
(21.2×23 cm), Windsor Royal Library 12429.
© 1991 Her Majesty The Queen.

ABOVE: *A Star of Bethlehem and Other Plants*,
c. 1505-08, red chalk and pen and ink, 7¾×6
inches (19.8×16 cm), Windsor Castle, Royal
Library 12424. © 1991 Her Majesty The Queen.

223

153

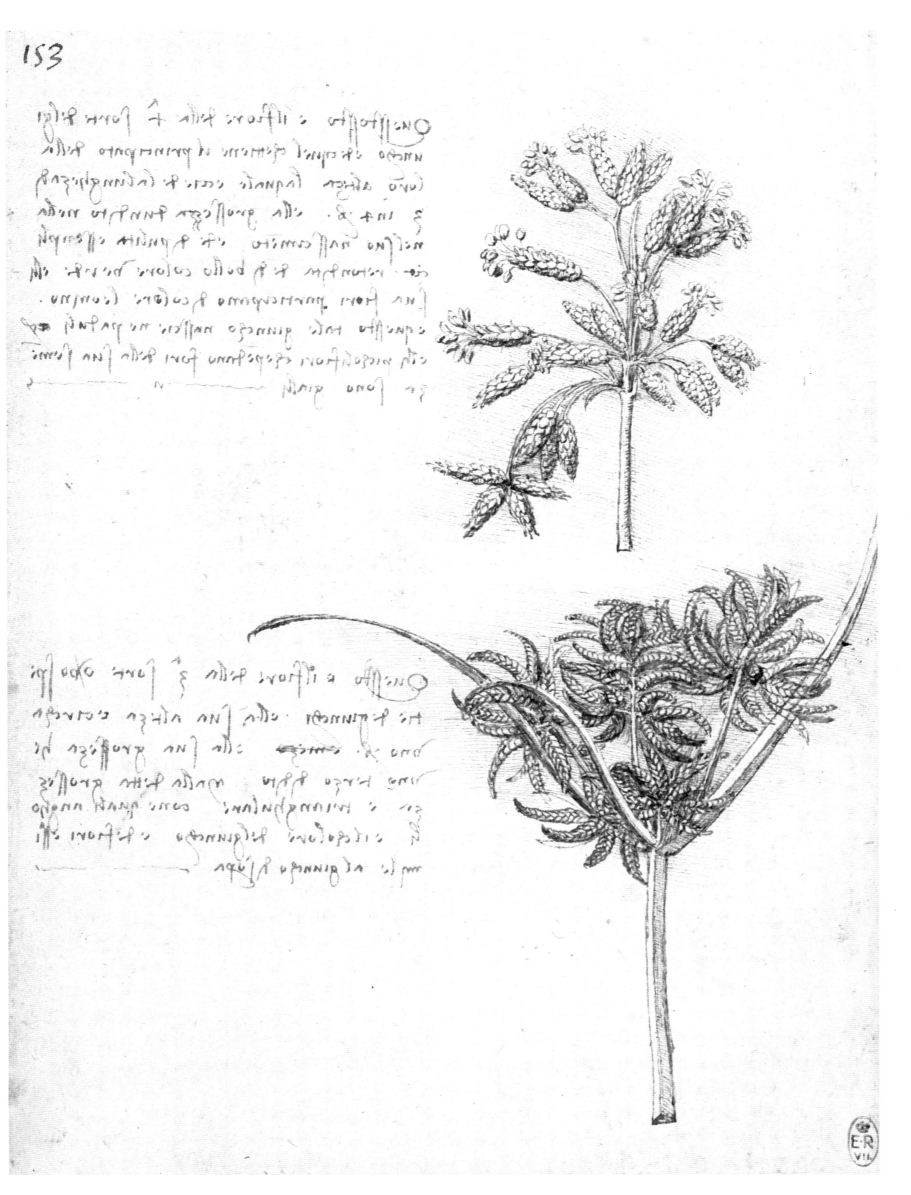

Leonardo's contemporary Andrea Corsali, in a letter dated 1515 written to Giuliano de' Medici, wrote of a group of people called *Guzzati*, who lived in India in the region between Goa and Rasigut, who refused to eat food that contained blood and who had agreed not to harm any living thing 'just like our Leonardo da Vinci.' In support of the claims that Leonardo was a 'gentle' soul, are his own prophetic riddles contain the recurring theme of man's destruction of nature.

Throughout his career Leonardo had made drawings of animals, both real and imaginary beasts, that were accurate studies of their movement and anatomy as well as being symbolic images.

Two sheets of drawings in the Royal Collection, and are related in style, layout and the theme of animal motion.

At the foot of *Cats, Lions(?) and a Dragon*, c. 1513-14, the inscription reads

On bending and extension. The animal species, of which the lion is prince, because the joints of its spinal chord are bendable.

This inscription suggests that the two sheets may have been intended as part of Leonardo's proposed treatise on the movement of men and animals.

The earliest of Leonardo's studies of cats were drawn in the late 1470s or early 1480s in preparation for the painting of *The Virgin and Child with Cat* (page 55), in which the cat twists its body to escape from the infant Christ's embrace. These later studies take the twisting cat motif further in his examination of the sinuous movements of the animal, its twisting form giving rise to the curly-tailed dragon.

RIGHT: *Study of Violas and Methods of Soldering Lead Roofs*, c. 1487, pen and ink, 9⅛×6½ inches (23.2×16.7 cm), Bibliothèque de l'Institut de France, Paris.

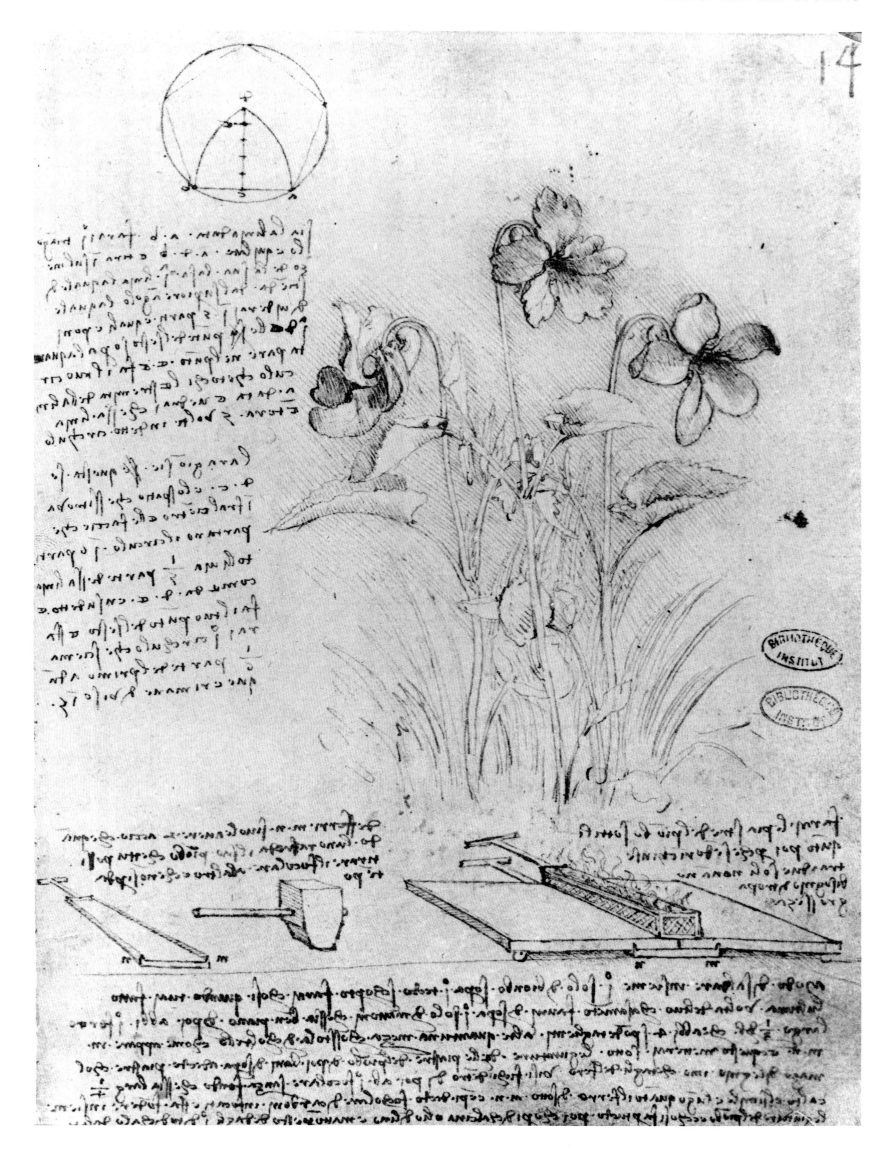

BELOW: *Studies of a Dragon*, silverpoint on white prepared surface, partly gone over with pen and ink, 6¼×9½ inches (15.9×24.3 cm), Windsor Castle, Royal Library 12370v. © 1991 Her Majesty The Queen.

RIGHT: *Studies of Cats and of a Dragon*, pen, ink, and wash over black chalk, 10⅝×8¼ inches (27×21 cm), Windsor Castle, Royal Library 12363. © 1991 Her Majesty The Queen.

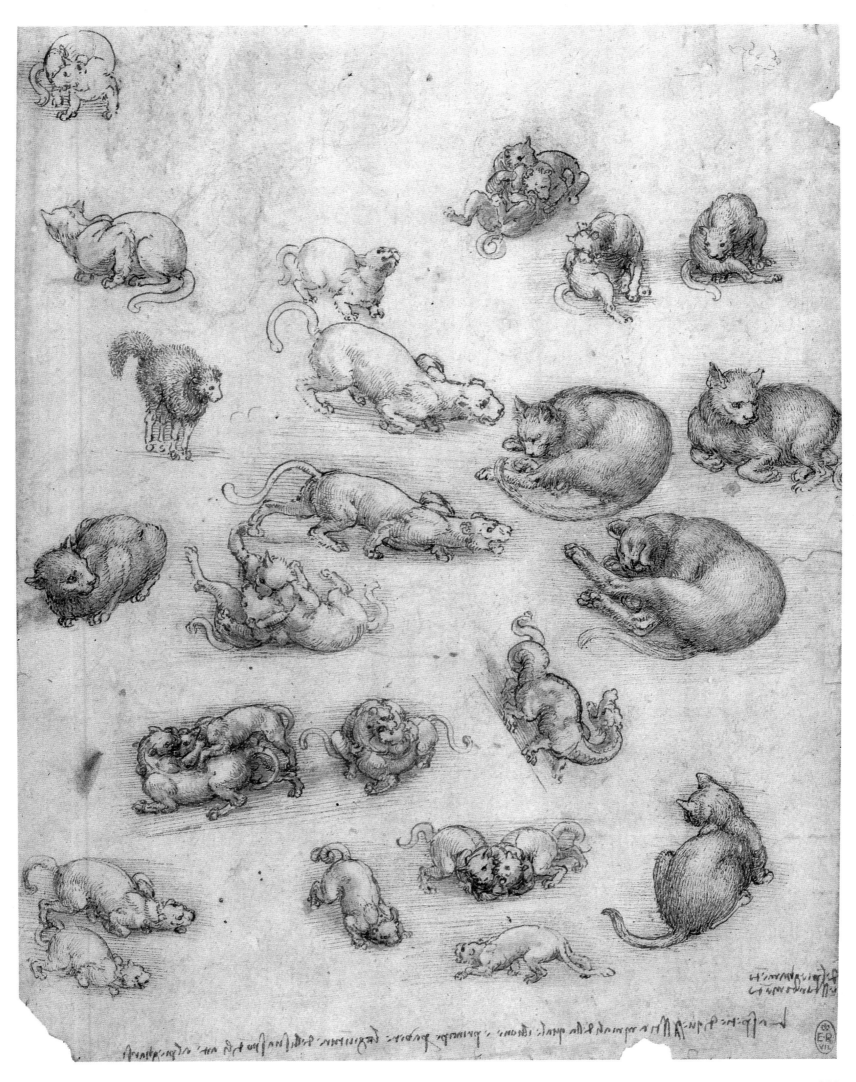

At the top of the sheet of studies of *Horses, a Cat and St George and the Dragon*, c. 1517, Leonardo has written:

Serpentine postures comprise the principal action in the movement of animals, and this action is double: the first is along the length, and the second across the breadth.

This series of drawings represents Leonardo's sense of the infinite possibilities that are presented by the movements of animals, especially when they are viewed from different angles. Although the mounted figure of St George was a popular figure in Milan, the drawings do not suggest that Leonardo was planning a painting on this theme, but was more likely adopted to represent better the idea of serpentine motion. The sheet of drawings of *Asses and an Ox* in silverpoint was, however, probably a study for a future painting on the theme of the Nativity.

As he was a clever and resourceful engineer and designer of masques, pageants and costumes for court entertainments in France and Italy, many of Leonardo's designs took the form of fabulous animals. For the festivities in Pavia in honor of François I, Leonardo devised a mechanical lion, which, after advancing a few steps, opened its mouth to reveal a mass of fleur-de-lys. Like his contemporaries, Leonardo drew his inspiration from traditional bestiaries. In his drawing of *A Dragon*, c. 1515-17, Leonardo depicts a more decorative monster which differs sharply from those on pages 229 and 231. Commentators have noted also that this dragon is wingless, rather like the Chinese version of the mythical creature. The drawing of the legs, body and head of the dragon suggest further that this may have been a design for a pageant costume to be worn by two men walking with bent legs to affect a more 'realistic' dragon gait.

It was the image of the horse, however, that was ultimately the animal that fascinated Leonardo throughout his career from his early work in Verrocchio's studio engaged on the Colleoni equestrian monument, through the *Adoration of the Magi*, the monuments for Francesco Sforza and Giacomo Trivulzio to the *Battle of Anghiari*.

BELOW: *A Dragon*, pen, ink, and black chalk,
8¼×10⅝ inches (21×27 cm), Windsor Castle,
Royal Library 12369. © 1991 Her Majesty The
Queen.

Chronology

	Leonardo's Life	World Events	Arts, Literature, Science
1452	15 April: Leonardo born near Vinci, Tuscany.		Metal plate first used for printing.
1453		End of Eastern Roman Empire with fall of Constantinople.	Hagia Sophia in Constantinople converted into mosque.
1455		Beginning of Wars of the Roses in England.	Gutenberg produces Mazarin Bible, first book printed with movable metal type.
1458		Athens under Turkish control.	
1460			Completion of Winchester Cathedral. Death of Henry the Navigator, Portuguese explorer.
1464		Louis XI of France establishes French Royal Mail.	
1468	Death of Leonardo's paternal grandfather in whose house he grew up.	Outbreak of war between England and France.	
1469	Leonardo living with his father in Florence, and presumably apprenticed in Verrocchio's studio.	Lorenzo 'Il Magnifico' de' Medici becomes leader of Florentine Republic.	Andrea del Verrocchio makes *David* sculpture; possibly his pupil Leonardo modeled for it.
1470			Alberti designs church of S Andrea, Mantua, Renaissance masterpiece.
1471			First European observatory built at Nuremberg.
1472	Registration of Leonardo as a painter with the Guild of St Luke.		Dante's *Divine Comedy* (1314) first printed.
1473	5 August: date of Arno drawing (page 15).		Birth of Nicolas Copernicus (d. 1543), mathematician, physicist, and classicist.
1474			William Caxton produces first printed book in English. Andrea Mantegna paints frescoes in Camera degli Sposi, Mantua.
1475		Peace of Piéquigny between England and France.	
1476	Anonymously accused of sodomy; Verrocchio, in whose studio he is still working, assists in his acquittal.		End of Timurid rule in Baghdad.
1477			Caxton produces Chaucer's *Canterbury Tales* (1388) in his press at Westminster. Botticelli paints *Primavera* in Florence.
1478	10 January: receives first recorded independent commission, for the chapel of San Bernardo in the Palazzo Vecchio.	Murder of Giuliano de' Medici, brother of Lorenzo.	
1479	28 December: draws hanged corpse of Bernardo Baroncelli, one of the Pazzi conspirators (page 19).		
1481	Receives commission for the *Adoration of the Magi* (page 56) for monastery of San Donato a Scopeto, Florence. Several payments are made to Leonardo, up to September.		Pietro Perugino and Pinturicchio at work painting Sistine Chapel of the Vatican.
1482	Leonardo goes to Milan, precise date unknown.	War between Papal States and alliance of Ferrara, Venice and Naples.	Portuguese establish settlements on the Gold Coast.
1483	25 April: Leonardo and Ambrogio and Evangelista da Predis commissioned to produce *Madonna of the Rocks* altarpiece for the Confraternity of the Immaculate Conception in Milan.	Accession of Richard III of England and disappearance of boy king Edward V and his brother. Accession of Charles VIII of France.	Cancelleria begun in Rome (completed 1513).
1484			Botticelli paints *Birth of Venus* in Florence. Discovery by Portuguese of the mouth of the River Congo.
1485		Death in battle of Richard III; accession as Henry VII of Henry Tudor.	Verrocchio begins work on Colleoni monument in Venice (page 7). Alberti's treatise on building, *De re Aedificatoria*, published posthumously.
1486			Rediscovery of Vitruvius' *Ten Books of Architecture*, Roman treatise. Clear glass supercedes colored glass around this time.
1490	Makes designs for festivities for marriage of Glan Galeazzo Sforza and Isabella of Aragon.		
1491	Leonardo working on the technical problems of the 'Great Horse' (page 84).	Unification of France and Brittany through marriage of Charles VII and Anne of Brittany.	Erection of Gate of Salvation, Kremlin, Moscow.
1492		End of Mohammedan rule in southern Spain. Rodrigo Borgia elected as Pope Alexander VI. Expulsion of Jews from Spain.	Christopher Columbus crosses the Atlantic and discovers the West Indies.

	Leonardo's Life	World Events	Arts, Literature, Science
1493	Full-size clay model of the horse exhibited.		Trade war between England and Flanders. Columbus discovers Puerto Rico and Antigua.
1494			Luca Pacioli writes *Summa de Arithmetica*.
1495			Francesco di Giorgio invents military mine.
1497	The *Last Supper* nearing completion.		John and Sebastian Cabot discover Newfoundland and Nova Scotia. Michelangelo sculpts first *Pietà*.
1498	Leonardo paints the *Sala delle Asse* in the Castello Sforzesco, Milan. Leonardo receives a vineyard from Ludovico Sforza, perhaps in lieu of payment due.	Succession of Louis XII of France. Savonarola burned at the stake in Florence. Columbus deprived of Governorship of West Indies and brought back to Spain in chains.	Vasco da Gama, Portuguese seaman, becomes first European to find sea route to India. Columbus discovers Trinidad and mainland of South America.
1499	Leonardo leaves Milan as French troops invade.	Cesare Borgia, son of Pope Alexander VI, conquers Romagna.	Amerigo Vespucci and Alonso Hojeda discover Venezuela and Guiana.
1500	February: Leonardo draws portrait of Isabella d'Este in Mantua. Leonardo briefly visits Venice. April: Leonardo returns to Florence.	Louis XII of France conquers Duchy of Milan.	Erasmus writes *Adagio*, study of Classical proverbs. Dürer *Self-Portrait*.
1501	Fra Pietro Novellara describes, in letters to Isabella d'Este, Leoanrdo working on a cartoon for a Virgin and St Anne, and the *Madonna of the Yarnwinder* (page 110).		Publication of first hymnbook. Anglo-Portuguese syndicate make first voyage to North America.
1502	Employed as architect and engineer by Cesare Borgia.	Marriage of Margaret, daughter of Henry VII of England, to James IV of Scotland.	
1503	Begins working on the *Battle of Anghiari* (pages 104-09).		Michelangelo sculpts *David*.
1504	Death of Leonardo's father, Ser Piero da Vinci. Leonardo working on engineering schemes at Piombino.	Treaty of Blois: peace between France and Holy Roman Empire.	
1505		Martin Luther enters Augustinian monastery at Erfurt.	
1506	Leonardo returns to Milan to complete *Madonna of the Rocks*.	First national Italian troops – Florentine militia – mustered by Niccolo Machiavelli.	Rebuilding of St Peter's, Rome, begins.
1507		Pope Julius II proclaims Indulgence to assist with building of St Peter's.	First use of name 'America' on world map.
1508	Leonardo returns to Florence and accepts employment from the French king, Louis XII.	League of Cambrai: Holy Roman Empire, France, and Aragon against Venice.	Michelangelo begins painting ceiling of Sistine Chapel, Vatican.
1509	Working on geometrical and anatomical studies.	Pope Julius II joins League of Cambrai and Venice is defeated at Battle of Agnadello, loses some provinces to the Pope.	Grünewald, *Isenheim Altarpiece*, painted around this time. Watch, 'Nuremberg Egg,' invented. Erasmus writes *The Praise of Folly*.
1510		Luther in Rome as delegate of Augustinian order. Treaty between Pope Julius II and Venice.	Hieronymous Bosch paints *Hell* around this time.
1511		England joins league of Julius II, Aragon, and Venice against France, and invades France.	
1512		French driven from Italy.	Michelangelo completes the *Creation of Adam* in the Sistine Chapel.
1513	Leonardo in Milan, Florence and Rome. Piero Soderini has protective barrier erected in front of the unfinished *Battle of Anghiari* in the Council Hall of the Palazzo Vecchio.	Scots defeated by English at Battle of Flodden. Giovanni de' Medici elected as Pope Leo X.	Machiavelli writes *The Prince*, a study in political subterfuge. Discovery of Pacific Ocean by Vasco Balboa.
1514	Leonardo working for Giuliano de' Medici in Rome and Parma.	Treaty of alliance between England and France sealed marriage of Mary, sister of Henry VIII, to Louis XII of France.	
1515		France defeated puppet Sforza ruler in Milan and gained Parma and Piacenza from Pope Leo X at Battle of Bologna.	Hampton Court Palace begun by Cardinal Wolsey.
1516	Leonardo leaves Rome for France in 1516 or early 1517.		Sir Thomas More writes *Utopia*. Ludovico Ariosto writes *Orlando Furioso*, epic poem. Portuguese merchants and traders reach China.
1517	Leonardo settled at Cloux in the employ of Francis I of France. Cardinal of Aragon sees three pictures by Leonardo – a portrait of a Florentine lady (the *Mona Lisa*? page 131), a young St John the Baptist (the painting on page 142) and the St Anne (the painting on page 120).	Martin Luther nailed his 95 Treatises to the door of Wittenburg Castle Church in protest at sale of Indulgences.	Raphael paints *Fire in the Borgo* in the Vatican. Coffee first introduced into Europe.
1518		Peace of London allied England, Holy Roman Empire, France, Spain, and Papacy against Turkey. Luther refuses to recant.	Daniel Romberg completes Rabbinical Bible.
1519	23 April: Leonardo dictates his will. 2 May: Leonardo dies. 12 August: Leonardo buried at Amboise.	François I of France and Henry VIII of England candidates for Holy Roman Imperial Throne; Charles of Spain succeeds as Charles V.	Hernando Cortes lands in Mexico at Vera Cruz.

Five Grotesque Heads, c. 1490, pen and ink,
10¼×8 inches (26×20.5 cm), Windsor Castle,
Royal Library 12495r. © 1991 Her Majesty The
Queen.

Select Bibliography

Baxandall, M *Painting and Experience in Fifteenth-Century Italy* (Oxford, 1972)

Beltrami, L *Documenti e memorie riguardanti la vita e le opere di Leonardo da Vinci in ordine cronologico* (Milan, 1919)

Boussel, P *Leonardo da Vinci* (Secausus, NJ, nd [c. 1989])

Byam Shaw, J *Drawings by Old Masters at Christ Church, Oxford* (2 vols; Oxford, 1976)

Clark, K *Leonardo da Vinci* (London, 1939, 1947, 1988)

Clark, K and C Pedretti *A Catalogue of the Drawings of Leonardo da Vinci at Windsor Castle* (3 vols; London, 1978-79)

Clark, K and C Pedretti *Leonardo da Vinci: Corpus of Anatomical Studies at Windsor Castle* (3 vols; London and New York, 1979-80)

Eissler, K R *Leonardo da Vinci: Psychoanalytical Notes on the Enigma* (London, 1962)

Emboden, W A *Leonardo da Vinci on Plants and Gardens* (London, 1987)

Fletcher, J 'Bernardo Bembo and Leonardo's Portrait of Ginevra de' Benci,' *Burlington Magazine*, (December, 1989)

Friedenthal, R *Leonardo da Vinci: A Pictorial Biography* (London, 1974)

Goldscheider, L *Leonardo da Vinci* (London, 1943)

Gombrich, E *Studies in the Art of the Renaissance*, IV; Oxford, 1986)

Gould, C *Leonardo, the Artist and Non-Artist* (London and Boston, 1975)

Grossman, S 'Ghirlandaio's *Madonna and Child* in Frankfurt and Leonardo's Beginning as a Painter,' *Städel Jahrbuch*, VII (1979), pp 101-25

Heydenreich, L H *Leonardo: The Last Supper* (London, 1974)

Heydenreich, L H *Leonardo da Vinci* (2 vols; New York and Basel, 1974)

Humble, R *Warfare in the Middle Ages* (London, 1989)

Keele, K *Leonardo da Vinci's Elements of the Science of Man* (London and New York, 1983)

Keele, K and C Pedretti *Leonardo da Vinci, Corpus of Anatomical Studies at Windsor Castle* (3 vols; London and New York, 1979-80)

Kemp, M *Leonardo da Vinci: The Marvellous Works of Nature and Man* (London and Cambridge, MA, 1981, 1989)

Kemp, M and M Walker, eds *Leonardo on Painting: An Anthology of Writings by Leonardo da Vinci with a Selection of Documents Relating to his Career as an Artist* (London, 1989)

Leonardo da Vinci (exh. cat. ed M Kemp, J Roberts, and P Steadman; London, 1989)

Leonardo da Vinci: Engineer and Architect (exh. cat. ed P Galluzzi, Montreal, 1987)

MacCurdy, E *The Mind of Leonardo da Vinci* (London, 1928)

MacCurdy, E ed *The Notebooks of Leonardo da Vinci* (London, 1938)

A P McMahon, ed *Treatise on Painting. . . by Leonardo da Vinci* (2 vols; Princeton, NJ, 1956)

Marinoni, A ed *Il Codice Atlantico di Leonardo da Vinci nella Biblioteca Ambrosiana di Milano* (12 vols; Florence, 1973-75)

Martinez, L *Power and Imagination: The City State in Renaissance Italy* (London, 1980)

Parker, K T *Catalogue of the Collection of the Drawings in the Ashmolean Museum* (Volume II: *The Italian Schools*, Oxford, 1956)

Parrochi, A 'Vecchio Col Molto Lungo,' *Antichità Viva*, XXIV (1982), 1-3, pp 128-30

Pedretti, C *The Codex Atlanticus of Leonardo da Vinci: A Catalogue of its Newly Restored Sheets* (New York, 1978-79)

Pedretti, C *Leonardo, Architect* (London, 1986)

Pedretti, C *Leonardo: A Study in Chronology and Style* (London, 1972)

Pedretti, C *Leonardo da Vinci: Fragments at Windsor Castle from the Codex Atlanticus* (London, 1957)

Pedretti, C *Leonardo: Studies for the Last Supper* (Milan, 1983)

Pedretti, C, ed *Landscapes, Plants and Water Studies in the Collection of Her Majesty the Queen at Windsor Castle* (London and New York, 1982)

Pedretti, C, ed *Horses and other Animals: Drawings by Leonardo da Vinci in the Collection of Her Majesty The Queen at Windsor Castle* (London and New York, 1987)

Popham, A E *The Drawings of Leonardo da Vinci* (London, 1946)

Popham, A E and P Pouncey *Italian Drawings of the 14th and 15th Centuries . . . in the British Museum* (2 vols; London, 1950)

Reti, L *The Manuscripts of Leonardo da Vinci in the Biblioteca Nacional of Madrid* (5 vols; New York, 1974)

Reti, L ed *The Unknown Leonardo* (London, 1974)

Richter, J P, ed *The Literary Works of Leonardo da Vinci* (2 vols; London and New York, 1970)

Snow-Smith, J *The 'Salvator Mundi' of Leonardo da Vinci* (Washington DC, 1982)

Valentin, A *Leonardo da Vinci* (Paris, 1950)

Vasari, G *Lives of the Artists* (ed. G Bull, London, 1971)

Zarnattio, C, A Marinoni, and A M Brizio, *Leonardo the Scientist* (London, 1981)

Zubov, V P *Leonardo da Vinci* (Cambridge, MA, 1968)

Index

Acknowledgments

The publisher would like to thank Martin Bristow, who designed this book, and Pat Coward who indexed it. We would also like to thank the following agencies, individuals, and institutions for supplying the illustrations:

Alte Pinakothek, Munich/SCALA, Florence: page 49
Archivio di Stato, Florence/SCALA, Florence: page 15 (above)
The Bettmann Archive, New York: pages 21, 22, 23, 26, 28, 30, 31, 103
Biblioteca Ambrosiana, Milan: pages 149, 152 (above), 157 (below), 158, 162, 164, 165, 167 (above), 168, 170, 171 (both), 173 (all three), 175, 178, 179, 180, 181, 182, 184, 185 (all three).
Biblioteca Nacional, Madrid: pages 151 (below), 152 (below), 153 (both), 154 (below), 156 (below), 157 (above right and above left), 166 (both), 167 (below), 172
Biblioteca Nazionale Centrale, Florence: page 155
Bibliothèque de l'Institut de France: pages 177, 227
Bibliothèque Nationale, Paris: page 156 (top)
Bodleian Library, Oxford: page 187
Castello Sforzesco, Milan/Foto Saporetti: pages 100, 101
In the Collection of the Duke of Buccleuch and Queensberry, KT, Drumlanrig Castle, Dumfriesshire: pages 110, 111
Collection of the Earl of Pembroke, Wilton House Trust, Wilton, Salisbury, Wiltshire: page 136
Courtesy of the Governing Body, Christ Church, Oxford: page 40 (above)
Czartoryski Museum, Kraków/SCALA, Florence: page 2, 76
Devonshire Collection, Chatsworth House, Derbyshire, Reproduced by permission of the Chatsworth Settlement Trustees: page 137
Galleria dell'Accademia, Carrara, Bergamo/SCALA, Florence: page 27
Galleria dell'Accademia, Venice/SCALA, Florence: pages 106, 126, 147
Galleria Borghese, Rome/SCALA, Florence: page 140
Galleria Nazionale, Parma: page 73
Galleria Palatina, Florence/SCALA, Florence: page 14
Galleria degli Uffizi/The Bettmann Archive, New York: page 24
Galleria degli Uffizi/Foto Ottica Europa: pages 15 (below), 63
Galleria degli Uffizi/SCALA, Florence: pages 10, 11, 35, 36, 38-39, 51, 56-57,

58-59, 60-61, 66, 78-79
Hermitage Museum, Leningrad/SCALA, Florence: pages 53, 54
Kunsthistorisches Museum, Vienna/The Bettmann Archive, New York: page 25
Musée de l'hôtel de ville, Amboise: page 33 (below)
Musée Bonnat, Bayonne/SCALA, Florence: page 19
Musée du Louvre/Réunion des Musées Nationaux: pages 33 (above), 40 (below), 41, 44-45, 52, 83, 102, 104-105, 120, 122, 125, 127, 128, 129, 130, 131, 132, 133, 134, 135, 138, 142, 145
Museo Bargello, Florence/SCALA, Florence: page 141
Musée du Louvre/SCALA, Florence: page 37
Museo di Firenze com'era, Florence/SCALA, Florence: page 18
Museo Mediceo, Florence/SCALA, Florence: page 17
Reproduced by Courtesy of the Board of Directors of the Museum of Fine Arts, Budapest: pages 84 (below), 85, 108, 109
National Gallery of Scotland, Edinburgh: page 43
National Gallery of Art, Washington DC/Ailsa Mellon Bruce Fund: page 46/Samuel H Kress Collection: page 50
Ospedale degli Innocenti, Florence/SCALA, Florence: page 67
Palazzo Pitti, Florence/The Bettmann Archive: page 16
Palazzo Reale, Turin/SCALA, Florence: pages 1, 32
Palazzo Vecchio, Florence/SCALA, Florence: 6, 29, 106-107
Pinacoteca Ambrosiana, Milan/SCALA, Florence: page 80
Pinacoteca di Brera/SCALA, Florence: page 20
Pinacoteca Vaticana/SCALA, Florence: page 68
Santa Maria delle Grazie, Milan/SCALA, Florence: pages 88-89, 90-91, 92-93, 94-95
Santa Maria Novella, Florence/SCALA, Florence: pages 12-13
SCALA, Florence: page 7
Windsor Castle, Royal Library. © 1991 Her Majesty The Queen: pages 9, 47, 84 (above), 86, 87, 97, 98, 112 (both), 121, 123, 124, 139, 143, (both), 144, 148, 150, 151, (above), 154 (above), 160-161, 163, 169, 189, 190, 193, 195, 197, 199, 200, 201, 202-203, 205, 206, 208, 209, 211, 212, 213, 214-215, 216, 217, 218, 221, 222, 223, 224, 225, 228, 229, 231, 232, 233, 236